Life and Death at the Mouth of the Musselshell

• Montana Territory – 1868-1872 •

FEATURING THE DIARY OF C. M. LEE, GUNSMITH, MERCHANT

Edited by H. Duane Hampton

Life and Death at the Mouth of the Musselshell
• Montana Territory – 1868-1872 •
FEATURING THE DIARY OF C. M. LEE,
GUNSMITH, MERCHANT

Edited by H. Duane Hampton

Copyright 2011 by Dale A. Burk

ISBN 1-931291-89-6

Library of Congress Control Number: 2011932597

Published in the United States of America

First Edition

ALL RIGHTS RESERVED
No part of this publication may be reproduced, stored in a retrieval system, or transmitted in any form or by any means without the prior written permission of the copyright owner or the publisher.

STONEYDALE PRESS PUBLISHING COMPANY
523 Main Street • P.O. Box 188
Stevensville, Montana 59870
Phone: 406-777-2729
Email: stoneydale@stoneydale.com

Dedication

To those who came before us.

Acknowledgments

Even a brief foray into the past produces a suprising number of debts to those who assisted along the way. Dale Johnson first called my attention to Lee's journal and Mary K. (Horstman) Miller read innumerable Montana newspaper accounts, gleaning small bits of information concerning indivudals mentioned in the journal. The late David Walter provided a constant stream of information and encouragement, while Fort Benton's historian, Joel Overholser, supplied reams of steamboat data. Molly, Glenda, Lory and Becca at the Montana Historical Society provided paths to photographs included herein. Daniel Gallacher and Alan Newell contributed computer equipment along with continual support and encouragement. Jun Wang, a visitor from China, answered constant queries about the mysteries of computer technology and Matthew Hampton applied his knowledge and technology to the maps of the Musselshell country. Without Dale Burk's enthusiasm and commitment, C.M. Lee's journal would remain in the shadows. My thanks to all.

List of Illustrations

Illustration No. 1, Assiniboine Lodge 18

Illustration No. 2, Wolfer's Cabin 21

Illustration No. 3, C.M. Lee Journal Cover 23

Illustration No. 4 C.M. Lee Journal Entry 24

Illustration No. 5, C.M. Lee Journal Entry 25

Illustration No. 6, Diamond City 26

Illustration No. 7, Fort Benton 34

Illustration No. 8, Liver Eating Johnson 54

Illustration No. 9, Steamboat 85

Illustration No. 10, Fort Clagett 95

Illustration No. 11, Helena 116

Illustration No. 12, Fort Musselshell Stereograph 171

Illustration No. 13, Fort Musselshell, Close-up Picture 172

Illustration No. 14, Sketch of Mussellshell Site 211

Maps

Map No. One, The Sawyer Expedition 16-17

Map No. Two, 3-D View of Mussellshell Area 48-49

Map No. Three, Overview of Montana Territory 80-81

Map No. Four, Close-in Perspective of Mussellshell Area........ 112-113

Publisher's Note: *We are indebted to Matthew Hampton, the author's son, who is a professional cartographer/GIS analyst and has been creating maps since he was in the 4th grade, for these maps. He currently lives with his family and many pets near the end of the Oregon Trail where he enjoys exploring the wilderness.*

Table of Contents

Dedication 3

Acknowledgments 4

List of Illustrations 3

Maps 4

Introduction 9

The C. M. Lee Diary 27
    1868 27
    1869 45
    1870 63
    1871 121
    1872 161

The Fort Musselshell Photo 171

Biographical Sketches 173

Notes 202

Appendix
    •*Life at the Muscleshell, 1869-1870,* by Peter Koch 208
    •*Account of the Attempt to Build a Town at The Mouth
      of the Musselshell River,* By Lt. James H. Bradley 219

Bibliography 228

Afterword 235

Introduction

When Cornelius M. Lee came to the recently formed Montana Territory in 1865, he came to a land and to a variety of cultures that were experiencing rapid transition and consequent turmoil. The Native American who roamed the eastern plains and western mountains thought that the land was his, and it was, for a time. In the west were the plateau peoples: the Flathead, the Pend d'Oreille (Kalispel) and the Kutenai. In the eastern portion of the Territory, a constantly changing matrix of plains people contested with one another for dominance: the Shoshones pushed south by the Blackfeet (Piegan); the Gros Ventres (Atsina) and Assiniboine coming in from the north; the Crow (Mountain and River) attempting to hold their own south of the Yellowstone River; the Cheyenne and Arapahoe making seasonal forays northward; from the east came the numerous Sioux (Lakota and Dakota).

The intrepid Lewis and Clark had traversed the land at the beginning of the century, and behind them came other white men seeking wealth in the form of furs. The resident Indians (with the exception of the Blackfeet) maintained an uneasy peace with the invading whites until the beaver thinned as a result of over trapping, and the fur hunters changed their quarry from beaver to buffalo. The American bison determined a major portion of the Plains Indian's culture, and any impact upon the bison had a resulting impact upon the Indian's way of life.

In 1832 the steamboat *Yellowstone* reached Fort Union, located at the juncture of the Yellowstone and Missouri rivers. Twenty-seven years later, the *Chippewa* steamed 200 miles farther up the muddy Missouri and the following year, 1860, the same steamship, accompanied by the *Key West,* reached the ultimate head of navigation, Fort Benton. Steamboats on the Missouri River were also to affect the Indian's way of life.

Bison robes, tanned by industrious Indian women, had always been part of the fur trade, but with fewer beaver in the streams and improved water transportation they became an increasingly important aspect of commerce. Before long, some imaginative pioneer discovered that a bison carcass – partially flayed and poisoned with strychnine – could produce 30 to 60 dead wolves and coyotes. Bison and coarse fur: the combination speeded the process already underway, a process that would painfully transform and ultimately overwhelm the Plains tribes.

With the buffalo disappearing in increasing numbers, old, traditional tribal boundaries and alliances changed. The increasingly aggressive Sioux came from the East and met resistance formed by existing tribal elements – the Blackfeet, the Gros Ventres, the Assiniboine, the Crow, and the Cheyenne. And then someone discovered gold in the western mountains.

Virginia City arose when prospectors found recoverable quantities of gold at Alder Gulch; the miners developed crude towns called Bannack, Helena, Diamond City, and Copperopolis in response to the exploitation of other mineral discoveries. Each new strike brought an increased number of white men into the area, which in turn increased the pressure upon the original inhabitants. Their resistance to that pressure led to cries for protection from the far-off federal government, and westward marched the military. First, in 1866, came a small detachment of soldiers posted at Camp Cooke – a ramshackle affair constructed where the Judith River flows into the Missouri; then came a larger establishment called Fort Shaw on the Sun River. Soon, military commanders, farmers, merchants, ranchers, and politicians began clamoring for better transportation links to the East and markets.

The Missouri River route to Fort Benton, thence overland south to the mining districts, was fine when there was sufficient water to float the steamships; unfortunately, this occurred only during one or two months in early summer. To the south, the Bozeman Trail connected Virginia City with Fort Laramie on the Oregon Trail, but it was long, torturous, and contested by the Cheyenne. The vast distances separating the rapidly developing mining frontier from traditional sources of supplies convinced Congress to appropriate money for the building of a wagon road stretching from the mouth of the Niobrara River on the lower Missouri River to Virginia City, Montana Territory. Selected to conduct the road expedition was James A. Sawyers of Sioux City, Iowa. He rapidly formed a road-building crew of 53 men, 15 wagons, and 45 teams of oxen. A military escort, a 36-wagon freight train, and 5 emigrant wagons combined to make a moving group of over one mile in length. Thirty-one-year-old Cornelius M. Lee and a group of other young men from Sioux City, Iowa, used the expedition as a method of working their way west to the recently discovered gold mines in Montana.

Carrying subsistence for six months, the Sawyers Wagon Road Expedition began its journey where the Niobrara River empties into the Missouri on June 13, 1865, and reached its destination, Virginia City,

Montana Territory, on October 12. During the four-month trip, Lee, who had left his mother and a gunsmith business behind in Sioux City, walked the 1039.7 miles beside his team of oxen. The young gunsmith-turned-bullwhacker kept a meticulous diary. He indicated miles traveled every day, types of soil and topography encountered, suggested that Sawyers was an inept leader, noted that the smell of bear determined that he was unable to eat the meat of that animal, and indicated his thought that the Indians encountered along the way acted in good faith, while the white man seemed to lack the understanding and ability to treat them fairly. He also thought that the Indians were better negotiators than they were fighters. The first portion of the Lee diary ends with the arrival of the expedition in Virginia City.

Lee's diary was used effectively by Susan B. Doyle in her *Journeys to the Land of Gold*, (Helena: Montana Historical Society Press, 2000) and by David Wagner in his *Patrick Connor's War (*Norman: Arthur H. Clark Co., 2010.) Sawyer had been a Lieutenant in the Sioux City Volunteers, the unit in which Lee served during the Civil War. This earlier relationship may have served as a basis for Lee's rather harsh comments concerning Sawyer's leadership or lack thereof. (See Map on pages 16-17.)

The Niobrara road 'engineered' by Sawyers and his crew never experienced heavy emigrant or freight travel. Sioux City did not become the eastern terminus for the Pacific Coast trade as its merchants had hoped. The Sioux and Cheyenne Indians had something to do with the failure, and so too did the rough terrain that lay between the two terminal points. More important in the lack of development, however, was the completion of the transcontinental railroad four years later.

Technology ultimately solved the transportation dilemma of territorial Montana. In 1869 the Union Pacific and the Central Pacific linked East and West, and freighters headed north from the railroad at Corinne, Utah, to the gold camps in Montana. Later, in 1882, the Northern Pacific reached Bismarck, Dakota Territory. This last development stimulated trade on the Missouri River for a time, but ultimately the rails pushed westward to the mining districts. Then came James J. Hill's Great Northern Railway and, with it, the gradual destruction of the last excuse for river transport on the Northern Plains. Before this occurred, however, Montanans were forced to rely upon the long overland trails or to the existing supply line represented by the shifting waters of the Missouri River.

Seasonal fluctuations of the Missouri's water level determined that steamboats could only reach the head of navigation at Fort Benton a few months out of each year. Merchants in the mining districts looked down river for a docking area that would allow more constant steamboat use of the river. They found that steamboats could reach the point where the Musselshell River emptied into the Missouri a month earlier and delay their departure a month later than was possible at Benton. Newspaper editors in Helena eagerly predicted lower freight rates and a more regular schedule of supplies once a new overland route connecting their city to the Musselshell site were established. Army officers urged that all military supplies for the territory be shipped on the Missouri as far as the Musselshell, then sent southward overland to provision the forts then being established to protect the Bozeman Trail.

The first attempt at white settlement at the conjunction of the Musselshell and the Missouri occurred when a group of Montanans formed the Rocky Mountain Wagon Road Company in early 1866 and surveyed a route connecting that point with the new towns of Copperopolis, Diamond City, and Helena. The planned freight business failed to develop, and when the big log structure the company had constructed as headquarters was swept away by the flooding Missouri two years later, the company terminated its activities in the area. Another group of prospective traders made a fresh start that same year – 1868 – operating under the title the Montana Hide and Fur Company. Helena investors dispatched ten men with directions to establish a trading post and to lay out a townsite. At least two saloons resulted. 'Colonel' George Clendenin, representing soon-to-be transportation and merchant prince Thomas C. Power, arrived to build a rival trading operation. During the summer of 1868 the small settlement at the mouth of the Musselshell took form and trade with the Gros Ventres and the Crow commenced. Warfare with other tribal entities also began.

Unfortunately, the establishment of these trading ventures coincided with a sharp reduction in the number of steamboats plying the Missouri. Previously, and tied closely to the discovery and mining of gold, the number of steamboats docking at Fort Benton reached the number of 39 in 1867. Carrying mining equipment, machinery, supplies and passengers up the river, the boats moved gold bullion, furs, hides and passengers downstream. The completion of the transcontinental railroad, combined with the decline in mining production, determined that steamboat traffic declined rapidly – with only six boats reaching Benton in 1874.

Traffic increased gradually thereafter as supplies from the East moved northward from Benton to the new settlements on the Canadian prairies. But this was too late for the traders at the Musselshell.

All of the plans and resultant activity concerning transportation routes to the developing mines were made with scant regard for the Native American over whose lands these roads must necessarily be constructed. The 1851 Fort Laramie Treaty recognized the Musselshell region as Crow, Blackfeet, Gros Ventres and Assiniboine land; four years later Isaac Stevens, in a treaty with the Blackfeet, identified this area as a common hunting ground and left it up to the various tribal elements as to who would gain the most use.

Alliances between these elements changed as intertribal relations grew more complex. Later, the Sioux, pushed westward by white settlement, the River Crow, and the Assiniboine all contested the white man's right to settle and to use their hunting lands. Conflict came with the increasing number of traders and hunters. While the white men were cutting wood, wolfing, hunting, or simply setting around the cabins playing cards for gingersnaps or canned fruit, the Native American was trying, at times desperately but ultimately futilely, to hold what was his. The geopolitical world of the Northern Plains twisted, turned, and finally readjusted. The federal government dictated reservation boundaries, confined the Indian within those boundaries, and deemed the Whiteman triumphant in his destruction of what had been.

The Assiniboine were a once numerous tribe previously centered in the woodland and prairie regions of south-central Canada and described as 'one of the largest, boldest, handsomest, most able buffalo hunting, gregarious, picturesque, peripatetic, and most individualist and iron-willed of all the Northern Great Plains Indian Tribes' (James Larpenteur Long, *The Assiniboines* (Norman: University of Oklahoma Press, 1961) xix,xx). These people had early contact with French and English traders. Moving west and south the Assiniboine changed subsistence from fish and fur to bison as they established trade relations with Missouri River tribes and incorporated the horse into their changing culture.

Intermittent warfare and trade with the Blackfeet and Gros Ventres accompanied their transition to a nomadic plains people, but it was disease – smallpox – that determined subsequent tribal relations on the Great Plains. The 1781-1782 epidemic, according to explorer David Thompson, reduced tribal populations anywhere from one-half to three fifths of their former numbers (Long, *History of the Assiniboine*

18). Pushed southward by recurring pestilence and drawn thereto by a plentiful food supply and trade, the Assiniboine joined the swirl and movement of other tribal elements on the northern plains.

While the Assiniboine were moving South, the Sioux were moving West. Originally settled in the lake and forest lands of the upper Mississippi Valley, the several tribes of Sioux began their westward migrations in the 18th century, displacing resident Omaha and Cheyenne peoples. And then they, as had the Assiniboine, discovered the horse. Their culture rapidly transformed itself, and by the middle of the 19th century, the various Siouxan groups were to become a major obstacle to white settlement and travel on the plains.

Previously moving westward from the upper Mississippi were the Crow (Absaroka), who eventually called the Yellowstone River area their home. The River Crow roamed north of the river; the Mountain Crow claimed the area south of the river. Great traders, the Crow represented the bridge between the Indians south and north and the River Crow were to play a major role in the lives of the small settlement at the mouth of the Musselshell.

Another group – misnamed Gros Ventre by early French traders – were the Atsina. Algonquian in language and closely related to the Arapahoe, the Gros Ventres reflect the great western migration of Indian peoples prior to the arrival of whites. Also moving out of the Minnesota region, the Gros Ventres rapidly adjusted to the new plains environment and allied sometimes with the Blackfeet and sometimes with the Assiniboine in opposition to other tribes and to the invading white man.

By mid-century, a series of alliances, sometimes temporary, promoted a modicum of stability. The Assiniboine could now count as allies their former enemies, the Gros Ventres and the River Crow, but remained antagonistic toward the invading Sioux. The smallpox-decimated Blackfeet remained at war with the Crow but now seldom traveled east to the Musselshell. It was into this uneasy alliance system that Cornelius Lee and his friends attempted to build a town called Musselshell.

Frequent raids by frustrated tribesmen disrupted the trade between the Musselshell and the mining towns, and the expected freight business between those areas failed to develop. Other men attempted to establish other towns and other steamboat landings; Kerchival City, Hawley, Pouchette, Little Rocky, Leesburg, Musselshell City, Carroll

– all represented, for a brief time, the promise of future prosperity and stability. Names and places changed during this frontier period on the Missouri, but the results remained the same: fewer steamboats, smaller freight loads, and finally none at all. Abandoned log buildings fueled the last few steamboats, and the ever-changing channels of the muddy river eventually claimed the settlement sites.

The town at the mouth of the Musselshell was different from the others only in the fact that its life, faltering though it was, found its way into Lee's journals – and there he recorded it, faithfully, day by day. In addition to providing a rare literate glance of this developing period, Lee's journal provides a basis for a few general statements pertaining to this early Montana frontier.

Of the more than 200 individuals mentioned by Lee, some biographical material has been found for two-thirds of them. Most were male (only four women are mentioned), most were young (average age: 30.5 years), many died violent deaths either during the years covered by the diary or shortly thereafter. Only two were black, at least 30 were foreign born, 41 are identified as having come from northern states, 15 from the South, all were transitory, many lived with Indian women, some lived and traveled with Indian bands, most were woodcutters and wolfers, a few gained subsequent recognition, most faded from historical view. If there is one constant that runs through the daily entries, it is one of motion: men arriving, men departing, steamboats coming, steamboats going, Indians visiting and trading, Indians fighting; bison here today in great, grunting numbers and gone tomorrow, migrating antelope by the hundreds, no antelope for months on end.

Most of the men mentioned by Lee made their living by cutting and cording wood to sell to steamboats as they made their annual journey up river. Wood on the Missouri sold for $2.50 to $15.00 per cord, the price determined by type of wood, cottonwood, pine or cedar, and distance upriver from civilization. The wood yards above and below the Musselshell usually received $14.00 to $15.00 per cord, and a fully loaded steamboat required one-half cord per mile on its up-river trip. An industrious individual could make money. But it was perilous work. Joel Overholser, in his *Fort Benton*, wrote that 'Newspaper files yield numbers, more than 50 woodhawks killed in a decade, probably double and possibly three times as many unreported were slain by Indians'. (p 349)

Many individuals combined their woodcutting with 'wolfing,' an

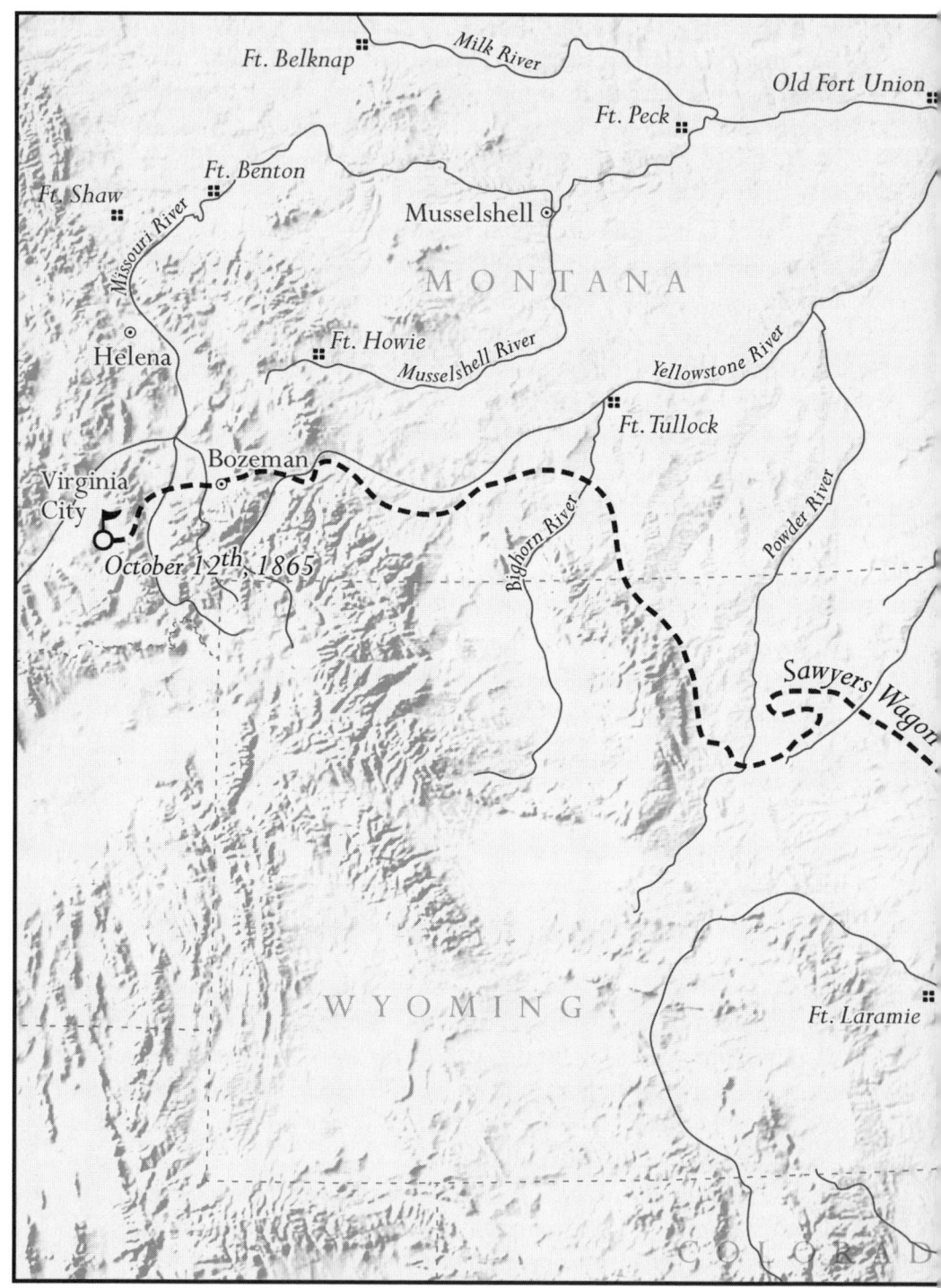

Map No. One – The route of the Sawyer Expedtion in 1865. Map courtesy Matthe

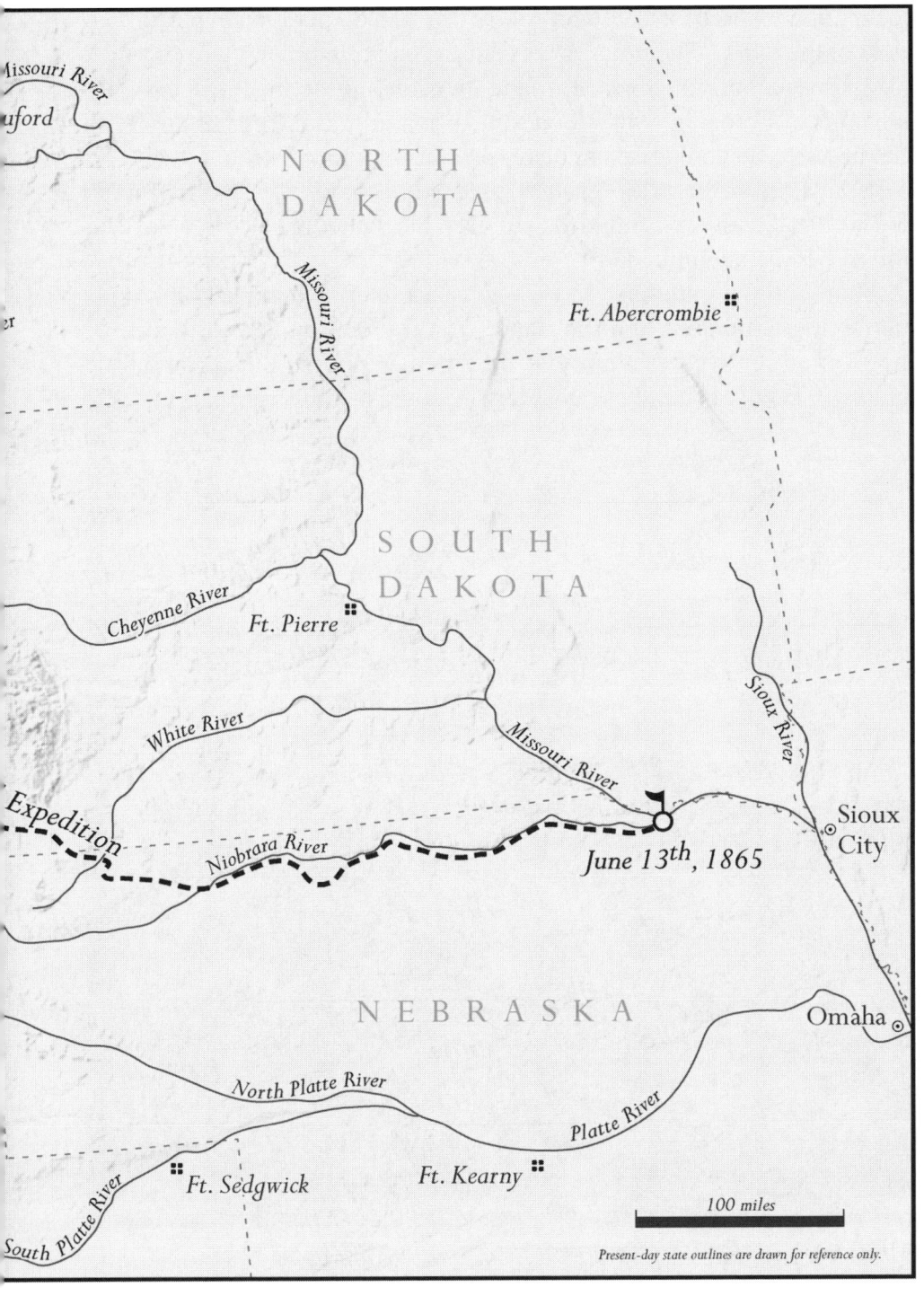

occupation wherein strychnine, selling for $16.00 per ounce, performed most of the work. The process was simple and effective. A wolfer killed a buffalo, partially skinned it, made incisions in the meat, mixed one-half ounce of poison with blood and sprinkled the flayed carcass with the mixture. He could reasonably expect his bait to kill 40 to 60 wolves. Wolf hides sold for $2.50 each at the trading posts. Of course, Indian dogs, other carnivores and birds suffered the same fate as the wolf. But only the Indian complained.

Late in the fall and early winter, antelope, bunched in bands numbering a hundred to a thousand, would group on the north side of the river and proved easy prey to the rifleman. Their skins brought the hunter 50 cents each and occasionally he could sell hindquarters and one

Lodge of Assiniboines, circa 1878-79. Photograph by W. E. Hook. Courtesy Montana Historical Society Research Center Photograph Archive, Helena, Montana.

loin for an equal price. Buffalo were usually available. Their tongues sold for .50 to .75 each, were pickled, dried, and shipped downriver. So numerous were they at times that tremendous waste resulted in their killing. One of Lee's contemporaries later wrote that the buffalo on the Musselshell were so plentiful that 'it was as if some Broddingnaggian pepper box had been heavily shaken over the immense plains and each grain a buffalo.' A Gros Ventres interpreter drew perhaps a better simile when he retorted: 'The country is one robe.'

As steamboat traffic waned, the Indians and their trade determined the success or failure of the attempt to build a town. An occasional group of Flathead and Pend d'Orielle appeared; one band of Arapaho came, but it was the Gros Ventres, the River Crow and the Assiniboine targeted by the traders. The invading Sioux bands: the Santee, Yankton, Yanktonai, Sisseton, and Wahpeton appeared all too frequently to fight, not trade.

The interaction of these tribal elements with one another and with the people settled at the mouth of the Musselshell constitute the basis of Lee's journal. Many of C. M. Lee's days – and even weeks – were uneventful, and a number of entries reflect the monotony. Other days, however, were filled to overflowing with an excitement, a very real danger and an enveloping fear that few modern persons living outside an active war zone have ever experienced. Tragedy is here, both human and environmental tragedy. Men kill one another, and the journal entries that report the event are matter of fact in tone; these men exterminate surprisingly large numbers of bison, antelope, and wolves. The journal describes 19th century entrepreneurs and laborers attempting to make a living in taming the wilderness, with little care or concern for the results of their taming. They were exploiters, pure and simple. They exploited the land and the animals, and the indigenous people. They even exploited one another.

Lee emerges from his journals as a strong, stalwart, steady type of fellow. There is little in the four years of daily entries that cast light upon his life prior to his coming to Montana Territory in 1865. He mentions writing to and receiving letters from his mother. He seldom missed making his daily entries and only infrequently do those entries stray from a reasoned discourse. Even when he dislikes one of his contemporaries, he refrains from writing malicious or injudicious remarks. He appears to have been relatively content with his life on the frontier and provides no evidence concerning his plans for the future. In relating the events as they develop, he avoids hyperbole and gives instead a straightforward accounting of daily activities, arrivals and departures, Indian attacks and attacks upon Indians, the numbers of buffalo and antelope killed and wounded; he comments upon his cats, dogs, and chickens that provided him with nuisance, comfort, and eggs. In the process of this careful accounting, he provides us with a close view of a frontier community at work, and finally, of a frontier community failing.

The journal reflects the transitory and turbulent nature of the time, a time when little remained static. A log cabin, constructed to shelter woodcutters from the elements, might become firewood to produce power for a steamboat a week or a month later. Friendly Indians, in to trade one day, might become attacking enemies the next. Bison and antelope and steamboats appeared and disappeared with the changing seasons, and everyone, Indian and white, was constantly on the move. Days of high excitement and peril were followed by weeks of tedium and deadening routine. And in the end, all of the diligence, hard work, and planning fail to forestall the building of railroads to the south or to increase the number of steamboats moving freight up and down the river.

While others came and departed, Cornelius Lee stayed. He made one trip downriver as far as Fort Peck and none to Fort Benton, Diamond City or Helena. He records the failure of an attempt to establish a lyceum, the scalping of Jennie, the big fight with the Sioux wherein Liver Eating Johnson earned his name, and activities that include baiting and skinning wolves, playing the fiddle for the amusement of the rough crowd around him, cutting wood, cutting hay, and alternately trading and skirmishing with Indians. He moved across the Missouri and constructed a two story log building for his home and a shop for his gunsmithing business; a year and a half later, he returned to the south side of the river and rejoined the small settlement there. He notes the numerous violent deaths of Indian and White with equanimity; the same emotion is reflected in his comments about ice in the river, snow in the air or mud underfoot. Visiting Indians can be welcome, bothersome or threatening. His attitude toward the Indian reflect both his time and his place. If the Indian was peaceful and seeking trade, he was good. If he was attempting to defend his homeland, he was the enemy, and as the enemy, any and all actions against him were justified. He uses the term 'squaw' and woman interchangeably to denote Indian women. When a steamboat passenger objected to a grisly display of skulls on the dock

The interior of a wolfer's cabin. #79-32. Huffman photo. Courtesy Archives and Special Collections, Mansfield Library, The University of Montana.

at Musselshell, Lee responds in a callous but customary fashion: '…we will presume that she has never had any near or dear friend murdered, mutilated, nor outraged, or she would not speak so slightly of the efforts of brave men to preserve themselves from a similar fate, nor of their justly feeling proud of their achievements.' (Journal entry, May 21, 1869). So much for the reasoning individual. He receives letters, he writes letters, he hunts bison and antelope, plants a garden, repairs guns, and on Saint Patrick's Day, 1872, he is 'Alone by myself. Sit and read, cook and eat, feed the chickens and the dog'. Many days were the same, but many were not, and Lee was aware of the changing nature of river travel, overland transportation, and steamboat cargo that reflected the rapid transformation of Montana Territory.

But it was the Indian people, the people of all the different tribes, who realized the greatest turmoil and change. The period following the demise of the little settlement at the mouth of the Musselshell saw a rapid, and unhappy transformation of all the Indian tribes along the Missouri.

Following the great Sioux War of 1875-1877, the federal government acted rapidly and – in retrospect – foolishly, in an attempt to force the assimilation and acculturation of these previously free people. First came restricted reservations: Fort Peck Reservation became the forced home of the antagonistic Assiniboine and Sioux; other Assiniboine were grouped with the Gros Ventres at Fort Belknap Reservation; the River Crow rejoined the Mountain Crow south of the Yellowstone River. Then came the destruction of the bison and forced reliance upon Agency rations. Boarding schools and absolute prohibition of cultural and religious activities followed as did starvation and death and Protestant and Catholic churches. Soon, even the smaller and much restricted reservations were thrown open to white settlement and former warriors and wives of warriors were told to become farmers and be happy.

In the following pages, Lee's words appear just as he set them down in his journal. None have been changed and only the undecipherable ones have been deleted. These omissions are marked by ellipsis and, due to Lee's penmanship, occur only rarely. The spelling of proper names has been standardized and punctuation inserted only where ambiguity resulted from its omission. I have allowed Lee's grammatical and spelling idiosyncrasies to stand where they do not interfere with comprehension. I have followed the principle of economy of annotation, providing identification of place names and some explication of historical references and allusions made by Lee. I have appended brief (sometimes very brief) biographies of many people mentioned in the diary. An asterisk following the first mention of a name indicates that some information about that person appears in the appendix.

Lee's activities and whereabouts between his last journal entry and 1875 remain unknown..I assume that he continued his daily record keeping in other journals, but no trace of either additional journals or Lee has been found. His name does not appear in any subsequent census reports of Montana or neighboring territories. The existing Sioux City newspapers contain gaps sufficiently large to allow Lee to have returned there unnoticed by the historical record. He apparently returned to Iowa – to Hardin County and became a dealer in farm machinery. He did not marry, but lived with his mother until his death on November 17, 1888, in Eldora, Iowa. Peter Koch's Life at the Musselshell, with Lt. James Bradley's Account of the Attempts to Build a Town at the Mouth of the Musselshell River – appended – offer contemporary and corroborative views of both the place and the time. They remain, but the site of the small settlement at the mouth of the Musselshell has disappeared. What was not washed into the Missouri River or cut up for steamboat fuel has been, since 1939, inundated by the waters backed up by the Fort Peck Dam.

The first of the two extant journals contain entries beginning on June 11, 1865, and ending on October 15, 1865. The journal pages are unnumbered in a 4 ½ inch by 7 1'2 inch buckram bound ledger and relate Lee's overland journey with the Sawyer's expedition. The second, and larger, (7 ½ inches by 12 ½ inches, 240 pages) contains the entries provided here: beginning on January 11, 1868 and ending abruptly on April 19, 1872. The 12 December 1871 is the last entry in ink; subsequent entries are in pencil. Lee also ran out of journal space: the last few entries are penciled on the back and front boards of the ledger.

Joan Hasencleaver, Hamilton, Montana, placed both the Lee journals and a typescript of them in the University of Montana Archives some years ago. She had been given them by Betsy Ross Jones of Bethesda, Maryland, who, in turn, had been given them to her by her father, Samuel Ross. None of the holders of Lee's journals knew what became of him.

166

1841

Tom Bogy & I rode very merry
staying the afternoon. Part at
night I went over to get some
antelope skins of Billy Harris
& returned by myself.

Feb 16th Thursday. quite cold & softly
snow nearly all day, part of
the time you could hardly see
across the river. the boys Brothers
started early this morning. Bill
Harris was to start up to Little
Rock this morning. But Pise
his pony back in the point yet
although he took it over the
river last night when I went
over. four men on that side
now & myself all alone on this
side. With the dog who to stand
guard. my Henry Rifle & plenty
of cartridges.

Feb 17th Friday. Moderate. The Boys my went
up the Muscle to the first crossing 5 miles
distant and returned. the traveling
being so slipery that it was almost
imposible for the oxen to travel
George & C.B. came over the river &
in the evening talking of going
down the river on the ice tomorrow
after some wolves for me. & some skins
for him of the others.

Feb 18th Saterday. Warm, rained a little in
the morning, evening after it quit to
blow, George & _____ down the river
and all hands ascended to the

about 8 o'clock. at by we had got down
Mr. Symms point & began to rain again
& all but himself concluded that best thing
we could do was to go into camp point &
I got wet ourselves I knew there to getting
the same day. accordingly we done so
getting 2 ½ ourselves it mile no 7 & 5 my
on our return at one & were the old had
an intent in. It had rained &
snowing near all day. The snow was
near all gone from the ice when we reached
home just two before sundown. & the water
was running into the ice very easy to the
Gulf. & the Muscle Shoal was quickly
and rising, having all now broken up the
ice by the Mississippi had long run the ice
at its mouth. Jeffry was well & was
I treated to a Bottle of Whiskey of ole we
that was speedy devoured among seven
men.

Feb 19th Sunday. Warm. snowed a little last
night. Cloudy all day. & raining to night

Feb 20th Monday. Warm. Muddy as the Devil
a lot of the Boys went up from our camp
to some Prairie to the right of the right of
the creek & killed 16 wolves. Indians
Spies of them. They also killed a Bull & two
bought the smell of Spring, wait.
when they went out. Judd & hill
Norris were nearly two days shooting away a
lot of Cartridges.

Feb 21st Tuesday. Warm. freezes little at night
Muddy or half during the day. 64.
Drew, Adams, Northup, Tyler & Long

Diamond City, Montana, circa 1870-1871. #946-724 Courtesy Montana Historical Society Research Center Photograph Archives, Helena, Montana.

THE DIARY

1868

January 11, 1868. Two years and three months ago tomorrow, I arrived at Virginia City1 in this Montana Territory. Today I am in Diamond City2, Meagher Co., Montana. I came to this place about the first of August 1866 and commenced the business of gunsmithing, in which I am still engaged. The winter of 1865 and 66 I spent in Helena. The fore part of the next summer, I spent in prospecting and running around over the country spending money. After finding I could not find any diggings that would pay nor purchase any without running too great a risk, I determined to go to work at my trade. Hearing that the gunsmith here was about to start for the states, I came and went to work. As I have had no adventures of special interest, I shall not be anymore explicit in reference to the past two year's experience, merely stating that I would have commenced this News dry but forgot to do so. The weather this winter has been very fine up to January 4th; during the night of the 3rd it turned cold and ever since it has been cold enough to freeze quicksilver. In fact, the temperature must have ranged from 35 to 45 below zero. Today it has moderated a little so that it is endurable.

January 12. Sunday. Still cold but not so severe as it has been. Nothing of particular interest. In the evening it snowed some.

January 13. Snowed but little last night. Snowing again in the morning. The weather still moderating, snow fell two or three inches deep. Mr. Lohmire, the mail carrier from here to Deep Creek on the Pony Express line from Helena to St. Paul via mouth of Musselshell, was in the shop today. He reported that he had been stopping at the post on the Musselshell the other side of the copper mines waiting for mail, but none came. As a party were going to start for the mouth of the Musselshell in a week or so, he came over here to make arrangements to go down with them and see what was the matter, whether there was no mail or if the Indians had killed the last rider that went down two months and a half ago and should have been back in four days.

January 14. Still good winter weather. Bill Puett* and two or three others started across the range yesterday hunting.

January 15. The weather about the same. I am getting seriously in the notion of going down to the mouth of Musselshell River on the Missouri, as there is a good prospect of a town being started there this spring that will grow rapidly and soon be a rival to Helena and be the permanent head of navigation, for all seasons. For seasons when the water is low, boats cannot get above this point but a short distance to where the rapids begin. Near the mouth of the Musselshell River is the best point for a town and a good landing. So far this winter there has been very little snow. Far less than the average up to this time for the last two or three years back.

January 16. Weather still about the same, if any difference a little more pleasant. Today I traded a double barreled rifle to Frank Bennett, one of the Musselshell party for a fine little mare valued at $65. This party is preparing to start down the Musselshell as I mentioned, to build a large warehouse on the Missouri. Their business here at present is to collect some feed for their horses and to hire a few hands

January 17. The weather about the same as yesterday. In the afternoon, rode up the gulch to where Jim Grubb* and his party were to work on their drain. Got home just at dark.

January 18. Nice and pleasant today. The Musselshell party started over the range today. Bruer* [Brewer] himself went over to Helena. He is the one that has the contract of building the warehouse at the mouth of the Musselshell on the Missouri.

January 19. Sunday. Nice and warm. Thawed considerable. Had my roan mare brought up from Stubbs Ranch and sent them both with Pat Dunlatty, for him to keep on his ranch. Late in the afternoon Doc Hardin* [Harding] and Miss Matilda Kline were married by Squire Garrigan* at Bracketts to the surprise and consternation of a host of admirers of the fair bride, who were hoping for her possession themselves, but lacked the courage to ask the momentous question and kept delaying until an outsider stepped in and bore away the prize. In the evening they were duly chivareed. When Doc came out like a man and invited the boys into the Montana Bakery and treated them handsomely.

January 20. Nothing of importance. The late marriage the universal topic of conversation among all parties.

January 21. Still fine winter weather.

January 22. Same as yesterday. The stage comes in on runners now, but not a great deal of snow.

January 23. Not much difference in the weather yet.

January 24. Snowing a little.

January 25. Snowed 3 or 4 inches last night. Windy today and the snow drifting. Greenwood* and Asa Newman over from Copperopolis3. They say they are getting out some splendid quartz now on the St. John Lode.

January 26. Sunday. Clear and still, but tolerably cool. Got a letter from H.E .Dimick,* St. Louis.

January 27. Cold nights, pleasant during the day.

January 28. Same as yesterday.

January 29. Moderate.

February 6. The weather has been very fine and pleasant during the last week. Last Thursday and Friday Dave Winner was here from Helena. He is about to start for St. Louis with the intention of bringing out a stock of goods to Benton or Musselshell in the spring. On Friday the quartz mill at New York Gulch was sold, at this place, at auction for debt. The masons in this place are making great preparations for a Ball on the evening of the 21st, which affords all the excitement there is to enliven the monotony of the days by causing little private dances occasionally to practice for the Grand Occasion.

February 3. I traded off my house and lot here in Diamond City to James Heard for a lathe, my intention is to leave this place this spring and either go to Benton or the mouth of Musselshell on the Missouri.

February 9. Sunday. Last Friday was very cold and stormy; snowing and blowing, today it is pleasant but still cold. Times are very dull here now, nothing being done in business or mining matters, except in the latter there are some drain ditches being run up the Main Gulch in which men are at work most all the time. The drain opposite here is doing well and has struck good pay, in fact did so last fall. At present Huntington and Heard are raising dirt to wash in the spring. The next drain is on bedrock but have not struck pay, but passed through some ground that prospected very well. The next one in which Jack Barger and Jim Grub* [Grubb] are interested, is also on bedrock and getting very good prospects. Still farther up there are more drains in operation with more or less favorable results, especially just above Blacktail Gulch they are taking out good or were before the cold weather closed them up.

February 10. Pleasant.

February 16. Sunday. Nice and warm; the last week has been very fine weather indeed for this season of the year. The snow is disappearing fast. No incident of any importance has occurred during the week. Everything is supremely dull. Today the place has quite a lively appearance, the day being very fine, a good many outsiders are in town.

At this point I neglected my journal entirely and am now writing it up from memory alone at Musselshell on the Missouri River, where I have built me a shop and am gunsmithing again. I left Diamond City sometime in March and went to Deep Creek4 and stopped with Davis* and John Fattig*. I had a couple of ponies and spent the time until about the 14th or 15th of April traveling around with them and Enos*, a half breed, and his family trapping and hunting. At the above date we were camped on Cammas Creek 15 or 20 miles from Diamond City. Leaving one of my ponies at camp, I went into Diamond, where I learned that old man Higgins* had that morning started 'cross the range for Musselshell. Remaining overnight, I started back to camp again the next morning and found great excitement in camp among the women and children for the men were all gone. I soon learned the cause from Enos's wife, who was a halfbreed and spoke English very well, that the Blackfeet had visited them during the night and got away with 8 horses, for Enos two, for Asa Newman 3, Henry Crittenden* and CM.Veits* one, and mine, that I had left. In a short time they all returned having followed the trail down Deep Creek as far as they thought prudent. Newman was on his way to Diamond and Veits had just started out for Musselshell with Higgins*. Higgins was also present, but only around a short time before I did. Camped overnight at the same place again and in the morning rolled out for Musselshell. I put my pack aboard the wagon and mounted my remaining horse, but Veits, having but one horse, was still worse off but with a resolute spirit he placed his luggage aboard the wagon and determined to foot it. Plenty of buffalo, had fine sport on the road hunting them. Our guide Jo Hayes* got off the course and took us way in on the Musselshell near to the right of the direct course. We struck the Mussel some 50 miles from its mouth, but had no idea where we were at the time. A party of Crow Indians came to us the same day that we struck the Musselshell River. We were well armed and had our weapons ready for instant use or I think they would have been very impudent. As it was they contented themselves with begging a little grub and trying to bluff me into a trade for my pony for an inferior thing that he rode but I failed to see it. Finally we succeeded in getting away from them, much to our relief you can bet. We were about two weeks coming down near the 1st of May. We had not been here but a short time before the Indians made a raid into the point below the place, while Jack Freebairn* [Freeborn] was herding and ran his horse off, mine, Elick Cameron's, and 3 or 4 mules for Higgins, and no Indians hit. No help for it though except you keep your horse tied up to a post. Still, it is anything but encouraging. At the time, a party of Whites were out hunting up the Musselshell and could have recaptured every horse, as they were cached in the brush close to where the Indians crossed with the horses, but were afraid to open fire for fear of being outnumbered, and allowed them to pass undisturbed. On the 6th day of May the ship Cora[6] arrived and unloaded a lot of her freight leaving it with Bruer [Brewer] and Whitson* in the building for the M.H. and F. Company [Montana Hide and Fur Company].

May 14. A detachment of soldiers, 100 men, under Col. Nugent* arrived from Camp Cook[7] in mackinaws. They camped just below town and soon began building a stockade, a hundred yards square. During this time I had been laying round doing nothing waiting for some favorable opportunity to build. Finding this was not likely to occur. Jack Freebairn [Freeborn] and myself concluded we would venture to cut a set of house logs for ourselves in the first point up the Musselshell, three quarters of a mile distant and get a span of Higgins' mules to haul them in with. We chopped one day and thought we would haul the next. So the next morning we started out with the team. This was on or near the ---- day of ------. We made one load all right, Jack going in with the team and I staying out and chopping. Jack had just arrived for the second load. Just as the wagon stopped and before Jack had stepped from the wagon, I thought I could hear some unusual noise, and looking round could see nothing. But seeing from the manner of the mules that they must see something, I quickly stepped to their side and through an opening in the timber I saw 5 or 600 yards distant a party of 10 or 12 Sioux on horseback and coming for us at full speed, a singing their ahi ayi, or battle song. Quickly telling Jack what I saw, I said, "Let's cut the mules loose." No sooner said, than done, he dropped the tuggs and I the neck yoke, and as it was impossible to get out of the point with the mules, as the devils were coming in so as to cut off retreat in that direction, we abandoned the mules and broke for the banks of the river 150 or 200 yards distant. Jack, being the most powerful man, besides having a little the start, arrived there in advance a very little and jumped down the bank 12 or 15 feet high, and I after him, where I proposed running along the stream under the bank. As I was picking myself up from rolling over after striking the ground, says Jack, "No, let's cross," and into the water he plunged without waiting for an answer. Of course, I had to follow suit, as it was not a time for standing on trifles. Jack had hardly got half way cross before he stepped into a hole and stumbled and to catch himself plunged his gun under water twice in succession. Fortunately the water was only a little over knee deep and about 15 or 20 yards wide. Jack had got within a few feet of the opposite bank and I had got about the center of the stream when Bang, Bang! went the Indians guns on the bank behind me, and I saw the water around Jack, at whom the shots were fired, as he came in sight first. Instantly wheeling where I was, I threw my rifle, a double-barreled one, up to my face in time to catch sight of a lot of dusky faces as they let fly their arrows not over 30 or 40 yards distant. Then hastily dropping out of sight, for my sudden hostile attitude had somewhat surprised them and confused their aim, as they all flew on all sides of me, except one which was fired with a deliberate aim by an Indian off to one side of the others, before I could bring my rifle round to him, then I was compelled to stoop almost into the water to allow the arrow to pass over my head. Raising, I fired quickly as the Indian was going out of sight, but without effect. Cocking the other barrel, I stood my ground while Jack passed over a narrow into the edge of the willows. The Indians, after falling back, fired several shots at Jack as he was going to the willows without touching him. I called to Jack to stop and show fight as that would let me out without getting shot in the back. After reaching the willows he did so by holding up his gun in anything but a backwoodsman's manner, but it answered the purpose and I reached the friendly willows in safety, where I recouped and we pulled off our boots which were full of water. While the Indians, the most of them, were breaking for camp at full speed for the stock there that were out grazing within a few hundred yards of the soldier's quarters, a few of them going up the Musselshell to cross above us. While I was standing in the water, I saw the mules running for home as hard as they could go and several Indians after them. While in the willows we were comparatively safe, as it is something that Indians seldom do, to venture into the brush after anyone and we were sure of assistance in a short time. Mighty glad we were to hear the firing commence at the soldier's quarters, thus we knew the Indians were engaged elsewhere. We had got half way down when a squad of soldiers and citizens made their appearance, going out as they supposed to hunt up our dead bodies. We soon made known our whereabouts and assured them that we were all safe and sound, then plunged in and waded back again among friends. Surgeon Hitz*, the fort surgeon, was among them and showed us his instruments, kindly intimating that he had expected the pleasure of offering his services to us, as a surgeon of great skill and ability. Thanking him kindly for his deep interest in our behalf, we politely assured him that we preferred to take his word for his scientific attainments than be obliged to submit to a personal demonstration. Although the Indians came within 300 yards of the stockade, none of them were killed. They got no stock but the two mules and harness they got from Jack and me, that they headed off and drove back.

In the other volume of this truthful narrative, the scene closes with an account of the somewhat wonderful escape of myself and comrade. Jack Freebairn, from a small party of hostile Sioux on the Musselshell a short distance up the river from the burg of Musselshell.

It was but a short time after that when they made another raid into the point below town and between the Musselshell and the Missouri Rivers after a couple of soldiers that were herding the government stock. The first notion we had of it was a terrific yelling by one of the soldiers followed by a few shots. A party of soldiers and citizens hastily rushed to the rescue but were too late to be of any assistance to the herders who were nowhere to be seen; in collecting the stock which the Indians had not disturbed, the body of one of the soldiers, a native of Canada, was found dead and several arrows sticking in it. Some in the hands and arms and some in the back. Those in the hands and arms were evidently shot while he had his gun to his face in the act of firing at them, disabling him so he could not use his gun, a breech loader, causing him to turn and run when they shot him in the back. The other body could be found nowhere. Tracks and a few drops of blood could be found down the bank and leading into the water Soldiers and citizens alike assisted in hunting for the missing one. His name was Cook8. This happened on ------.

During the early part of the summer old man Higgins shot himself through the arm by [page torn] ---- wing his Henry rifle from under his ------the arm, merely cutting open the sleeve until it passed the elbow where it entered and came out high up towards the shoulder, passing through the center of the arm, shattering the bone and inflicting a very severe wound. Being an old and grey-headed man, fears were entertained that he would never recover, but he was a man of great ----- and fortitude and finally recovered, but his arm was somewhat stiff when I last saw him in the spring of 1869 as he passed this place on a steamer on his way to Diamond City where he has a store. One of his attendants, while he lay wounded at this place, went out one morning just after a slight shower, to get a bucket of water and slipped into the river and was drowned. He was a Dane or Norwegian and could not swim.

One Sunday a party who was indulging somewhat in drink, and were about to get up a shooting match to see who was the best shot, when Buck Barker's* gun went off accidentally and almost instantly killed Frank Bennett. This occurred in the early part of May before the arrival of the soldiers. He was buried on the bench above the place and was the first of a burial place for this place.

No more desperate adventures occurred near here during the summer. After killing the soldiers, the Indians left us undisturbed. They attacked a couple of men near Fort Hawley9 above here, but they got

The busy port of Fort Benton, Montana Territory, photo taken circa 1878-79 Photograph by W.E. Hook. Courtesy Montana Historical Society Research Center Photograph Archives, Helena, Montana.

the worst of that. John Johnson* and Henry Keiser* (were the men). Johnson got wounded in the leg, but they shot and killed four or five of the devils, and they let them alone after that. Johnson was brought down here where he received medical attendance from Surgeon Hitz.

During the summer Col. Nugent, the commanding officer here, made himself quite contemptible and offensive to the citizens by a very arbitrary exercise of his authority in expelling several citizens from the place and vicinity. John Kelly* he drove from his woodyard 'cross the river from this place for an alleged complicity in whiskey trading to the soldiers. Also at different times a Scotchman named Kennedy,* Waring*[Warring], and Jack Brown*. He also arrested and placed under guard for some time a German, Fred Watters. Finally, I think he was served notice from headquarters that such a line of conduct was not agreeable to them, as he changed his tactics and became quite a gentleman in his intercourse with the citizens here.

September 5. The Colonel and his command started up the Missouri for Camp Cook again, cordelling their supplies in a mackinaw. Col. George Clendenin, Jr.* and Major J.S. Bruer also accompanied them, the two latter intending to return again soon.

I shall endeavor on the following page to give an abstract of the arrivals and departures of the steamboats at this place during this summer, as the navigation of the Missouri is becoming quite an object the last few years.

September 6. Sunday. At this date I am determined to once more begin to keep dates correctly and to write my Journal daily as it occurs. How long I will persevere in the practice I cannot promise but will make the beginning with a good will. I might as well state at this point as any other that I have succeeded in getting me up a substantial log cabin which I now occupy as a gunshop and boarding house. Albeit I am not only shopman but landlord and lady and the only boarder. But that is nothing after you get used to it.

September 7. Busy at work building a bastion around the door of my shop for protection in case of an attack by Indians as we are not very strong since the departure of the soldiers.

September 8. Fine weather. Completed my bastion. In the afternoon some Indians arrived from down the Musselshell: three bucks and three squaws. One of the bucks was a Sioux, but expressed himself very friendly towards the whites, said peace had been declared and the Sioux had taken the white man by the hand. Some of the boys at first were determined to shoot him but concluded not to do so. At dusk they moved down in the point and camped for grass for their horses. Capt. Andrews* and Whitson* are busy at work on the M.H. and F. Co. stockade and one of their own, but progress slowly. James McGinnis* is busy at work on a stockade around the back portion of Clendenin's buildings. In a few days we will be in a condition to stand a severe attack from any party of hostile Indians that are likely to be here.

September 9. Today the Indians crossed the river saying they were going to Milk River and started off in that direction. Shortly after they left a party of our boys started down the river on the other side with a team to kill some meat, intending to be out all night. They soon discovered by the trail that the Indians had not gone as they said they would, but paying no more attention to it they passed on. When arriving at the hunting ground some miles further they found the trail where the party had passed into the point where they intended to hunt, and also seeing the game running in different directions, a sure sign of some unusual presence. The boys called a halt to consult. While doing this an elk made his appearance a short distance off in the edge of the brush. Johnson dropped him in his tracks with his never failing Spencer. Thinking discretion the better part of valor, they hastily loaded the meat and returned home where they arrived about 9 o'clock. About sundown a mackinaw arrived loaded with men from the mines. All were strangers to me. A couple of them are for this place to take charge of the M.H. and F. Co. establishment. Their names are R.R. Gates* and W. Thompson* John Fisher* succeeded in killing an old bull 'cross the Musselshell this evening late, but it was poor.

September 10. Quite a frost this morning; the first this season here. A stray horse came in today from up the Musselshell. He has a couple of slight bullet wounds in his neck, has a government brand on, and is in fine condition. A party of wolfers left here some time toward the end of last month, for whom considerable anxiety is felt. They intended to go up the Musselshell or out to the Black Butte10. Our new storekeepers are busy taking an invoice today. The mackinaw is also laying over.

September 11. Our esteemed fellow citizens W. Jenkerson* and Doc Gleason took their departure down the river on the mackinaw today. Peace go with them. The wind blew violently today from the west all day. Fisher and Keiser brought in 6 wolf skins today that they killed by poisoning the buffalo Fisher killed.

September 12. This morning it was pleasant and calm. In the

afternoon it "blowed" like the devil from the north. I am still busy at my house preparing for cold weather. George Grinnell* killed a large pelican today in the river. They are a curious looking beast – 8 feet and 3 inches across the wings from tip to tip.

September 13. Sunday. Snowing a little all day.

September 14. Cloudy and chilly; rained a little. Snow nearly all gone.

September 15. Snowing again this morning, cold and cloudy all day. The boys on the other side killed three buffalo bulls on McGinnis' point today. Busy today making me a stove. In the evening set it up. Did first rate considering it was not finished.

September 16. A little more pleasant. A herd of buffalo passed up the bottom close by today. Johnson, Fisher, Keiser, and McGinnis went out to try their hand. Killed one and crippled two or three others. Finished my stove. It is very pleasant these long, cold evenings.

September 17. The first ice of the season this morning. The M.H. and F. Co. are at work this morning on their stockade for the first time since the new arrivals.

September 18. Cool. Rained a little in the afternoon. Johnson killed a blacktail up in the hills this morning, says the hills are covered with their tracks. Fisher and Keiser, or as Fisher with a patronizing air calls him "the boy," went 'cross the Musselshell to put up some hay they cut yesterday. They were frightened by the running of a big herd of buffalo that they could not see in the brush close by them. Thinking it was Indians they cached themselves. They thought it was too late to go to work before they discovered their mistake. Then they went hunting, but were unsuccessful.

September 20. Sunday. Warm and pleasant yesterday and today. A mackinaw and a couple of small boats passed down the river today. Most of the men were from Benton.

September 21. Cold and windy last night but several of the boys went down to McGinnis' point today to hunt some bear that were in the habit of coming to eat off the buffalo carcasses there. Johnson says that when nearly there, he and Pomp Dennis* went ahead to see how matters were, found everything still and quiet, no bear there, then called the rest all up and had them quietly take their positions. They waited but a short time before a bear made his appearance, but thinking from his position the other boys did not see it, he was waiting for a better shot when bang went Pomp's gun and away went Pomp in an opposite direction and bang, bang, went Ed Sharp's* [Schaff] and Warring's guns. Both after firing their guns retreated in the same hasty and energetic manner that Pomp had. By this time, the noise and confusion had brought several bear out of the brush in plain sight, and he, Johnson, getting a fair aim at one with his Spencer, fired and brought him down, but jumped up again and ran for the brush, when a second shot brought him down again. Still he reached the brush and escaped. These bear will nearly always when shot, whether badly hurt or not, fall down, and if an old bear, woe to the man that is in sight and reach that he can see. They will invariably go for a person. On looking around, Johnson says that all of his party that were visible were up in the trees, or getting up, as fast as possible, and with some difficulty he persuaded them to come down as the bear had all left.

September 22. Moderate during the afternoon. Warring, one of the bear hunters, came in and told me his side of the story. He says that after they got there and saw no signs of the bear, they all thought that they would not be apt to come, so each man strayed where chance led him without any attempt at concealment. He, himself, very deliberately setting his gun against a tree, proceeded to pick and eat gooseberries that grew in abundance there. Sitting down on a log to take it perfectly easy, he had sat but a short time before the crackling of the brush aroused him and warned him of the approach of some huge animals. At the same time the other boys, judging from their actions were laboring under some strong excitement. Anxious to discover the cause of all this apparent panic he seized his gun and carefully raised himself up to see over the low brush in which he was sitting, and the first thing that attracted his attention particularly was a bear, who had likewise come to a perpendicular position and was taking a deliberate survey of the situation of affairs, and evidently not yet anticipating any danger. Before he, Warring, could make up his mind whether to open the fight or fall back in good order, bang went somebody's gun and down went the bear squalling and rolling like all creation. And almost simultaneously with the downfall of the first, a second one and still closer, raises mysteriously to an upright position to see what was to be seen. Thinking that to retreat now would be hopeless, he raised his gun and fired with a hasty and uncertain aim at the center of the bear's body between the shoulders, and down went Mr. Bruin making the woods reverberate with his terrific cries. Without waiting to see fully the effects of his shot, he, with more haste than grace, lay down his gun and began the ascent of a small tree that stood convenient. After getting up a short distance, he turned his head to take a survey of the situation and discovered the third and largest bear of all. At the same time he saw Johnson still on the ground in a belligerent attitude and R.R. Gates; the latter was like himself industriously engaged in climbing a small tree that stood temptingly convenient. But what afforded the greatest relief was the discovery that Gates was much nearer the ground and consequently more likely to receive Bruin's first advances. So, feeling somewhat more assured of personal safety, although at the possible sacrifice of a friend, he confidently called out to Johnson to shoot, give him hell, and other encouraging expressions. Johnson shot and down went the bear, but jumped up again and ran off into the brush where the others had gone. After a short consultation of all hands they concluded that bear meat was not very good eating after all, and as one of the party sagely remarked, the damn bear might have reinforcements a short distance off in the brush. So they returned bootless and somewhat crestfallen at their bad luck. Warring says that they look so big and savage that a man can't face them if he wants to if his legs have any regard at all for the personal safety of his body.

September 23. Pleasant. Today the steamer, *Fanny Barker*11, passed down the river, the last boat of the season. She had a good many passengers, among them I saw A.W. Puett.* She passed about 9 o'clock in the forenoon; stopped only a few moments. I got a letter from mother dated August 2nd, been since August 29th in getting from Helena to here.

September 24. Rainy; heavy frosts every night now. A double decker mackinaw passed down; some thirty on board and some few women and children.

September 27. Sunday. The last few days have been nice and warm like Indian summer. Quite smoky today. The party of wolfers arrived all safe and sound. They succeeded in getting some 320 wolf skins and three bear skins, and a few antelope skins. They were troubled a good deal with bad weather, keeping their bedding wet and making it impossible to dry their skins readily, but all kept well and hearty most of the time. They were near or at the foot of Black Butte. Right at the foot on the east side they found a spring of good running water, where always before it was supposed there was none. A few days after their arrival at their hunting ground they had a slight skirmish with a small party of Indians, whom they supposed to be Blackfeet – 17 in number. When they approached within hailing distance the boys ordered them to stop and send one of their number up to talk. They paid no attention and continued to advance, when a shot was fired over their heads pretty close to them which caused them to scatter and run in every direction, firing their revolvers in return. The boys then began firing in earnest with their Henrys and Spencers but with no other effect that they could see except to cause some tall dodging. One of them got behind a hill at long range and fired a few shots with what appeared to be a Springfield rifle, but did no damage.

September 28. Pleasant as usual. Today the Crow Indians arrived from Peck12. They crossed the river below and camped on the other side. They say they had a big fight with the Sioux three days ago near what is called Round or Black Buttes13. They lost one man and killed some 20 of the Sioux, but lost over a hundred head of horses. The Crows are very much afraid of the Sioux and are going to the little Rocky Mountains14 to get away from their range. Several white men came with them: Jake Leader,* Tom Stewart,* and Baker.* The first was the Crow talker of Fort Hawley for a long time.

September 29. Pleasant. Every nook and corner is full of Indians today, so you can scarcely turn around, and goodbye to anything lying round loose. Oh what inveterate beggars; it beggars description!

September 30. Pleasant. The Indians still round picking up and begging. Although at peace with the whites some of them are very insulting and overbearing. Weapons have been shown several times on both sides, but more for a Buncombe than anything else. Their chiefs are talking to them several times a day to keep them quiet. They keep me quite busy repairing their guns and pistols. The former are generally smooth bore muskets and flint locks. They use a gun or pistol as though there was no such a thing as breaking it. Good robes are scarce among them yet as it is most too early in the season.

October 1. Pleasant. The Crow camp left today, all except a few bummers and squaws that are living with Jake Leader and Tom Stewart. As soon as the camp was gone, some of the squaws mounted the highest places they could find and began to look for Sioux that they expected would be after the Crow camp. But let them come, we are pretty well prepared for a fight. The stockades are nearly all completed and my house is well supplied with loopholes and in short rifle range of all the others that are so situated as to protect each other. October 2. Pleasant. Lohmire and John Cochran* arrived today from Thompson Gulch15. They came across the country on foot with a pack horse. Had no trouble or difficulty on the road until they arrived near Fort Hawley where they struck a party of Blackfeet who let them pass after begging the most of their grub without offering any violence. Times are very dull in the mines they say.

October 3. Pleasant. A mackinaw arrived today, eight men on board bound for the States. They left Benton late last Wednesday, ran all night part of the time.

October 4. Sunday. Pleasant, but smoky; in fact, it has been more or less smoky all this fine weather. Henry McDonald* and Add Armstrong* started out wolfing on foot with two pack horses, to be gone 12 or 15 days in the direction of the Black Butte, wherever they could find wolves.

October 6. Wet and rainy today.

October 8. Pleasant. Hauled a little wood today. Tabor* from Little Rocky16 arrived today in a small boat with two men. He tells a big story of knocking down 7 Indians with an axe handle; maybe so and maybe not as he is an unconscionable liar. In the evening a large mackinaw arrived bound for the States. James Heard of Diamond City was aboard her, he says he is disgusted with this country.

October 9. The mackinaw lay over last night and I sent a letter to Mother by Heard. Col.Clendenin is expected every day with his winter supply for men and Indians from Fort Benton.

October 10. Reports have been circulating for several days of Indians having been seen lurking around, which is more than probable. Fred Walker and Baker came in today from down the river on the other side and say they saw 18 or 20 Indians last evening on foot, evidently a war and stealing party of Siouxs or Assiniboins. These men were wolfing down there and concluded they had better suspend operations for a few days.

October 11. Sunday. Pleasant. Tabor, Ichivy,* [Ivey] a wood yardman with Fisher and Ed Ayers,* left here today to go to Little Rocky – all carrying heavy packs.

October 13. Moderately cool. Another mackinaw today, three men on board. They came all the way by river from the Beaver Head, had their boat hauled round the falls17 which cost them $15.00. Large mackinaws they charge as high as $60.00.

October 14. Pleasant. Col. Clendenin arrived today from Benton. He left here when the soldiers did. Lt Canfield* also arrived from Camp Cook with two flat boats loaded with bacon mostly, and a guard of 20 men, on his way to Fort Buford18, I believe, where the Indians ran off all their stock. No news of importance except of high prices in general and of provisions in particular.

October 15. Cool nights lately, but pleasant during the day. Lt. Canfield shoved out bright and early this morning. During the day McDonald and Add Armstrong arrived from their wolfing trip. They got some 40 skins and were out only 30 or 40 miles towards the Black Butte. Saw no signs of Indians.

October 17. Pleasant. George Grinnell started for the Milkriver Agency19 today in company with a party of wolfers from the other side who intend to stop on Beaver Creek. Two more mackinaws today – one the largest of the season, some 30 odd persons on board. The other a small one, only 3 men. The first passed early in the morning, the other towards night.

October 18. Sunday. Pleasant. Capt. Andrews was quite sick last night, delirious part of the time; is better today.

October 20. Still pleasant. Two wolfing parties started out this morning for the Judith Basin20, to be gone some six weeks. Capt. Andrews, C.R. Veits, and Henry McDonald with a wagon and one yoke of cattle is one party. Lohmire, Add Armstrong, and John Johnson with a span of horses is the other party. The two parties will bed together for protection in case of Indian difficulties. R.R. Gates, Pomp Dennis, and Joe Martin went off with them intending to go to Helena; to be gone some six weeks or two months.

October 21. Pleasant. Went hunting in the Hills today with Williams.* Found three dead wolves which we appropriated the skins.

October 23. Very pleasant. Plenty of antelope around now.

October 25. Sunday. Pleasant as usual. Went hunting with three others on the other side of the Missouri. Saw only a few blacktail deer.

October 26. Fine day. The trees are about bare of leaves now. A petition is being circulated here to send to the P.M.General in regard to the new Post Route now advertised from Abercrombie21 to Helena. The petition prays for the route to pass through here and across the county to Helena by Diamond City.

October 27. Fine as usual and clear of smoke. Most of the fine weather has been smoky.

October 28. Jake Leader and Tom Stewart went out hunting up the river on this side, while Warring and Whitson* started up on the other side. During the day a couple of Arapaho Indians came in on the other side. What they are after no one knows. About sundown Jake and Tom returned and said there were Indians on the 4th point above here. They heard considerable shooting and a few Indians, then concluded they did not want any fresh meat.

October 29. Fine. Warring and Whitson came in after dark; killed an elk on the 4th point above on the other side, but saw no Indians except the two here whom they met shortly after starting out.

October 30. Fine. Williams, who is cutting wood in the hills, says that some Indian was watching him today, and at noon he swore he would kill him if he was there, but he was not there so he was not killed.

October 31. A little cool last night. Busy daubing my house perfectly tight.

November 1. Warm. Went hunting cross the river. Killed an antelope.

November 4. Pleasant. George Grinnell, Dennis Halpin* and Charley Rogers arrived on the other side.

November 7. Snowing a little. Went hunting with three others on third point below on the other side. Killed two blacktail just at dark and camped; had a cold, damp sleep in the snow.

November 8. Sunday. Snowed a little all day. Had a big tramp, but killed nothing; returned towards night and stayed at George Grinnell's.

November 9. Cool, ice running in the river this morning and feels decidedly like winter might be approaching slowly.

November 10. Still colder. Went hunting 'cross the Musselshell with Williams, killed a deer, saw a good many.

November 12. Warmer. Snow nearly all gone; slush ice in the river.

November 13. Thawing. Col. [Clendenin] and Tom Stewart killed some buffalo on the other side of the Musselshell.

November 14. Cool. McGinnis, Tom, and a lot of squaws went out to get the buffalo meat killed yesterday. In the afternoon Jim Wells* arrived in a mackinaw from Benton with provisions for George Grinnell and some stuff for Col. from Power* at Benton. They were barely able to get here for the ice.

November 15. Sunday. Cold. Plenty of ice in the river. McGinnis and party arrived about noon with what meat the wolves had left of their buffalo. Several men came down with Wells to get work here.

November 17. Cool. Wells, Tabor, and Dexter,* who came down with Well on the14th all started for the Milk River Agency, also George Grinnell and Ed Schaff, for the Pouchette[22] with a team after meat. In the afternoon the wolfing parties that went to the Basin arrived, but only got 140 skins among them. The buffalo and wolves were leaving they said when they got there.

November 18. I and Williams went out to see a bait we had put out; found only two wolves 'cross the Musselshell in the hills. Williams killed a deer.

November 20. Cool. Col. [Clendenin], Veits and Henry McDonald started out on horseback to put out some baits.

November 22. Sunday. Cool. McDonald and Veits returned today.
November 24. Cool. Pomp Dennis arrived last night. Bruer [Brewer], Gates, and the rest of his party are at Little Rocky where their boat is "froze" in the ice. Pomp reports good times in the mines. In the afternoon Capt. Andrews, Veits, McDonald and Secord* a went down the river to cut hay; rather frosty for hay. George [Grinnell] and Ed Schaff arrived late with a load of meat.

November 26. Moderate. In the afternoon Bruer, Gates, Joe Martin, and two strangers arrived. They footed it from Little Rocky where they stored their stuff.

November 27. Pleasant. Last evening Veits and McDonald missed their horses. This morning in company with a half dozen of the boys they discovered, by their trail, that the Indians had got them. They followed the trail onto Crooked Creek Ridge then gave it up as a bad bargain as they were likely near Black Butte.

November 28. Warm. I forgot to mention that on the 25th we had quite a spirited mass meeting in regard to destroying the soldiers' stockade23. It is considered as very dangerous to the general safety in case of an Indian attack.

November 30. Pleasant. The river is still clear of ice at this point. Veits and F. Smith* started down the river in a boat on a hunt. Fred Watters and Bill Norris* lost their pony a few days ago on the Pochette, Fred having him out at the time. Saw no Indians.

December 1. Pleasant. Bruer and party started up the river. Think the river would be clear of ice above by this time.

December 2. Snowed a little last night. Bruer and party returned forenoon. Later F. Smith and Veits returned, having killed a couple of blacktail and a whitetail.

December 4. Moderate. Veits and Smith went down the river again to hunt.

December 5. Snowed a little in the morning.

December 10. A little snow on the ground. Today a couple of white men and a Mountain Crow24 squaw came in down the Musselshell with 5 ponies. They came from the Mountain Crows, I think. Their names are Davis* and Charley Morrison.*

December 20. Sunday. Quite cool. The Missouri is still open at this point. Last Monday a party went up the – Musselshell with a team after meat. Bruer, Capt.Andrews, Whitson, Veits, Smith, and Gus Tyler*; gone three days and killed four bulls and a couple of blacktails. No news from the outside world, to change the monotony of things nor any Indian alarms. All the woodchoppers and wolfers are getting quite careless. A couple of inches of snow.

December 27. Sunday. Quite cold. The river blocked up here on the 23rd. On the 24th it broke up again and moved down the river some distance. On the 25th it was all tight again except the channel which is still open. To cross you have to go to the mouth of the Musselshell. There it is closed across. Christmas passed off very quietly, a little tanglefoot was destroyed on the other side; nothing serious resulted from it.

December 31. Snowed all yesterday and last night. Today the 5 horses belonging to Davis and Morrison are missing.

1869

January 1. Cold. New Years passed off very quietly. Jennie* [Smith] brought me a piece of peach cobbler that she made that was far excellent and made me think of home and feel lonesome. Davis and Morrison struck out after their horses.

January 10. Sunday. Moderate. A few days ago Davis and Morrison returned without any horses. They followed the trail to where the small party that stole their horses joined the main party.

January 17. A party of wolfers, nine in number, arrived here today from Black Butte with 10 horses, a wagon, and two yoke of cattle. The Flathead Indians25, they say, are in the vicinity of the Black Butte, but they are friendly. Party all left for the Black Butte again, except Johnson, the man that owns the team. I was down the river hunting with Cash Veits during the week between the 10th and 17th, but had poor, poor luck; killed only an elk and a few antelope and left them lay as they were too far off. On the 13th I came across Jim Wells from Milk River, lately from Peck who told me that the party that had started from Milk River some time ago to try and raise a lot of goods from a sunken steamboat26 below Peck had been attacked by some three hundred Sioux ten miles below Peck and four of them killed and one severely wounded, and the balance barely escaped with their lives by getting into the brush. Wells himself being one of the number says he has hardly got over the scare yet. W.H. Tabor was one of the killed. During my absence, a party of Crow Indians were in here and succeeded in getting into my house bastion, but were discovered before they did any mischief except to steal a little meat.

February 3. Fine weather now. Clendenin, Capt. Andrews, F. Smith, and Warring are all putting up ice. No Indian alarms at all.

February 4. Bruer, Veits, Williams, Gus Tyler, and Whitson started out to the Basin to wolf with ox team. Whitson intends going through to Helena.

February 5. Cold today. Provisions are scarce here now and high: flour from $20 to $25 per sack, coffee 65 cts. a pound, sugar 50 cts., bacon 50 cts., and salt 25 cts., and game scarce close by.

February 6. In the evening the Lyceum, which has been operating here for two or three weeks, met and had their usual amount of spouting and recrimination.

February 11. Very pleasant the last few days. Add Armstrong started for Benton.

February 12. Today an ox got into an air hole in the river and came very near going under. It belonged to the Norwegian, Johnson. Wells and Grinnell are busy nowadays putting up ice.

February 13. Cool. The Lyceum failed tonight on account of a game of freeze out for a can of fruit; consequently I presume it has died a natural death.

February 14. Sunday. Valentine day; nice and warm. According to the old adage I fear we will have some bad weather yet.

February 19. Been nice and warm lately. Snowed and "blowed" furiously this morning, soon quit, and this evening is cold as Greenland.

February 21. Sunday. Still cold.

February 22. A little moderate; trying to snow. Scott and Snider of the Black Butte wolfing party came in today and say they lost their horses a few days ago by the Indians, and think that Davis here was with the Indians, but they are mistaken. In the evening Capt. Andrews and Gates went down to the third point to arrest Davis on suspicion. They brought him up, but he could easily prove himself innocent.

February 23. Moderate and snowed a little.

February 25. Gates, Warring, Joe Martin, and Bill Norris started for Helena and Diamond City today, also Johnson. Scott and Smith returned to their camp. Martin and Norris packing their blankets on their back; Johnson asking too much to haul them on the wagon.

February 27. Pleasant lately. Hauled some coal today I found up in the hills some time ago.

March 6. Pleasant. Went with Pomp Dennis with a team to the Pochette on the second and got back last night. It turned cold the first night out and remained so until today. Killed six buffalo and antelope. Brought only two of the buffalo in; too cold to hunt.

March 7. Sunday. Pleasant. Capt. Andrews, Smith, Howard, and Fisher started up the river to get out pine wood.

March 11. Snowed last night, most all disappeared during today. Jim McGinnis and I took a circuit on the other side of the river after some bulls that came in sight, but only wounded some of them. In the afternoon a Crow war party of 15 came in from above.

March 12. Warm. Capt. Andrews returned today from above. The Crow party still around, a perfect nuisance.

March 14 . Sunday. Cold as Greenland. The Crow party left today.

March 16. Thawing a little today. Bruer, Veits, Williams, and Gus Tyler got back today. Had poor luck, only got two wolves; none in the country where they were so thick last fall.

March 18. Warm. Started up the Musselshell after meat in company with Clendenin, Bruer, Veits, Gus Tyler, and Jack Masterson, the bullwhacker. About two miles up killed a bull and discovered somebody coming towards Musselshell that had the appearance of being a white man, but could not attract his attention at all although in plain sight not over 500 yards distant, and did not wish to fire upon him. Finally concluded he was some crazy white man as his tracks showed he was wearing boots. We dubbed a small branch putting in here as Surprize or Crazy Man's Creek. Went a few miles farther and camped.

March 19. Warm. Saw no buffalos. Started down the river again. Killed four more bulls today. Camped near a bait of Veits where he found 40 dead wolves, which he and Bruer began to operate upon. Rained a little on us last night.

March 20. Warm; rained a little on us again. Returned home and found that our crazy man was no other than the Norwegian, Johnson, who started for Diamond City the 25th of last month with Gates and

This 3-D presentation of the Mussellshell River at the point where it joins with the recorded in this book took place. Note the harshness of the terrain along

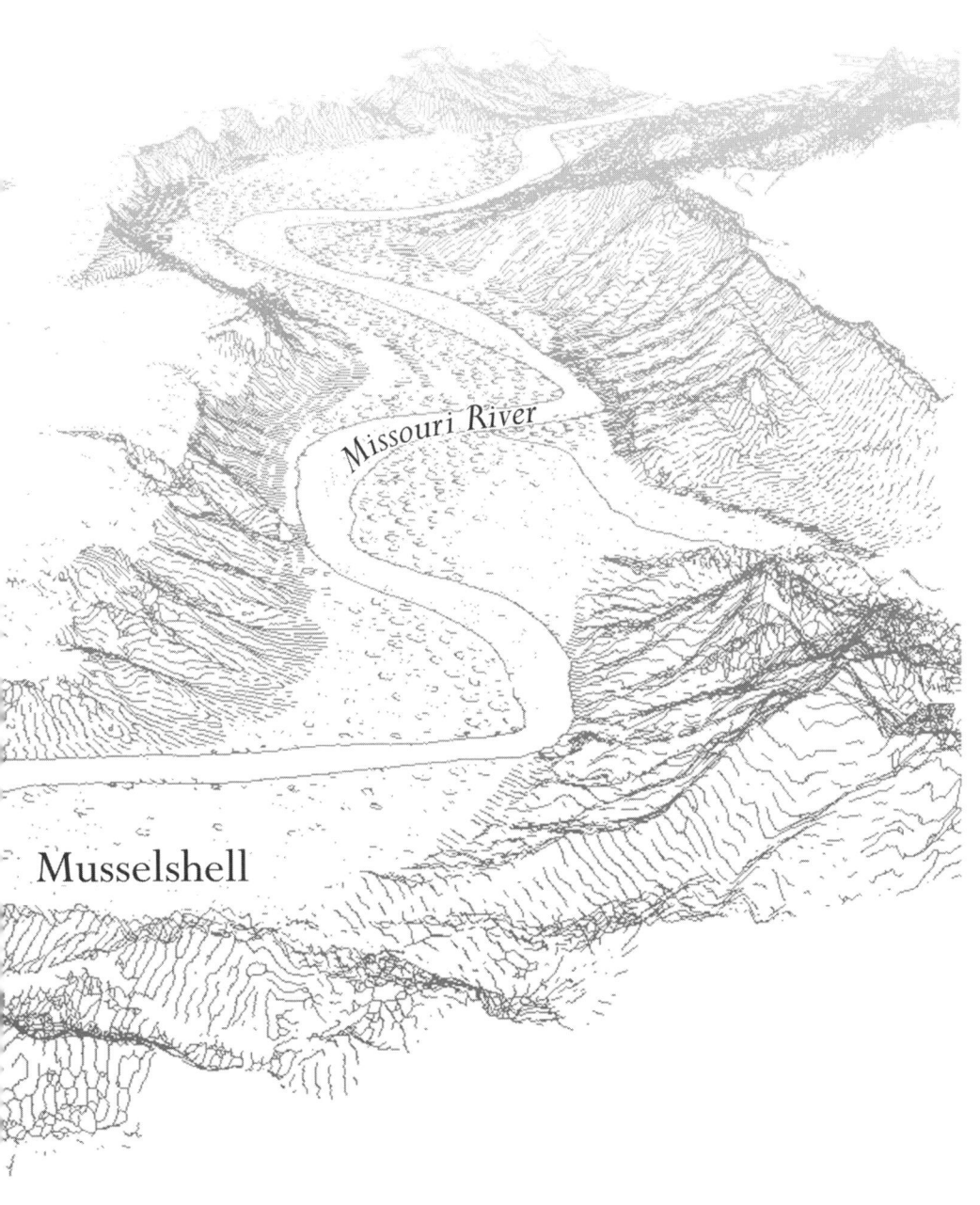

*...uri River gives one a birds-eye view of the landscape around the area the events
...er course – known as the Missouri Breaks. Map courtesy Matthew Hampton.*

party. It appears that the first or second night out, Johnson lost his cattle and the whole party shouldered their blankets and went to the Black Butte wolfing party. When Johnson stopped, the balance went on through. We also found the whole of the wolfing party in here, having had a fight with 5 or 75 Crows, killing and scalping one of them, they made the best fight they could until dark, then left everything and came in here, feeling mighty hostile, you bet, towards the Crows whom they think stole their horses also. As near as I can learn, the fight was mostly caused by a Flathead half breed in the party of wolfers that the Crows want to kill, as they and the Flatheads kill each other whenever they can.

March 21. Warm. Today the ice went out of the channel of the river. Early in the morning, parties crossed on the ice and by noon it was all open.

March 22. Warm. Three teams and 6 men were busy today hauling logs from the first point up the Musselshell. One team, Jack Masterson, Tom Stewart, Jake Leader, and Charley Morrison were out in the timber. Capt. Andrews, with his team, was just coming in loaded about half a mile distant, and Bruer, with his team, was going back empty a few hundred yards away from the stockades, and everybody laying around heedless of danger. Jennie, the only white woman in the place, and two Crow squaws were out about as far as Bruer's, but in low place to one side of the road where they could not be seen from here, on their way in. A party of 4 or 5 Sioux Indians on foot raised their yell on the hill to the right of the road about half a mile distant, and rushed for the teams and women. I was just coming out of the shop with a loaded gun to fire at a target as the alarm was raised; then the Indians were about half way down the hill, and scattered in every direction. Bruer had abandoned his team and was making good time in the direction of the M.H.&F. Co. stockade. Capt. Andrews' team was apparently standing still, while he was making towards the Musselshell River closely pursued by 10 or 12 devils that came in behind him. While the women could not be seen, Bruer, I saw fire a couple of shots with his Henry then disappeared behind the stockade. I rushed back into the shop and seized some more ammunition and a couple of revolvers. By this time nearly every man in the place was out with his gun. Some of the Indians were within 300 yards of my house and were scattered all over the bottom. One of the squaws had received a shot through the thigh, and Jennie, in stopping to assist her to her feet had received a shot through the neck that stunned her and had been scalped not over two hundred and fifty yards distant. As a lot of us passed behind my house, we met the two squaws coming in at the top of their speed, but none of us had any idea of Jennie being there. We saw the Indian raise up and strike at something with his coup stick, then break and run as Veits opened on him with his Henry rifle, while I began firing at some across the flat. At the same time the firing became general from all quarters and the men fast approaching the Indians who instantly began to retreat as fast as they came. In a few moments Capt. Andrews came in safe and sound and began to inquire for Jennie, which was the first intimation any of us had of her being outside of her house. She was soon found and brought in still alive but shot through the side of the neck and scalped. At the same time a party went out to the timber and got the Col.'s oxen. They were just in time as the Indians were driving them off as they came up. On their way out they were found by the party that were in timber at the time of the attack, who had escaped by crossing and recrossing the Musselshell. The Indians kept firing at long range but their ball did not come in heavy. Nobody hurt but the women. All of the cattle are wounded. Some of them will die or have to be killed. During the fight, a couple of Crow Indians of the last war party came in on the other side causing some alarm over there. They report 300 lodges of Sioux at Round Butte some 50 or 60 miles below and that the country is full of their war parties. Also they stole a lot of horses, but the Sioux overtook them and they had to leave them and escape the best they could, and could not tell where the balance of their party was. The Sioux today shouted to us that they were two hundred strong and would give us a fight again tomorrow27.

March 23. A little cool. Eleven more Crows came in today on this side of the river. No Sioux today. Capt. Andrews killed one of his oxen. Jennie has a good prospect of raising another scalp and says if she had had a revolver she would have had the Indian's scalp instead of his having hers.

March 24. Warm. The Col. killed one of his oxen. The others, I think, will recover. The other two Crow Indians came in mounted, they having tried their hand the second time and succeeded, feel quite jubilant over it. Everybody is getting well fixed for a fight.

March 25. Warm. Jake Leader and Tom Stewart are busy putting up their house, which they had about finished hauling the logs for at the time of the raid. After dark the Crow party left taking nearly all the squaws with them that have been staying here this winter; nobody sorry.

March 27. A little cool. Several of the squaws came back early this morning, gave out or could not keep up. They say they ran into a party of Sioux.

March 29. Pleasant. Henry McDonald came in from Joe Bushaney's* [Bushaway] place 40 or 50 miles below, and says that Long,* Foster* and Bill Jordan* were killed at that place on the 16th by what they thought to be Assiniboins. While they were out chopping cord wood close to the house. Long was scalped. A man called Big Dan as severely wounded and only saved by Joe coming to the door with his gun in his hand and covering his retreat. Plenty of game on the river.

March 30. Cool. A party went down to the third point to see what had become of those there. While they were gone they made their appearance at Grinnell's all night having seen no Indians.

April 1. Cool. Scott, Snider, Joe (the Flathead, half breed), Theodore,* and Straun started for the agency.

April 3. Joe Bushaney and Hartz arrived with Big Dan who is nearly recovered.

April 5. Cool. Bruer and Veits began to haul Williams his wood.

April 7. Still a little cool. Late last evening Joe Martin, Bill Norris, Whitson, Greenwood, Tom Tate, and Johnson, the Norge, arrived from the mines, all except the last.

April 14. Quite pleasant lately. One year ago today I left Diamond City for this place. Gates and Warring arrived today in a mackinaw. Proposals are advertised for material for this place to build a post, hope it will not fall through.

April 15. Bruer and Veits went to Jenk's point to bank wood. Considerable of whiskey drunk today at Warring's as he has a fresh supply now. Grinnell, Fisher, Tom Stewart, Coonie, Capt. Andrews and a few others were slightly on it.

April 27. Pleasant. Nothing of great importance lately. Greenwood and Tom Tate began helping me today to build an addition to my shop.

April 29. Pleasant. About 9 o'clock today a few Indians made a raid to get the only horse belonging to the place, which was hobbled and close to where Stewart and Davis were loading wood on the bank of the Musselshell River. They ran Stewart and Davis in and got the horse, but in crossing the Musselshell River it mired down and the party that rushed out from here began putting in the Henry and Spencer balls so close that they were compelled to abandon it in the mud, no better off than they came. Stewart thought they were Assiniboins from their talk as they were close to him and he heard them speak to each other.

May 1. Quite warm. Jim Wells, Dennis, John Johnson, Ross,* and a couple of strangers arrived from the agency. In going, the party ran into a lot of Assiniboins and came near having a fight with them, which is the reason they did not return sooner. As they came past Well's point they saw a big fire last night. Thinking there were Indians, they raised a company here and went there at daylight this morning. When they got there they had nothing but burnt logs to contend with and returned quite crestfallen.

May 3. A petition being circulated for a Post Officer and Col. for Post Master. The river is very low yet. The prospect of a post being established here is dull. Most of the loose men are talking of leaving. I have been busy lately in building a larger shop. Everything is dull now and waiting for steamboats.

May 8. Warm lately and the river slowly rising. Cloudy today. About 9 o'clock this morning Davis and some squaws were out on the bank of the Musselshell River getting wood when they were fired upon by a party of Indians and run in by them, one ball passing through Davis' squaw's clothes and barely touching the skin on her arm. At the first alarm nearly every man seized his gun and gave the devils chase for a half mile where some 40 of them cached themselves in a small coolie that runs into the Musselshell River, evidently for the purpose of allowing our party to pass them and cut them off. But instead of doing that our party instantly surrounded them and kept up such a fire with their breech loaders that an Indian could scarcely show his head nor the balance of the Indians could not come to the rescue. Not knowing the force in the coolie exactly, our boys kept crowding up slowly until two of them were shot: Jake Leader through the head and killed instantly, and a moment afterwards, Greenwood received a shot in his left shoulder that lodged in his body. This slightly checked, the balance some 12 or 15 in number, until a reinforcement of 8 or 10 good men from the other side arrived, and they determined to settle old scores right there. About this time it began to rain hard, but no one paid any attention to the weather as all were armed with breech loaders using metalic cartridges. After skirmishing around two or three hours it was evident that there were no Indians in the brush opposite the coolie in which the Indians were secreted across the Musselshell. Three men succeeded in gaining a point in the brush not over 75 or 100 yards distant from the mouth of the coolie where they had a good view of the situation of the Indians and opened a deadly fire upon them. At this stage of the action the situation of the Indians was desperate indeed .The long rain had rendered their flintlocks nearly useless and destroyed the elasticity of their bows. For a few moments only did they stand this raking fire, then made a desperate rush to escape. Several hit the dust in a short distance and not a few were seen to stagger and fall as they ran, those escaped into the brush. Six were found dead in the hole. In all, there were thirteen of what can with safety be called, good Indians. When the boys made the last rush upon the Indians, several of them were still able to sit up, but no questions were given or received. A rifle or revolver placed along side of their head soon terminated their earthly career, and perchance before the body was done quivering, the scalp was dangling at the wampum of some desperate individual who was anxious to preserve some trophy of the fight. John Johnson set the example of mutilating by cutting off the head of one that he declared was his meat and by cutting him open and taking a piece of the liver to put a taste in his mouth. The example was contagious, for I assure you they were men that had no tender sympathies for poor Mr. Lo or any of his family. In fact, most of them had buried the mangled remains of friends or comrades too often to not retaliate. The only alternative an Indian fears the more terrible the retaliation, the sooner he is ready for peace28.

"Liver Eating" Johnson. Photo by John Fouch. #943-008. Courtesy Montana Historical Society Research Center Photograph Archives, Helena, Montana.

    May 9. Today a party went out and examined the brush on the other side of the Musselshell River and discovered the Indian's camp with all their baggage. So terribly frightened were they that they never stopped to pick up a thing. From appearances they must have been laying in wait for several days to get a favorable opportunity. Nearly everybody today has plenty of Indian trophies that they are busy cleaning and drying. Capt. Andrews is busy as he says, advancing the interests of science, by boiling and cleaning the skulls of the dead Indians. The balance of the carcass being left to feed the wolves. Among the relics of the battle are 13 scalps, 6 or 8 guns, a lot of bows and arrows, butcher knives, tin cups, canteens, buffalo robes, war bonnets, and a lot of their medicine bags, besides the clean and grinning skulls. Greenwood, I think, is not dangerously ill, though seriously wounded.

May 10. Pleasant; the Missouri rising slowly.

May 14. First boat of the season, steamer *Deer Lodge*29 arrived. She left Sioux City April 6th. The river is in good stage. Several men left here on the boat for the upper river. Among them was Mr. Orcutt* who has been stopping with us for some time. One, a boy, got off the boat for the M.H.&F. Co. house. Capt. Andrews had his Indian relics systematically arranged and labeled and exposed to the public view on the levee. They were a great curiosity to Pilgrims and steamboatmen.

May 21 or 20, not sure which. Fine weather. *Importer* arrived, T.C. Power and family on board with some friends. They are deadly opposed to the prosperity of this place. After looking at Capt. Andrew's show of relics Mrs. Power remarked that she would like to see the savage that cleaned those skulls. In charity for her, we will presume that she has never had any near or dear friend murdered, mutilated, nor outraged, or she would not speak so slightly of the efforts of brave men to preserve themselves from a similar fate, nor of their justly feeling proud of their achievements.

May 22. Steamer *Nile*30.

May 23. *Cora*. May 24. *Ida Reese*, also *Fanny Barker*; 15 or 20 men landed from the Cora to cross the country. Bought a yoke of cattle of Smith and Andrews. The river still rising slowly.

May 25. Raining.

May 26. Raining, muddy as the devil.

May 27. Rainy a little yet.

May 28. Clear. The Pilgrims from the *Cora* started this afternoon.

May 29. Steamer *H.M. Shreve* arrived with freight for me from St. Louis31.

May 31. Warm. Greenwood left for camp Cook on the Huntsville, Capt. Andrews for the states on the *Nile*. Tom Stewart also left for the Crow camp with his squaw on the *Huntsville*32. Bill Martin reports seeing a party of Indians on horseback coming this way above here. Everybody has their gun and ammunition in a convenient place ready for use.

June 15 Cash Veits and McGinnis left on the steamer *Sallie* bound for home.

July 15. I have been slightly neglecting my journal lately but there has nothing of importance happened except the arrival of a few boats until today. When John Johnson, Ed Schaff, Fred Watters, Charlie Morrison, and myself were compelled much against our choice to participate in a little adventure with a few hostile Indians in the point below the place. Ed and Fred were hauling poles and the balance of us went along as kind of an escort. We were all armed with breech loaders, and while the two were loading, I stood looking around with a glass. When Johnson called my attention to some object in the willows which he declared to be an Indian. I looked at it with the glass and so did he, but in the uncertain light it was in, it was a matter of doubt with us what it was. So Johnson shouldered his gun and started for it declaring that he would find out what it was. He had gone hardly a hundred yards when some men that were at work building fence near town raised the yell of Indians and began firing. I shouted, "Indians! Indians!" to Johnson, and broke for the wagon some two hundred yards, Charlie Morrison being with me. Fortunately we discovered the guns of the boys with the wagon and carried them with us and delivered them to the owners who came to meet us. The Indians that had raised the alarm were coming from the Musselshell way above us for the purpose of cutting us off from town. After the four of us came together we all broke for a big pile of cordwood some 100 yards or more distant. On the way to it [we were] thinking the devils were getting unpleasantly near. I stopped to fire a shot or two with my Henry rifle. Momentarily checking them, I saw one of the devils return the compliment by raising his gun and firing at me, but his ball passed out of hearing from me. By this time the others were getting to the woodpile in advance of me. When within 10 or 15 yards of the friendly woodpile a spent ball or buckshot struck me in the left thigh, but as my running was unimpaired and if any odds slightly improved thereby, I concluded I was not much hurt. The only effect being a slight stinging sensation. As soon as we got behind the woodpile we began firing at the Indians as fast as we could, who instantly turned and fled from us a good deal faster than they pursued us. I turned the attentions of my Henry to two that were making gigantic strides in the direction of some brush on the bank of the Musselshell; with what effect I would hardly tell any more than I thought it improved their running as much as their shots did mine. At this moment Johnson came up to us, he having run way to our right; as we came up he was limping slightly and said he was shot through the leg. He was bleeding profusely; one of the boys passed him a handkerchief with which he bound his leg himself. Johnson said he stopped to shoot and his gun misfired and while trying to shoot, some Indian behind him shot him through the leg, almost knocking him down when it struck him. The citizen of the place rallied to the rescue on the double quick and fired a few shells over our head into the brush. A party of 8 or 10 men came within shouting distance and called for us to come away, and with difficulty we made them understand that one of our men was wounded and we wanted help. With their assistance we carried Johnson up and drove up the team which had stood quietly chewing their cud during the melee. Johnson's wound proves to be severe but not dangerous as the ball barely missed the bone and the main artery.

July 16. Friday. This morning some woodchoppers came from the 4th point below on the other side and said they were attacked yesterday about two hours before sundown, who fired four shots at them, then ran. Two shots passed through old man Schultz killing him instantly. The Indians did not fire over 20 steps. A party went down to assist in burying Schutty. Our skirmish yesterday was about 2 o'clock so I think there must have been two parties of Indians.

August 5. Thursday. Nothing of importance lately except dry weather. This is the driest season that has been known for several years. The river is very low. Steamboats are having a desperate time indeed. This morning Edward Everett came in on horseback and nearly dead for water and says that he is one of the guides for the surveying party under Capt. Clift* ordered by Gen. Hancock to survey a road from Fort Ellis[33] to this place. The party is now at the Black Butte afraid to venture this way on the account of water, as they can find none on the road in this direction, and that he himself nor horse has had water for two days. It will be necessary for somebody to go from here to lead them in and show them water. I volunteer to go for one and the two stores hire Henry Keiser to go with me and he persuaded Bill Norris to go also. Getting everything in readiness to start after dark, as we do not like to venture out in daylight. [We'll] take Everett's horse along with us.

August 13. Friday. Arrived safely back at Musselshell with the surveying outfit. We found the party on the morning of the 8th near

Black Butte. We saw one of their scouting parties on the 7th but could not tell positively what they were, as they might be Indians we allowed them to pass out of sight, then discovered by their trail what they were and pursued as rapidly as possible some 10 miles until dark. During the afternoon the sun was eclipsed almost totally; quite dusky for a few moments. The weather is very smoky, so much so that you cannot see much more than a mile even with a good glass. At daylight we started on the trail again and went near eight miles farther and found the camp. Capt. Clift was preparing to start in a few moments with a horseback party to go through. After eating some breakfast that they kindly furnished us, the train started on and came 10 miles and returned back to the water, while I was ahead looking for a road. It was so very smoky that it was impossible to see or rise landmarks at any distance at all, and very hot and sultry. After finding the train had left us, I and Henry concluded we would go to the spring on Piney Ridge by ourselves, as we were both getting very thirsty. This was the first time I ever experienced any suffering from thirst, and I hope the last. The effect upon me was peculiar; a parched tongue, lips, and throat were disagreeable but not painful, but they were accompanied with an almost ungovernable desire to vomit, and in the last few miles I had to dismount several times to do so. For an hour after getting to the water my stomach felt to be in a very unsettled condition and only by a strong effort that I could refrain from vomiting. After refreshing ourselves we started to return; lay out on the prairie without knowing where the train was. On the morning of the 10th we took the trail and found the train all where we had started from the morning before, they having become frightened on the account of water. Once more the train pulled out, went 10 miles to Piney Ridge Spring, road very good except the last half onto the ridge. Good water but hardly enough for so many men and animals; two companies cavalry and six 6-mule teams. The amount was a good deal improved by digging. On the 11th the train lay still while a party went ahead and dug out a spring 10 miles on the road. On the 12th, drove to the dugout and camped. Found plenty of water by more digging; slightly alkalied.

  August 13. Drove in here. Followed what is known as the Crooked Creek Ridge, 21 miles by the roadometer. Our arrival was hailed with pleasure by the citizens who were about to get up a party to start out and see what had become of us, as we were absent 3 or 4 days longer than anyone supposed it would require. The officers of the party speak in very favorable terms of the road and the country through which it passes. Its favorable qualities being second to none in the country; grass, wood, and water in abundance, and a comparatively level country to pass through with a rich and fertile soil. This has been an uncommonly dry season; the whole country nearly is dried up. Between here and Black Butte water would be scarce for a slow ox train, but horses and mules can easily make plenty of water every night.

August 19. Capt. Clift issued a notice describing a reservation at this place and warning intruders not to encroach upon it. In the afternoon the trains moved out a couple of miles and camped on the Musselshell in readiness to start the next day.

August 20. This morning Col.Clendenin's ox and Mabbet,* McDonald, and Levi Protzman* of the Skin and Grease34 left with a loaded team for Helena on the new road with Clift to show the Helenaites that the road is practicable. Also a party started for the Colonel to go to the Crow camp with Tom Stewart on the Pochette.

August 22. Sunday. Very warm. The tracking party returned this morning and said they were run off last evening by a party of uninvited Indians and that they abandoned everything.

September 7. A lot of wolfers left today leaving the place with only 6 white men and two Negroes in it (Hoover* with me).

September 10. Went hunting up river; returned in Bill Mason's mackinaw.

September 14. J. Lee and a small party of Rappahoes arrived yesterday and left today. They were going to the Grovent [Gros Ventres] camp. They killed a pig on the other side for Jennie.

September 16. The first heavy frost of the season. Last season it was on the 10th of this month.

September 18. Rained.

September 19. Sunday. Pleasant in the afternoon. I discovered a couple of blacktail on the hill across the Musselshell with the glass, and in company with Gates, Mills, and the Negro, Charley, I went and killed them both at very long range. A little exciting as we are looking for Indians everyday now.

September 20. This morning Joseph Lee and Harry Hovey [Hoover] thought they saw an Indian across the Missouri when they were down on McGinnis' point. Steamer Throckmorton arrived; Steamer *Columbia*35, Capt. Throckmorton, I should say. Been laying above for a long time, had almost to dig his way down, only 17 inches of water and his boat drawing 18 when light.

September 23. Myself, Joseph Lee, Harris,* H. Hovey, and Williams all went hunting up the river. Killed nothing. J. Lee found a horse in the third point above on the other side. Rained in the afternoon and all returned wet and muddy. Hovey took a little boat up as far as the third point and that let him out on boating he says.

September 25. Col. Clendenin arrived with mackinaw from Benton. Thomas Bogy with him. The river very low.

September 29. Yesterday afternoon J. Lee, H. Hovey, Williams and myself started up the river hunting. Laid out last night by a fire on the third point above on the other side. We were considerably startled in the night by a buffalo swimming the river close to us, then going back when he saw our fire. Thought it was a bear at first. Early this morning went to the next point above and were in fine spirits at the prospects of getting a supply of fresh meat as we had just killed an elk and found plenty of them, when we were startled by the report of the brass piece at Musselshell 15 miles distant. The knowledge that nothing but Indians would bring it into action coupled with the fact that there were but six white men and two Negroes in the place were anything but agreeable subjects for reflection. Hastily constructing a raft we placed our meat and two men upon it and started down the river as fast as a still current and a just-rising heavy wind could carry us. Arriving at Musselshell we learned that early in the morning they were startled by some random shots below town. Rushing out to see the cause they discovered some 30 or 40 Indians, mostly mounted, within gunshot. In a very short time R.R. Gates, an employee of the M.H.&F. Co. opened on them with a shell, to their evident annoyance. A few shots drove them entirely away; could not tell if any Indians killed or not. They were very glad to see us returned all safe.

September 30. Pleasant. The Col.'s two pigs were found; one dead and the other badly wounded. It is also evident that they wished to draw the men out and then make a rush upon the place.

October 7. Plenty of flies yet about the house.

October 9. George Grinnell arrived with teams from the Agency with some freight for me from Steamer *Sally*.

October 13. Flies around yet. Last night Bruer [Brewer], Bill Norris, H. Keiser, and Charley Morrison started with wagon and two horses cross the country to Diamond and Helena. Col. Clendenin and Grinnell left horseback for the Agency, all leaving after dark last night.

October 14. Today Warring and Thompson arrived from Benton,

sickness of W. delayed them. They brought quite a stock of liquor and cigars, also reported an ox train coming cross the country for some freight left here by Steamer *Tempes*t36.

October 15. Pleasant. About noon the train arrived; some 30 odd wagons, two hundred head of cattle under Mr. Edward Swan* who was principal owner. They were 16 days on the road from Helena. Levy Protzman was with them. Corraled at the corner of my shop. This is the first freight train for Musselshell. God forbid it should be the last.37 In the evening Pomp Dennis started for the Col. at the Agency. A small party of Crow arrived with Tom Stewart.

October 17. Sunday. Cold. Snowing and blowing. The first snow this season. Last year it came on the 13th of September. The Col. and Pomp arrived. The Col. had started on his return.

October 21. Quite cool lately. Swan train has been loading since Tuesday morning.

October 22. Cool. Swan's train started out, also the Col. with teams for the Crow camp. Andrew, the Negro, Tom Stewart, and 11 Crow Indians with him. I shall also start in a few moments to go with him.

November 6. Returned again today. Found the camp on the head of Armell's Creek 75 miles from here. On the 26th of October about 90 lodges of them there. Remained at camp three days and started on our return. Met Swan at the Black Butte, Brouckel with him. Pomp, Little McDonald, Drew Denton*, and Lohmire were there also, wolfing. Six Crow Indians came in with us as kind of an escort. Had very fine weather on our trip except the first few days which were very cold. Left the wagon on the ridge as we came in.

November 7. Sunday. Very windy. Brought the wagon in today. There are a couple of lodges of Rappahoes [Arapahoe] here now; been here for some time.

November 14. Sunday. Pleasant. Rained and sleeted considerable during the week, but has nearly dried up.

November 16. Yesterday Dick Harris and Fred Watters started down the river in a small boat; got upset. Fred went on to his cabin and Dick undertook to come back and lay out all night; quite cool. He came in about noon from up the Musselshell and said he got lost and ran into a band of 75 Sioux; but guess not.

November 17. Snowing this morning; hardly daylight yet and just had my breakfast. Snowed but little and soon gone.

November 24. Pleasant lately, scarcely freezing nights. The river is raising a little. The Rappahoes still here.

November 25. Cyprian* [Matt] and a couple of Grovents arrived from Milk River.

November 26. Bill Norris arrived last night from Helena. He left Bruer and a party of men at the Crow camp on the head of Armell's Creek and came in above from there on horseback. He has been appointed U.S. Marshall to take charge of the Steamer *Taconia*[38] laying at Peck.

November 27. Grinnell and F. Smith started out after meat. Cyprian and most of the Rappahoes started for Milk River, the balance started for their main camp. In the afternoon Norris started for Peck in a skiff by himself. The ice running pretty thick today in the river.

November 29. Cold and snowed a good deal today. Just at evening, Mr. McNeal*, a deputy U.S. Marshall arrived and took possession of the M.H.&F. house in the name of the law. He came down the river in a small boat, two men with him: Whiskey Smith and James Burdick.

November 30. Cold. Bruer and party arrived from Crow camp later in the evening. Ice running very thick today.

December 1. Cold last night. The river closed from shore to shore this morning.

December 2. A little moderate; snow about all gone.

December 4. Moderate. Grinnell crossed the river on the ice. He says a party of Indians passed up the river on foot on the other side of the river; hostile, of course, or some of them would have been in here. The Col. discharged his Negro, Andrew* [Jackson] yesterday.

December 5. Sunday. Moderate. Skating today with Levy Protzman. Indians around and no mistake. The Col. saw fresh sign of them today on Crooked Creek[39]. Also Abner Babb saw a couple towards evening in the hills between here and Crooked Creek.

December 6. I was still in bed this morning when a rapid firing up the river startled me. I sprang up already dressed as I had lain down with my clothes on and seized my rifle, a Spencer, and some ammunition and ran out onto the bank of the river where the men were fast collecting, and soon learned that the Indians were on this side of the river and trying to cut off 4 men who had horses on the first point and had gone to bring them down. But they were a little too late as the horses were gone when they got there. The firing on the other side of the river was done to keep back the Indians, as the boys ran along under the banks on the edge of the ice. A party of us started up the river on the run, but soon met the boys all safe. Indians soon showed themselves all round but I think only for the purpose of making a demonstration in favor of those up the river with the horses. The boys also think they killed one of them as he was seen to fall. Strange to say, they never fired a shot, in fact they had but little chance to do so but at long range. In an hour they all left. When the Col. and a party went up to the first point and found his cattle all right; safe and sound.

December 7. Nothing worth relating.

December 11. Moderate. A small party of Grovents arrived today and say the camp is coming.

December 15. Pleasant lately. today it snowed a little and turned cold. Several lodges of Grovents arrived. Whiskey is their best holt. The smallpox is about done among them; a good many of them are badly scarred with it and make anything but a prepossessing appearance.

December 17. Snowy and blustery this morning.

December 19. Sunday. Snowing a little all day. Two or three inches deep now, I expect on the level.

December 21. Cold.

December 25. Saturday. Moderating, been cold as the devil.

December 27. Moderate. Thaws considerably during the day. The Grovents are still here and doing considerable trading: horses and robes for whiskey, although there is a heavy penalty against it, there are plenty that will trade it to them.

1870

January 1st, 1870 – Saturday. Mild and pleasant. A few days ago a party of 8 Crows came in with 50 head of horses and mules that they stole from the Sioux on the Yellowstone. They only stayed overnight, are very much afraid of the smallpox of the Grovents. This morning Col. Clendenin, Charlie Morrison, and Big McDonald* started for Benton by way of the Crow camp which is supposed to be on Armell's Creek somewhere near the head.

January 2. Sunday. Very nice and warm but damned muddy. John Fattig, G.R. Davis, Henry Keiser, and Gus Tyler arrived from the Crow camp at the mouth of Armell's Creek instead of the head, where the Col. started for, also Doc Clendenin* from Little Rocky.

January 9. Sunday. Warm. Bill Norris arrived from Peck yesterday. He lost his Marshall papers by upsetting his boat going down and has to go up the river to see about getting some more. A good many hostile Indians around Peck. They made a dash in there a few days ago but did no damage. He says he followed the trail of a war party most of the way up here and thinks they must be near waiting a good layout of whites or Grovent horses. Cyprian, the Grovent talker, also came in from Milk River a few days ago and brought the mail. He returned yesterday. The Grovents are scattering their camp along the river opposite here. They have camped all along at the head of the point. Considerable talk of T.C. Power selling out here to Farwell of Peck; hope it is so.

January 13. A little moderate today; been cold as the devil for a few days. Some of the Grovent lodges are moving up the river after buffalo.

January 20. The Col. and McDonald arrived from Benton. They left Charley Morrison at Camp Cook sick of smallpox.

January 23. Sunday. Pleasant. Today the Grovents all left for up the river. They were burning considerable of cordwood and the boys over there were talking so strong about it that they got frightened and started off. Nobody is at all sorry. The Col. and Grinnell started for the agency this afternoon on Milk River.

January 24. Warm; snow nearly all gone, a few days ago there were nearly six inches on the ground, the most I have seen at any time in this part of the country. Bruer started up the river on the ice today with a load of goods for the Crow camp, several men going with him.

January 25. Thawed a little. Some of the Grovents still hanging around.

January 26. Thawed a little. William Johnson, the Norwegian of last winter's notoriety, arrived today in company with John Kennedy*. They came in from Black Butte with a few furs. A small party of Crows also came in. Porcupine and Two Belly being with them. In the evening Jack Brown arrived from Browning40 with a big paper mail.

January 27. Snowed a little last night. Thawed today.

January 28. Warm, froze very little last night. Johnson and Kennedy left, also Two Belly and staff left for their headquarters.

January 30. Sunday. Warm and looks like rain; froze none the last two nights.

January 31. Warm, a good deal of water on the ice. The Col. arrived this morning alone, he got separated from George by the latter losing a glass and going back to look after it. In the evening George arrived all right, having found his glass and went back to the agency and stayed overnight.

February 2. Warm; snow all gone; mud nearly dried up.

February 4. Pleasant. White Eagle* and a party of Grovents in today. In the evening the buck and squaw known as the -------- took their robes, four in number, over to -------- and traded them for -----, which they brought to me to know if there was any ------ in it. I told them a little; they thought a hook. The Indians all drunk in the evening. [Spaces were blanks in journal.]

February 5. Pleasant. White Eagle and his party left again.

February 6. Sunday. Pleasant. Frank Smith and Doc Clendenin arrived with team from Little Rocky, also the Col.'s team. Bruer remained above still trading with the Crows. Late in the evening Jim Mabbot, William Judd,* Bill Norris, and Lohmire arrived; the first three from Helena.

February 7. Pleasant. In the afternoon D. Halpin, J. Cochran, and Charley Morrison arrived. Charley shows no signs of the smallpox. Six lodges of Rappahoes and a few of them Grovents came down the river today and camped on the Musselshell above us.

February 8. Warm. Boyd started to Browning yesterday. Johnson and three others came in today on foot, said the Crow Indians stole their horses at Piney Ridge spring. Also Jack Frost* and comrade came in from Mountain Crow camp on the Yellowstone. Bill Norris and Dick Harris started for Peck.

February 11. Turned cold and "blowed" furiously in the morning. The six lodges of Rappahoes left, taking 4 horses belonging to parties stopping here. Just now 8 or 10 of the boys mounted and followed a little after noon though it was bitter cold.

February 12. Moderated again towards night. Col. started up the Musselshell to Crow camp. The boys returned with the stolen horses [this] afternoon. They overtook them early this morning. They quickly returned the horses. Before the boys got to their camp they met them with them. A couple of smoke or fires visible today, Indians I presume.

February 13. Sunday. Cool. All the strangers left today. Judd fell over the river bank last night and broke his collarbone.

February 14. Valentine day. Pleasant. Clear and cloudy but chilly.

February 15. Cool with a little snow. R.B. Gates, McNeal, and Levy Protzman started for Helena in the storm. The Col.'s and Big McDonald's horses are missing today. McD. found that a white man took them up Crooked Creek supposed to be the fool Babb. Jack Brown came in from

Browning with mail.

February 17. McDonald found his horse killed up Crooked Creek and the Col.'s alive. Babb was in the other day and McD. bawled him out. Of course, he denies everything. Brown went back to agency. Sent letter to Dimick41. Boys came tonight. D. Halpin and Mabbet ran a foot race by moonlight for Bottle Bitters. The Col.'s team arrived from camp, he remaining in camp.

February 20. Sunday. Moderate. The Col. returned last evening with the two Crow chiefs, Horseguard and Two Belly. This morning Bogy went out in the Col.'s place as he left a stock of goods there. A good many of the Crows are also coming in now as the Grovents are all gone. Reed is also expected everyday to distribute a lot of provisions among them.

February 21. Warm. A good many Crow Indians in today. Their camp is about 7 miles up the Musselshell River. Grinnell and party out after meat with 6 horses; to be gone several days on the Pochette.

February 22. Snowing this morning, but soon quit and began to disappear. Some of the Crow Indians brought in some scalps and a hand of some Indians they had killed this morning on Crooked Creek. Seven of them, Flatheads and Ponderays [Pend d'Oreilles] undertook to steal a lot of horses from the Crows this morning a little before day. The Crows turned out and followed them. Aided by the snow, they soon overhauled them and made short work of them, killing all of them.

February 24. Warm; snow all gone. Plenty of Crows around now. Their camp is about 5 miles above on the Musselshell. The are expecting Reed* [Alonzo] here everyday from Milk River with a lot of flour and sugar and other things to distribute among them.

February 25. Warm. The river shows it plainly. Plenty of Crow Indians around. Some of them are in mourning now for three of their number that were killed by the Flatheads yesterday. I think all of their relatives have a big spell of crying.

February 27. Sunday. Warm. The river has risen nearly four feet in a few days. The ice is broken loose all along the shore. Some parties crossed the river by means of a boat from the ice to the shore. Tom Stewart came in this morning with some of the Indians from Mountain Crow Agency42. Also the long looked for Reed arrived, says his wagons will be in a day or two. The roads are very bad. Jim Wells with him; the bad roads caused a good deal of delay.

February 28. Moderate. Nothing unusual except the arrival of a couple of squaws that were with the party of Rappahoes that left here about the 12th, said they were tired and foot sore, scarcely able to walk. They say that five days ago they were attacked by the Sioux and all the rest killed but them for all they know. Tom Stewart says that he thinks it was the Mountain Crows that cleaned them out.

March 2. A little cold today and yesterday; snowing a good deal today. The wagons arrived with flour and a little sugar for the Crow Indians. This afternoon 49 sacks of flour were given them and some sugar. The balance will be given some other time. The place is so full of Indians now that a person heartily wishes every one of them dead. Such beggars! The city of Paris never saw the like. Tonight the shop is clear of them for the first time for several days. My friend. Arrow Chief, and squaw, finding my coffee was about gone, thought he would go where they had plenty of it. While I did not endeavor to dissuade him from it.

March 3. Snowing this morning and a little during the day. Major Reed's teams started back for the Agency. Pete Koch*, Bill Martin, and party came up today.

March 4. Cold; froze hard last night. The river is falling rapidly again the last day or two. Major Reed and Wells started back to the Agency. A couple of inches of snow on the ground now.

March 5. Cold this morning and trying to snow. The Indians are still running around and stealing every opportunity they get to do so. I understand they have taken considerable from Col. Clendenin. I do not give them much chance about my place. My friend Arrow Chief and squaw invited themselves to partake of my hospitality last night. During the night he kicked the squaw out of bed and gave her a few gentle taps over the head and left her crying on the floor for an hour, for some reason which I imperfectly understood. Such another squalling I thought the house was full of Sioux and were scalping her. Today the Crows drove off Grinnell's, Judd's, Mabe's, and Oleson's* horses, Olesen seeing them go. The boys then corralled a lot of the Indians in the Skin and Grease House and sent for Horse Guard. The Crows denied it bitterly. The boys finally let the Indians go as they could make nothing by keeping them.

March 6. Sunday. Thawed a little during the day but soon turned cold again. The Crow camp moved up the Musselshell a short distance. They are getting very hungry for buffalo meat. Jennie's favorite squaw brought me my little dog today that some of them stole a few days ago. The boys found most of their horses except Olesen who is out two yet. The Crows finding they were discovered in their thieving probably turned them loose again to be found the best way they could.

March 7. Cool but sunny; so was yesterday. A few Indians still around last night. Yesterday for the first I learned that Reed had posted some notices that he had received information of trading and trafficking with the Indians with whiskey and without license. (He) warned everybody that property found engaged in this business would be confiscated. The supposition among the citizens is that this is a plan of the Col.'s to frighten outsiders into selling him their robes cheap. As far as I have been able to learn, they nearly all swear they will see him in hell before they sell him a robe under any such compulsion. It is evident upon the face of the notice that Reed does not wish to confiscate property or drive matters to extremities with the people here and the only advantage in such a notice upon such general information as alleged in the notice, that is likely to accrue to any person is in their being able to buy up and haul all the robes that are liable to confiscation in anybody else's hands besides the Col's. That he is at the bottom of it is almost self-evident. Whether Reed is playing into the Col.'s hands or is merely doing as he is to give parties a chance to do away with anything liable to confiscation and at the same time do his duty is a matter of conjecture only, among the not posted. Olesen came in today with his horses. It appears now that no one is sure that the Crows took them at all.

March 8. Warm; thawed a good deal. The Col. is just preparing to get out a little ice, rather late, I think, and poor ice at that as the river is liable to break up in a week or 10 days.

March 9. Snowing this morning, soon quit and was nearly all gone by noon. Snowing again before dark; cloudy and dismal. I forgot to mention yesterday that a Rappahoe and a Grovent arrived here that belonged to the outfit that was reported to be cleaned out. They say that the Mountain Crows attacked them, killed two of their men, and stole nearly all of their horses somewhere near the Yellowstone. Now they were on the Armell's Creek somewhere above us having a rough time. The papooses and squaws all having to walk. In the fight they killed a Crow they say, and wanted to kill a Crow buck that is here but the whites told them to go slow.

March 10. Cold; snowed last night and nearly all day today. The Col. busy getting up ice, bull whacking himself. Some Crows at Skin and Grease left today on account of the Rappahoe, though he left yesterday morning.

March 11. Clear and cold; two inches snow on the ground. Nothing important that I have heard of.

March 13. Sunday. Cold and snowing a little nearly all day; freezing hard for a few days.

March 14. Clear and cold; everything still and quiet.

March 15. Clear and cold today; thawed a very little in the sun where the wind did not blow. Doc Clendenin and Warring started up the Little Rocky day on foot.

March 16. Cold today; a small part of Crow Indians came in late last night. They found plenty of buffalo but a short distance up the Musselshell. The camp will probably be here in a short time again trying to trade with F. Smith for robes.

March 17. St. Patrick's Day, be Gad. Not quite as cold as yesterday, but cloudy most of the day and snowing again this evening. The Indians took their departure again today, very nearly perfected a trade with F. Smith. I am getting anxious to see warm weather and for the river to break up. It has been a long time since steamboats.

March 18. Still cool but thaws a little. Bill Martin and Pete Koch came up from their woodyard. Nothing new. Was over to see Frank about trading.

March 19. Same as yesterday.

March 20. Sunday. Tolerably pleasant. Everything is quiet about the place. Today I effected a trade with A.F. Smith for his share of the two ranches across the Missouri from here, or from Musselshell.

March 21. Quite pleasant, snow melting rapidly. Smith took 98 of my robes to the other side of the river. Col.Clendenin started alone for Fort Benton, a horseback taking Mabbot's and Judd's horses with him. Today is one year since the ice broke up here last season. The Col. intends to come down with a boat as soon as the ice is out of the river. I hope "she" will go soon for I am getting tired of this cold weather and dread the mud we will have for a few days.

March 22. Nice and warm. Today is the anniversary of our first Indian raid last spring, when Jennie lost her hair and got wounded in the neck. She still wears her head covered, but is strong and hearty, and able to lose another scalp if unavoidably necessary for her to do so. The first geese of the season flying over today, saw two or three flocks. Delivered all my furs to Smith; he hauled them across the river on the ice. Nothing exciting or marvelous.

March 23. Nice and warm. The Musselshell broke up and carried out ice nearly or quite across the Missouri, which is also beginning to rise this afternoon. The snow is nearly all gone and the mud drying up rapidly. Today someone came very near getting up a panic by reporting they saw Indians across the Musselshell on the hills. I got my glass and soon quieted the alarm by discovering a lot of antelope quietly grazing on the top of one of the hills where they saw their Indians come up and look over. Frank Smith is busy building him a boat in readiness for the ice to go out.

March 24. Warm, cloudy afternoon; froze but little last night and night before. Missouri rising rapidly all day. It is about as high now as it was any time last season. No crossing on the ice today as it is almost impossible to get on and off the ice. The Musselshell keeps piling the ice out onto the Missouri. A flock of geese passing over occasionally.

March 25. The river fell a good deal last night. Cloudy and a couple of little showers of hail; the hail something like a pea in size. Warring returned towards evening, tolerably well played out. Oleson lost a horse in the river by drowning, with saddle and bridle. He was passing along the bank under the bluffs above here opposite Grinnell's stockade when the horse undertook to get a drink and got in over his depth and soon went under the ice. He is considerably discouraged by it.

March 26. Pleasant but cloudy. The Missouri is down as low as ever nearly and is open clear across nearly half mile above here. Grinnell and Cochran came over in skiff today.

March 27. Sunday. Raining this morning for some time and muddy as the devil. Pete Koch and party started for Milk River.

March 28. A little chilly; froze hard last night. The ice, I see, is piling up a little in places. Shot a goose that was flying over the bottom, with a Spencer rifle from my shop's backdoor. He did not like to fall but had to do so as it was shot through the body. Everybody had to run out and see what was up, with their rifles in hand, as we would not be at all surprised to have a brush with hostile Indians at any time. I think the Missouri River ice will go out tomorrow sure, as this evening it is quite mild, but dark and cloudy.

March 29. Froze very little last night. The wind a little cool, but sunny today. About sundown the ice in the Missouri began to start and crowd in under that that was fast and in a few moments it was all moving and grinding as far as you could see up and down the river. In the space of 15 or 20 minutes the water rose over two feet in front of the place on account of the ice gorging a little below. It is so rotten and weak there is but little danger of it gorging seriously. Last year it started out on the 21st of March.

March 30. Wednesday. Pleasant, except the wind which raises toward 9 o'clock is a little chilly. The ice made a terrible crashing last evening and this morning the bar of the island in front of us is covered with ice. The river must have risen 4 or 5 feet to have done it. Today the ice is running quietly in a steady stream, toward evening not near so much running. Boats crossed the river readily; very little excitement except a good deal target shooting all round by the boys.

March 31. Very pleasant and nearly calm, but little ice running besides what slips in from the banks where it lodged. The first arrival downstream, a boat from Little Rocky, Doc Clendenin, Drew Denton, and Rocky Mountain Charley*. Also Dennis Halpin came over from Milk River, a stranger with him named Joe.

April 1. All Fool's Day. Nice and pleasant. Got letter by Dennis from Scribner and one from L.M. Rogers. James Wells arrived from the agency, started yesterday morning. His business I have not learned yet.

April 2. Pleasant. Smith and Warring launched their boat today with the assistance of all hands. Wells had considerable of trouble settling his business today with Smith in regard to securing himself in his pay for his ranch, but was finally settled to his satisfaction. I was across the river on my ranches for the first time since purchasing. Grass is beginning to show and flies have shown two or three days.

April 3. Sunday. Pleasant days and warm nights. Doc Clendenin, Warring, and George Grinnell started down the river in a mackinaw with some 4 or 500 robes aboard bound for the states. Grinnell bilked a good many here out of what he owed them. By a scratch, I corralled him at the last moment. Wells and Halpin and Joe started back for the agency and I took possession of the ranches on the other side of the river that I purchased of A.F. Smith. I took some things over, but came back and stayed at the shop overnight; ran around a good deal and am quite tired.

April 4. Nice and pleasant. Moved over some more things early in the morning. Then I and Ed Schaff began to haul wood to the river bank. Hauled four loads, then quit to do some other work. Harry Hoover* and some others took a wagon and team up the river on the north side to haul some wood. This evening I am writing at my upper ranch opposite Musselshell. After this, I shall probably make this side my home most of the time. I expect to move my gunsmith tools over as soon as I can prepare a building suitable for a shop separate from the room I live in, as I have got tired of living and working in the same place continually. The river is very low, but I hope there will be water a plenty.

April 5. Quite warm. The grass looks quite green through the bottom. Was busy hauling and cording wood at the upper end of the point [where] the landing is. Just about the center of the point there is a small island that divides the water of the river in two channels during high water. At present the water all runs down the main channel next to the berg of Musselshell. Unless the water is up very high boats cannot land conveniently to get wood except at the upper end and a few a short distance at the lower end and below the island. Pete Koch, Bill Martin, and his party got back from the agency with their team today. I have understood that Hoover's party went to jump the point just above us for the sake of some hay ground on it.

April 6. Windy and chilly. Busy banking wood. I and Ed Schaff, my ranch partner, were cross the river at noon. Nothing new.

April 7. Quite warm, some thunder about sundown. Everything quiet.

April 8. Very windy, blowing upstream so that a sailboat would run rapidly upstream. The cottonwood buds, I noticed day before yesterday, were beginning to swell. Yesterday I and Ed stopped the gang way down to McGinnis' point to keep the cattle from straying. Finding they could not get down this morning we found them hid in the willows at the lower end of our point. Was over to town this evening after a further supply of grub. A little rain at dark.

April 9. Same as yesterday; very windy and chilly. Did not work in the afternoon but went over to town to do some blacksmithing for the wagon.

April 10. Sunday. Windy again; quite chilly last evening, a very little ice this morning where it stood in a vessel and exposed. This afternoon Col. Clendenin arrived from Benton with a mackinaw loaded with goods for his store here. He was accompanied by five others who are going to Fort Peck. Among them was a U.S. Marshall[43] and a District Attorney. Their business at Peck, I understand, is to sell the steamer *Tacony* that lays there in the hands of the law. George Boyd* was also with the party, also two other gentlemen who intended to bid upon the boat, I understand.

April 11. Windy as usual, but warm. Was over to town. The Peck party left in the afternoon in the big yawl that Col. has had charge of.

James Mabbot went with them; his business was to try and see Grinnell if he was at Peck yet. He took the necessary papers with him. T.B. [Thomas Bogy] got gloriously drunk.

April 12. Very warm; not much wind; this evening it is blowing furiously, but has rained none yet. I forgot to mention yesterday that one of the squaws at Col. Clendenin's, and known as Mrs. Bogg, died from the effects of venereal disease of long standing. The Col. himself has a squaw also that he keeps for his own use. He has become satisfied, he says, that to be a successful Indian trader a man must become as near an Indian himself as possible, a doctrine that he has put in practice as much as possible. There is but one man besides him that is living with a squaw. So far Musselshell can boast of but two half breed children, one the child of Jake Leader, an Indian interpreter of the Crow language, who was killed at the fight on the 8th of May last year at this place, and another the son of R.R. Gates, D.U.S. Revenue Collector at this place, which is now about a month old and was born here at the Col.'s place where the mother, who is known as Buckskin, is now stopping while Gates is above at Helena and not expected to return soon, if ever.

April 13. Snowing a little this morning and quite cold and blustery all day, so much so we did not haul wood. I went cross the river. A small party of Crows came in. Their camp is on Flat Willow and Box Elder. Today they learned for the first time what has become of a party of 29 of their warriors that went to steal horses of the Sioux late last fall. Heretofore they were always inquiring what we knew of them. Just lately we learned that they had a desperate fight with the Sioux and were all killed after a seven day's fight in which there were 15 or 20 of the Sioux killed also. The news went from Fort Buford to the states by government mail carriers, soldiers detailed for the purpose, then round to Helena and to Benton and Fort Browning from whence we received it. There is no communications at all between Peck and Buford during the winter except by hunters or Indians, and seldom those. From Peck news goes up the river and from Buford it goes down. The Crows would hardly believe the report at first because we always denied knowing anything about it before, and wanted to know how we came by our information. Finally Tom Stewart explained it to their satisfaction. McDonald came down today from his woodyard above here; he came horseback.

April 14. Cold and blustery. The Col. started for the Crow camp with a lot of goods, or rather, he sent Tom Bogy and Stewart. I and Ed hunted all day for our oxen; could not find them anywhere.

April 15. Cold and windy. Found our oxen and went to work in the afternoon. Yesterday a party of ten Crow Indians came from Peck, brought a letter to Judd from Bill Norris. 1200 lodges of Santees and Cut Heads44 below there a short distance. Fattig is down trading with [them], says they have sent or are about to send a big party to attack this place and to look out for them. The mackinaw with the robes stopped a couple of days, then pushed on down the river again.

April 16. Froze a little last night but warm during the day. Worked hard all day. In the afternoon, Jennie said she saw three Indians on the hill cross the Musselshell. A little later they had a little Indian scare at the burg. Little McDonald had a horse hobbled down towards the Musselshell. As he went after it, he met it with its hobbles broken and coming at full speed. He fired his Henry a few times and brought assistance, but no Indians were seen.

April 17. Sunday. A little cool and quite windy. Was over to the shop to do a little repairing for the boys. Three more Crow Indians arrived from Peck on foot. They report 150 mounted Sioux on the way to wipe out this place and that they will be here in three days, that they want to stay and fight them also so as to have some scalps to take to their camp. Ed is complaining of being nearly sick abed this evening. I stayed across the river last night at Judd's of the Skin and Grease.

April 18. Windy and warm. Found the cattle on the point above. Went cross the river in the afternoon with Ed. Brought over my possible box.

April 19. Quite warm. Cold last night. Plowed some for garden. Nothing of especial interest to record.

April 20. Pleasant. Quite a party came down from Little Rocky, panic stricken with the prospects of the country this summer. Several of them intending to leave. They came down on a raft. In the forenoon we finished plowing our garden spot.

April 21. Pleasant. Planted a lot of potatoes. I slept at Judd's last night and came over at sunrise. A party started for the mountains this morning consisting of Bruer, Little McDonald, Smith, John Williams, and old man Lawson, taking a wagon and span of horses. Musselshell has but 10 men and three squaws with two children, while this side of the river has three men and one woman making an available force of 13 fighting men only within supporting distance of each other. Frank Smith, Ed Schaff, and Jennie Smith moved into the upper stockade with me to be the better prepared for Indian fighting. As all parties are momentarily expecting an attack from the red devils and consequently everybody stays close at home.

April 22. Quite warm. A party of 15 Lower Grovents arrived today from below and passed Fort Peck. Letter from Mabbot to Judd, one from Doc Clendenin to A.F. Smith. The U.S. Marshall Wheeler, shot himself in the arm accidentally with a shotgun making severe wound. The steamer, *Tacony*, sunk from laziness, I understand, on the part of the ones taking care of it. Mabbot collected his pay of G. Grinnell, I understand. Doc did not know whether to shove on down the river or not as 12 or [more] lodges of hostile Indians are reported to be on the river a little below Peck. The appearance of the Indians almost created a panic this morning as they came up on this side of the river and carried a small flag of truce. Although they are friendly Indians, they were afraid of being taken for Sioux and fired upon. The Col.'s wagon returned last night without having seen the Crow camp or any part of it.

April 23. Very windy today and last night and slightly cool. I and Ed corded wood on the bank today. Those Indians left for Little Rocky, Bill Cutter* going with them. This evening I see another party over there; Crows, I think. Today for the first, the river is rising a little.

April 24. Sunday. Pleasant. A large party of Crow Indians at Musselshell in the morning. I went over and worked in the shop all day for them. They came in mostly for some flour at the Col.'s, left for them by Reed. They have mutilated themselves by cutting off their fingers and hair for their dead friends that were killed by the Sioux. They also destroyed a great many robes and lodges and reduced the size of a great many of their large lodges. They make a comical looking sight to see them with their fingers tied up and their hands and face all bloody, and their hair cut off close, and their face blackened with coal. Only those that have lost relatives do these things. Their main camp is somewhere near Little Rocky.

April 25. Pleasant. Stayed at the shop last evening; came over again before sunrise this morning, went back and worked in the shop, while Frank Smith worked in my place with Ed hauling wood. The most of the Indians left during the day, part of them returning to camp and a party going after the bodies of those killed by Sioux below Peck and to get revenge if possible without running too much risk themselves. The river is rising slowly; some three inches now.

April 26. Warm and windy. Hauled wood. Set stakes for water marks. Low water mark at the woodyard this spring is 18 feet and below the level of the bank. The Col. started a wagonload of goods to the Crow camp again.

April 27. Pleasant. Cattle down on McGinnis' point. Hauled wood. The river raised near two inches. A.F. Smith began to cut wood for us.

April 28. Pleasant, but windy. Went over to the shop and repaired the right hind wheel. The Col. told me that his Crow woman came back last night in the night sick with the smallpox and that the Indians that came in with her left a soon as they learned the nature of her sickness. The Col. is very much alarmed at the prospect of trouble with the Crow on account of the smallpox as they are terribly afraid of it and there will probably not be another Crow here for six months. He is also quite anxious for the safety of Tom Bogy and party that left for the Crow camp a few days ago. More particularly as he and Tom Stewart parted in a quarrel. Tom declaring in at the M.H.&F. Co. that he would do all he could in opposition to the Col.'s trade with the Crow Indians. The river is rising rapidly. This morning for the first, it is running through the channel on this side of the island.

April 29. The hottest day of the season so far. Had to set the wagon tire this morning, then went to point above and got the cattle and hauled 13 loads [of] wood [in] afternoon. The river has raised about a foot or more and still rising.

April 30. Warm. Today a party of Lower Grovents that have been living with the Crows for some time, passed down the river on their way home, making but a short stay at Musselshell for fear of the smallpox.

May 1. Pleasant. Last evening some persons or Indians stole one of the iron flat boats left in the Col.'s charge and took it down the river. Last evening I went over in town to stop and set fire to my coal pit again.

May 2. Quite warm. Came back cross the river. The first load of wood, the tire ran off the right front wheel. Had to stop and repair damages. The river rising rapidly, raised near 25 inches at the woodyard, above low water mark. In the evening the party of Crows arrived at Musselshell that went after the dead bodies of those of their tribe that were killed by the Sioux last winter. They had their bones carefully wrapped up in a good blanket or shawl and are going to take them to camp. It appears that the fight took place on this side of the Yellowstone near where the Powder River empties into it and on the top of a sharp butte which the Sioux surrounded and finally took by making a desperate charge upon it and according to the story of the Lower Grovents losing 25 of their own men in the attack. The Crows say that the bodies were stripped of flesh by the wolves and that the remains of several and one Sioux still lay on the ground. Mere Ah Sash, the Crow chief with the party, says that he relieved his feeling considerably by shooting a few times into the carcass of the Sioux. The Col.'s case of smallpox, he says, is doing as well as could be expected. The Crows are very careful to keep at a respectful distance.

May 3. Quite warm. Looked very much like rain last night, but only a very few drops fell. The river is rising very rapidly. Broke a hound and tongue; Batt went to work to repair it.

May 4. Rained a little this morning. Went over to the shop and repaired the wagon. Col.Clendenin's squaw died of the smallpox last night and was buried today. Tom Bogy also returned from a fruitless search after the Crow camp on Armell's Creek and did not see an Indian until they met Two Belly last evening with his party. In the afternoon a Grovent squaw came in from towards the Agency, but has very little to say and cannot tell where she came from or what she came for.

May 5. A little cool and windy. Old man Lee and Joe Synnix* came down from Little Rocky. Busy hauling wood.

May 6. Pleasant. Stayed at Judd's last night. Came over before sunrise with Uncle Joe Lee. Hauling wood all the time. The river rising rapidly, three feet of a raise up to this date. Steamboat *Cora* 2 years ago.

May 7. Pleasant but windy. The river still on the rise and the banks caving in fast at Musselshell in front of T.C. Power and the Skin and Grease. Big McDonald and Gus Tyler went above to bank some wood they have been cutting during the winter. In the afternoon I and Ed surveyed a little to see about getting water out of the river in a ditch to irrigate with but were sorry to find the bottoms none nearly level than we supposed. Not sure we can get water yet.

May 8. Sunday. Cool and very windy; today is the anniversary of our big Indian fight last year. Up to this date we have been unmolested, nor have we heard of any depredations being committed near here. I wrote this late last evening and was a little ------ as Frank Smith and Ed went to the point above today to hunt. Ed ran onto a tepee right in the thickest of the brush but saw no Indians, but might as well for he beat a hasty retreat to Frank and they both concluded that they did not want any meat and came home and reported what they saw and did. The bank is caving in very fast at Musselshell. The river, I think, is on a standstill.

May 9. Pleasant and not quite so windy. I am a little under the weather on account of my eyes, have been bothered some lately, the first for a long time. Some of the boys went above today to see Ed's lodge and as was expected found an old Grovent lodge but did not enter it as the flies were buzzing around very thick and thought there might be some dead Grovents in there that had died of smallpox. Found our cattle on the point below. The Col.'s could not be found. Received letter from Dimick, also one from John Fattig and heard the news that there would be 25 or 30 boats here this season, that the U.S. freight was to be shipped by the river and that some of the Lower Sioux Indians were coming two hundred lodges strong to clean us out.

May 10. Warm. Frank Smith and Ed hauling wood. I have been laid up with my eyes since Sunday. Joe Mosser* and Dean ------ came down on a raft from Little Rocky. The river falling.

May 11. Very warm. Frank and Ed hauling wood. Eyes still sore. Went over the river in the afternoon; the river falling still, some 5 or 6 inches.

May 12. Very warm. River falling slowly. Barely able to work myself today. In the afternoon Bill Martin, Oleson and Louis Larsen* came up with Bill's oxen to leave them in the point with us. They have about two hundred cord on the bank below.

May 13. Pleasant with strong wind from the north. Bill Martin's crowd returned below. During the afternoon a heavy smoke rose up below in their direction. I hauled wood in afternoon. I am troubled every morning with my eyes paining me so that I have to lay abed until near noon. The river is falling a little, I think. Frank worked for me forenoon.

May 14. Pleasant. Rained a little last evening. Hauled wood all day. At daylight this morning Big McDonald came and aroused us to cross the river. He had walked all night and left Gus Tyler sick at their yard, either mountain fever45 or smallpox. His business was to get medicine. I put him across the river; for a wonder, my eye did not pain me. A heavy shower about dark. From appearances during the afternoon it must have rained heavily up the Musselshell. The river rose an inch and a half last night. A year ago today, the Deer Lodge arrived from Sioux City.

May 15. Sunday. Pleasant. A heavy shower in the night. The river rose 4 or 5 inches; still rising. Was over to Musselshell, the bank still caving off very fast there. McDonald just started this morning back to

Gus Tyler, whom he left sick and alone night before last. The news about boats is still very discouraging; only ten reported to be on the way.

May 16. Cool. The river rising still. Three feet and 8 inches of a rise above low water mark. Hauled wood all day. Pete Koch and Louis Larsen came up from below. The smoke the other day came from a lot [of] Bill Martin's wood that was burning on their point. They have lost near 75 cords of wood they say, by fire. Our potatoes are coming up finally.

May 17. Cool. River rising. Went down to long point after some elk meat that Bill Martin sent word we could have. Took the team. I, Ed, and Smith going there. Seems to be a good many deer in the points now and some elk.

May 18. Moderately warm. The river has risen four feet and 3 inches above low water mark. Pete Koch returned home. Tom Bogy and quite a crowd were over today to see us. In the evening I went across the river and stayed overnight. I forgot to mention that yesterday a large mackinaw with a lot of discharged soldiers passed down early in the morning. No news of importance.

May 19. Same as yesterday. The river on a standstill. I had just reached this shore with the boat this morning about 9 o'clock when I saw a man running in Musselshell and yelling at the top of his voice. In a moment afterward I saw a party of 5 or 6 Indians horseback dash across the bottom. When I instantly gave the alarm and then stationed myself in a favorable position to wait until the Indians should come in range of my gun on the other side of the river, while Ed brought me the needle gun. In a moment a party of three ran in behind the bluff directly opposite and sprang off their horses. I fired with a five hundred yard sight and from the manner in which they threw themselves out of sight, I judged I had struck some of them. Frank Smith was out in the woods at work when the alarm was raised. We could give but little assistance after this to the other side except to fire a few shots at very long range. I fired a couple of shots in particular at somebody going up the hill in the direction of the Indians but did not touch him or alter his gait. During this time the boys in the burg were keeping up a very lively fire with their Henrys and Spencers at from five to 8 hundred yards distance, but the Indians were always on the move. In the course of an hour, they all crossed the Musselshell and passed along the bluffs down the river. I counted 35 mounted Indians and a few loose horses with the aid of a glass. Just after the Indians had disappeared behind the timber, they fired the brass

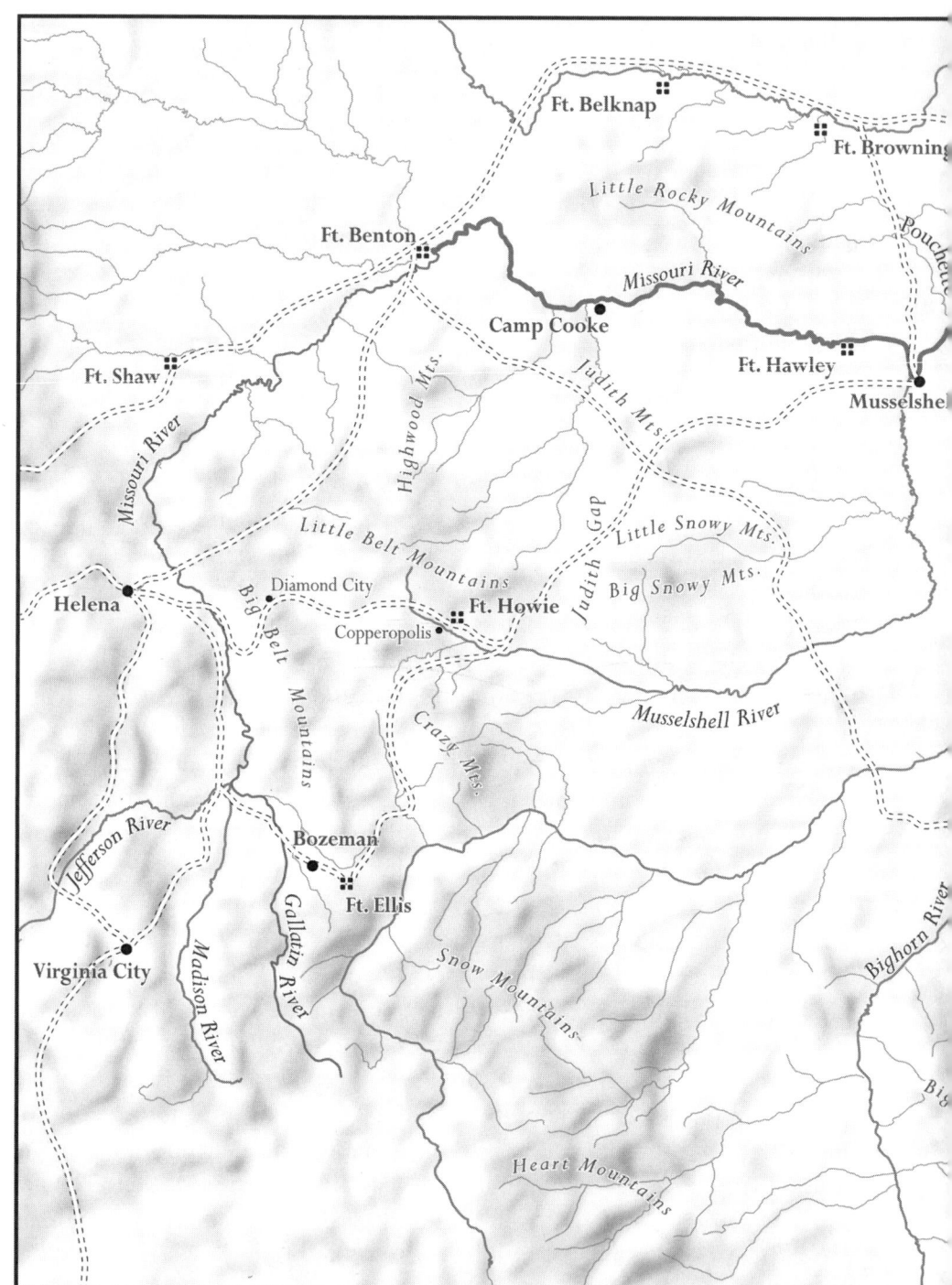

This medium scale map provides an excellent overview of the Montana Territ[ory] what was going on in the rest of the Territory at the time. Map courtesy Matth[ew]

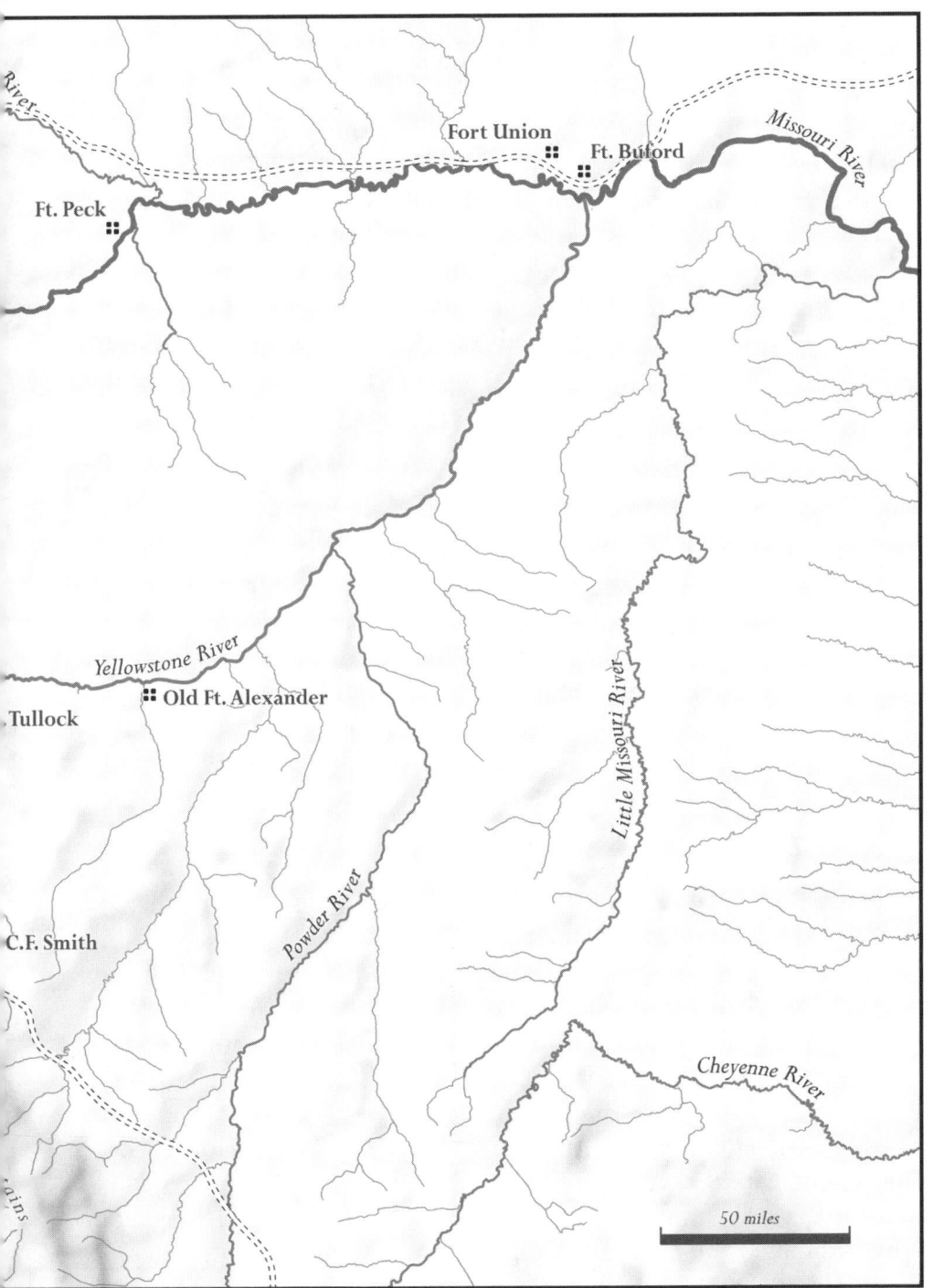

scape involved when placing the Fort Musselshell enterprise in context with
...pton.

piece at Musselshell and sent a shell that exploded over the timber near the mouth of the Musselshell, with no other effect, I think, than to hurry their departure. I saw a couple of them running up the bluffs way on the other [side] of the Musselshell River. After waiting a short time, I and Smith crossed the river to learn the particulars on that side. Judge of my surprise when I learned that the person I fired at crossing the bottom was no other than the half crazy Frenchman that has been stopping there for some time, waiting for a boat to go down the river. It appears that he was just packing up his blankets when the alarm of Indians was raised and regardless of the cries of the boys or the appearance of the Indians, he started up the hill on the Hawley Trail and walked right into the midst of a half dozen Indians who fired one shot at him and knocked him down with sabre striking him across the face with it and sticking a spear into him alongside of his nose, he going end over end down the hill dropping his pack, then getting up, he again struck out on the back trail into Musselshell. All the remarks he made were, "Oh Lord, this is terrible." Fortunately for him, the Indians pitched into him in plain sight of the boys, who kept up such a volley of lead that the Indians dared not follow him. His wounds proved to only be slight ones, and he would give no explanations of his conduct. After the fight, a party went out and got his pack and also found a good Remington revolver that the Indians had lost. On our return, we encountered an old buffalo bull just above the landing and had a little run after him and emptied our Henrys into him and around him at 3 to 500 yards but did not succeed in bringing him to the ground. The brass piece was fired two or three times after the Indians left, in hopes it might be heard by Bill Martin's and put them on their guard but the wind was unfavorable.46

May 20. Cool and cloudy with slight sprinkle of rain. The river rising nearly 4 feet and a half. Ed was fishing today and let the boat get away from him. He and Smith had a serious time getting it again; fortunately it lodged on the island and by building a raft they crossed to it.

May 21. Cool; sprinkled a very little. Was over to town. Some attachment papers were served by A.F. Smith on Mepferd.* [James Mefford] A party wants to go hunting in the morning in long point provided there is no boat. The Col. corraled his cattle over here again.

May 22. Sunday. Slightly cool. Steamer *Nick Wall*47 arrived this morning just after the hunting party landed and of course that postponed the hunt and they crossed back, but the boat only touched to land.

Mabbit, Bill Norris, Warring, and Louis Larsen, and nine of the boys had an opportunity to go aboard her. She was heavily loaded having 280 tons freight besides a few passengers. She reports but 7 or 8 boats on their way up, and no government freight coming. Warring says that Doc Clendenin got down safely and that there is no danger of George Grinnell ever coming here, also that Fort Peck is to be vacated and rebuilt either here, Little Rocky, or at old Fort Hawley. Mabbit says he got his pay from Grinnell or at least the most of it. The Steamer *Tacony* was sunk and sold as she lay for $350. Dick Harris went down the river and Bill Norris returned here strapped as usual. The steamer just touched at our yard in passing to land an old Indian, causing a great revulsion of feeling on our part as we expected to sell them some wood. Steamer *Deer Lodge* is expected tomorrow, T.C. Power and family aboard.

May 23. Warm. The river falling. Warring stayed here last night. Louis and French Joe went below. I and Ed went with them to point below after cattle. Found them all right and brought ours and Bill Martin's up. Worked until we broke an ox bow, then I crossed the river.

May 24. Cool; rained hard last night; muddy as the devil. Steamer *Ida Rees No. 2* 48 arrived; wooded with the Col. Durfee and Farwel on board. Farwel and Col. Clendeninn had a brisk little row at the woodyard opposite here. The principal cause of the quarrel was an anonymous letter sent to Peck and supposed to be done by the Col. sent by the party that took the iron boat from here some time ago. Embittered also by some old recollection, Farwel had decidedly the best of the fight, bloodying the Col.'s phiz and knocking him down a time or two to the great amusement of the bystanders. The Col. was very anxious to get hold of a pistol but no one accommodated him with one.

May 25. Warm and windy. Mabbot of the Skin and Grease is busy packing up everything to go above on the *Deer Lodge*. In the afternoon I and Frank went sailing up the river to Well's point to hunt, but got no game.

May 26. Warm. The river is falling fast lately. They have been firing the cannon at Musselshell this afternoon across the Musselshell River thinking, no doubt, they could bluff off any Indians that might be around, as some tracks were seen this morning, I understand, not far from the burg.

May 27 and 28. Warm. The river on a stand. Went over to town, concluded to start down the river and meet a boat with Mabbot and Tom Bogy. Came back and got ready and shoved out in Smith's boat about three o'clock in the afternoon. Shot a deer just at dark two or three points below Bill Martin's place. The evening very fine and pleasant. No moon, but there flecting from the Northern Lights made it quite light. Ran nearly all night, then ran ashore on the right bank and slept till daylight, then started again soon. Saw plenty of buffalo. Ran 6 or 8 miles and got breakfast. Killed a couple of buffalo bulls here that came to the river to get a drink. Shoved out again and met steamer *Deer Lodge* and boarded her 15 or 20 miles this side of Round Butte49. T.C. Power and family on her and some 15 or 20 passengers all told, who amuse themselves by shooting at all the game that comes in sight. Arrived at Bill Martin's woodyard near four o'clock afternoon. Steamer wooded a few cords, arrived at Musselshell at dark. Unloaded a little freight there and ran up to our yard where she lay all night and wooded with us. I am so hoarse with a cold, I can scarcely speak.

May 29. Sunday. Moderate. The river rising rapidly this morning. I could not speak at all for some time, kept improving during the day. Frank Smith went up on the steamer last night, also Joe Mosser, and Tom Bogy.

May 30. Cool. The river rising fast; began to rain in the forenoon and rained all day. McDonald and Gus Tyler came in about noon from their yard above. Said no boat had landed at their place yet. They thought someone had been saying they had the smallpox, that kept the boats from stopping with them.

May 31. Cool. Rained hard all last night and all day. Steamer *Nick Wall* passed down; just touched at Musselshell about sundown or a little before. It snowed until the hills looked quite white, kind of a slush snow, then quit storming anymore but was quite cool so that I am very much afraid our little garden will be destroyed.

June 1. Cool and a little cloudy. The sun rose clear, a little snow on the hills yet. The river is about four feet 7 inches above low water mark, the highest it has been this spring. Rained considerable during the afternoon. Lohmire came down yesterday on the *Nick Wall*. Gen. Sheridan50 and staff were aboard of her, I understand. She thinks of making a second trip from Sioux City.

June 2. The river rising rapidly; 5 feet of raise. Crossed the river to see Lohmire. Mills* and Sillcot* went down to Bill Martin's. Doing nothing nadays.

June 3. Pleasant. Rained very hard in the night. The river is 5 feet 3 1/2 inches high above low water mark this spring. In the afternoon

Frank Smith, Eph Hoover, and Mountain Charley arrived from above on a raft. Frank is laid up with a lame back.

June 4. The river on a stand. Steamer *Ida Reese No. 2* passed down in afternoon. She wooded at the Col.'s. Judd arrived on her. No robes shipped yet on account of the orders of Gen. Sheridan, in consequence of the smallpox last winter among the Indians in this country. Rained towards evening.

June 5. Sunday. Rained all night last night. Steamer *Viola Bell*51 arrived late last night and lay at Musselshell overnight. The river is falling a little, about an inch.

June 11. A very hard shower today towards evening. June 5th in the evening, the *Deer Lodge* arrived. On the 6th I went down to Peck on her. On the 11th the Steamer *Sallie* passed Fort Peck. Fred Watters was on her. I succeeded in getting a pair of field glasses and a robe of him;

Steamboats played a vital part of the history of the upper Missouri River and were significant to the way of life enjoyed at Fort Musselshell. Shown here is the stern wheel Far West, which had a illustrious history, including being the first boat up the Yellowstone River with General Custer in 1876. No. 955-112. Courtesy Montana Historical Society Research Center, Photograph Archives, Helena, Montana.)

during the evening he started down the river again of himself to go to the *Nick Wall* that is on a sandbar near Spread Eagle Bar.

June 13. Steamer *Bertha* and *Peninah*52 passed Peck. The former, I came up on. In the evening we lay at Round Butte woodyard. The *Peninah* coming in a few moments after us. Major Reed and Farwel also on board the *Bertha*.

June 14. Arrived at Musselshell at dusk. *Bertha* wooded at the upper yard. Before she had loaded five cords, the *Peninah* arrived at the lower yard and I went down to see her and oh, such mud, ankle deep all the time. Warring started to Helena on the latter boat, also several of the boys left for different places on the river. The *Bertha* lay overnight, but the *Peninah* shoved out and went on up the river. James Wells also went upon the *Bertha;* he arrived while I was at Peck.

June 15. Steamer *Viola Bell* passed down the river. Still rising; over six feet above low water mark.

June 16. Steamer *Ida Stockdale* passed up, left some freight for the Col. I remained at Musselshell last evening, did not return until the boat left. Then Frank was very much disappointed that he did not get to go up on her. Returned across the river again.

June 17. Pleasant. Worked in the shop repairing guns. The river still rising.

June 18. Hot today. Did a little on garden fence; keep the cattle up nowadays. Only four men in town now. This morning Bill Norris, Fox, and three Indians on horseback started for Fort Browning. One of the Indians was Louise, a Crow squaw, that Reed has taken a fancy to. She is just getting over the smallpox, from which her parents just died a few days ago. From the best information I can get, but few of the Crows have the smallpox yet.

June 19. Sunday. Very hot. Looking for Indians everyday.

June 20. Very warm. River falling slowly. Had another Indian raid today. Ed was lying down in the shade of a tree in front of the stockade, while I was inside reading and Frank and Jennie were in the stable, when Ed happened to turn his head and see a half dozen mounted Indians across the river directly opposite to us and going toward Musselshell at a moderate gallop. He watched them a moment without being certain what they were, if hostile or friendly, then shouted, "Oh Lee! Indians! Indians!" In an instant I and Frank were at his side with our Henrys in our hands, but so steadily did they go for Musselshell that we hesitated to fire until they were nearly out of range. Then they turned to the right and ran in behind the Skin and Grease stockade, wheeled their horses around and fired a volley into the buildings without a single man at the place seeing them. While they were galloping down, I could see some of the doors open as if to invite the Indians to enter if they only had the nerve to do so, and I fired a shot or two to try and wake them up, but to no purpose. Then I and Frank opened on the Indians with 900 yard sights as the Indians opened fire themselves, then rode off at full speed followed by a volley of heavy rifle balls. In a moment we saw the Col. slipping out from the Skin and Grease and run down home and proceed to load up the cannon in front of his place, but was so slow that the devils were clear out of sight up the Musselshell. Towards evening I went over to town and learned that everybody was completely surprised, that the Col. and party were talking of going hunting on the Musselshell toward evening as he said that the Indians never attacked the place this season of the year. The words were hardly out of his mouth when the firing commenced. Judd and Charley Morrison sprang into the bastion at the back end of the stockade and opened on them at a hundred and fifty yards distant; unfortunately not killing any. Judd failed to get a cartridge in his gun the first two snaps by being in too big a hurry to load and failing to throw the lever of his gun far enough forward and before he got ready for them, they were going as fast as their horses could take them. Nobody was hurt. Six men in the place were all they could muster, and one of them arrived yesterday and had just come in from on the Musselshell where he had been hunting. In the evening they fired a shell cross the Musselshell as a feeler.

June 21. Warm; looks like rain. In the evening Oleson and French Joe came up from below to see what the matter was as they had heard the 1st shot fired from the cannon in the evening. They report things quiet down their way, say they have seen a little sign of Indians.

June 22. Warm. Steamers *Sallie* and *Bertha* passed down today, the latter stopped at Musselshell and took the Col.'s and Judd's buffalo robes down the river. Not many passengers aboard either of them. The wood panic is so great that some yards above are selling pinewood for four dollars a cord. Both boats had a supply of it on board. There is one item of encouragement for next year for a good supply of boats then, that is, that none of the freight shipped by rail has reached Helena yet, while the river freight is coming along in good time, which I hope induce Montana merchants to ship by boats next season almost entirely. At any rate, circumstances will compel me to abide my chance for another season, hit or miss. The river has fallen a foot or more; above five feet above low water mark at present.

June 23. Moderate. River falling still. Pete Koch and Bill Martin came up this morning about daylight to get their oxen. They are going to move up here for the present as there is no prospect of doing anything there this season anymore.

June 24. Warm; a heavy shower last night. Nothing of importance except Ed let the cattle get away from him while he was herding them. Bill Martin and party came up last evening and slept in the lower stockade.

June 25. Warm; rained hard last night. Potatoes are doing fine now. Steamer *Peninah* passed down, stopped at Musselshell, took some government freight aboard. The Col. also went aboard her, going to the States, leaving Peter Koch in charge in his place with instructions to move his buildings. Eph Hoover also came down from Little Rocky, also Thompson.

June 26. Sunday. Warm. Yesterday and today there has been a large fire burning below somewhere by the smoke that rises in that direction. The river is falling fast, but is horribly muddy this morning on account of a heavy rain above. Warring came down from Little Rocky last evening. Looks very much like rain again this evening.

June 27. Warm; thunder and lightning last night but no rain. The river has fallen 18 inches or more. The Col.'s men have begun to tear down buildings in readiness to move their store farther from the river. No news of importance.

June 28. Pleasant.

July 3. Sunday. Pleasant lately with warm days and cool evenings. Smith is preparing to go down the river soon. The river is down again to about 3 1/2 feet above low water mark. Yesterday Bill Martin, Sweeney,* Missouri,* and Brady* came down from Hawley on a raft bringing a lot of meat. They said that they could see three fires the other day down the river when we saw the big smoke. Also report that sixty Sioux passed down the river on the north side a short time ago having been to the Crow camp and stolen a lot of horses.

July 4. Warm. The river still falling slowly. Very quiet fourth until near noon when we had another Indian raid on Musselshell. I went across the river about ten 1/2 o'clock; in an hour afterward, three others followed me. They had got in about 300 yards of the buildings over there when a party of mounted Indians made their appearance on the hill to the right of them, 5 or 600 yards distant and raised their war whoop and gave chase, and opened with their revolvers as they came up. Two of the boys lit out for the houses as fast as they conveniently could. The other, being behind in the start, dropped down in the sagebrush on the bank of the river and fired a shot or two as the Indians circled away from him to get out of range of the balls that were coming from Musselshell and from the two stockades on this side of the river. All three of them got in more frightened than hurt. At the same time that the horseback party made their dash, there was a party of foot men in the sagebrush back of the place and among the trees towards Musselshell River, and in behind an old shop building. They opened their fire as the boys ran out, but fortunately no one was hurt on our side. I was sitting in the store of T.C. Power and Co. talking with the man in charge when the alarm was raised by Warring shouting, "Indians! Indians! Look Out!" I snatched my Henry and ran out in front of the building and got one shot at the party running the boys in, with what effect I could not tell. The shell not freeing itself readily prevented me from running to meet the Indians, probably saving me from the sagebrush. After firing a few shots at the running Indians, I proceeded to assist in handling the cannon and throwing a few shells up the Musselshell where the Indians were retreating as fast as they could while they were in range of our rifles. As usual, in a short time they began to appear on the bluff cross the Musselshell, but a little farther off. We fired a few shells at them when they all disappeared. Dinner being about ready when the fight began, most of the boys went in to eat, while I and a couple of others took our station on top of the house to watch with the glasses. Soon saw several Indians over in the hills coming back again, most of them on foot. In a short time we detected the heads of three or four on the banks of the Musselshell apparently watching for some of their own party that we thought were wounded. Leaving the other two to watch, I went down and exploded a couple of shells apparently right where they sat causing them to disappear very suddenly. A lot of them (were) still on the hills cross the Musselshell. We explode a few more shells over their heads. Still they hung around. A reinforcement of three or four men arriving, a party started out to explore the sagebrush. One dead Indian was found about three hundred yards out, shot through the thigh and bled to death. He ran and crawled a hundred yards after he was shot. He had an old flintlock gun and bow and arrows, ammunition for about a dozen rounds for his gun. He had fired his gun and got the powder in for another charge before he got his own death shot. After scalping him, he was brought in and dumped into the Missouri. The Indians were watching our proceedings from the bluffs and appeared to conclude that it was useless to hang around any longer as they began to disappear. In a short time there was none visible. Everything considered, the fight made quite a lively little 4th of July celebration. From their actions we judged that there were some more of their number dead or wounded. Hope so at any rate.

July 5. Pleasant but cloudy; in the morning everything quiet. In the afternoon Drew Denton and Joe Synix came down from Little Rocky. Everything is quiet up the river; no Indians to be seen.

July 6. Pleasant and a little cloudy. Frank and Jennie are busy packing to go down the river on the Steamer *Stockdale* that is expected down the river today. (It is 10 or 11 o'clock now.) Towards evening the steamer arrived and landed on the other side at Gov. landing. Eph Hoover came over with a yawl having got off above. Everybody went cross the river but Ed. Jennie, Frank, Warring, and John McDonald all left on board for the States; peace go with them, as we will not have much peace here I am afraid for fighting with Indians and scarcity of grub this winter. Things are very dull here now and will probably remain so until steamboat time next year.

July 7. Pleasant; evenings quite cool lately; the river still falling. I and Ed busy cleaning up today. Bill Martin and his crowd moved their things up here today and started a hunting up the river in the afternoon, also Thompson crossed the river to go above with D. Denton and Synix when they go.

July 8. Pleasant, but cloudy with appearance of rain. River falling fast. Judd and a lot of the boys over to see us today. Judd, Charley Morrison, Joe McKnight,* and Johnny Cochran came in last evening at Musselshell. Everything quiet above. McKnight and Cochran came in on horseback; the others on a raft. Thompson, D. Denton, Joe Synix, J Cochran, and another, McKnight, I think, started up the river again this afternoon for Hawley and Little Rocky.

July 9. Pleasant. Bill Martin and party returned with a supply of meat. Charley Morrison came over from the other side.

July 10. Sunday. Cool. Rained nearly all night; a fine shower for the garden. Towards evening most of the boys crossed the river to hunt. A short time after they had gone, a herd of buffalo came to the river on the opposite side to drink. Ed, Brady, and myself crossed the river and approached them as they were going back into the hills again. By following up one of the large coolies that put into the river from between the hills, we approached within two hundred yards of the main party and were lying behind a little bank trying to decide which we should all shoot, as meat was our object. When a single cow appeared from a little ravine to our left, scarcely a hundred yards distant and stood broadside to us, in an instant the three guns were leveled at her heart and the reports followed in quick succession. She made a few quick bounds and stood sullenly still while the herd broke pell mell up the hill. At the same time I turned my Henry rifle to work upon them as they ran, firing 4 or 5 shots before they were out of sight over the hill. As they disappeared, one of them behaved as though he had received a severe wound. As the cow still stood on her feet a couple more shots near the heart settled her. Ed and Brady went to work to cut out some meat, while I shouldered my gun as guard and went onto the ridge. In looking round I soon found another wounded buffalo, a young bull; a few more shots settled him. They both proved to be in very good condition so early in the season. Shouldering our meat we hurried down the river and crossed the river and reached home at dusk just as the other party of hunters came back. They had succeeded in killing a blacktail and startling up a big bear on the point below the mouth of the Musselshell.

July 11. Pleasant. Was cross the river working and packing up my tools to bring over here. Bill Martin and crowd went below to their wood yard to be gone 5 or 6 days.

July 12. Warm and pleasant as usual. Saw a couple of buffalo bulls cross the river at the lower end of Jenk's point; did not go after them.

July 13. Very warm; the river still falling.

July 14. Evenings cool and nice but the days are as hot as the devil. Bill Martin and party returned. Brady and Missouri arrived early in the morning, said they were disgusted with the country and they were going to leave for civilization and began to arrange affairs accordingly. Quite a little storm of wind in the afternoon, with a little rain.

July 15. Missouri, Brady, and the emigrant started down the river on a raft early this morning bound for the States. Towards noon an Irishman named Jinny Grimes came down the river on a raft from Benton destitute and broken, trying to get to Minnesota near Fort Abercrombie where he had a mother and brother. He said they were living on farms, said he had been robbed of everything the other side of Benton by a party of Indians and whites. His story was a little confused in regard to it. We gave him some grub and an old musket. He started down the river but crossed over to the other side. The wind "blowed" hard from the west today most of the time. Went hunting in the evening to Well's point but got nothing.

July 16. Very warm. Today the first mackinaw of the season passed down; ten persons aboard. Two of them were women, and a couple of children.

July 17. Sunday. Very warm. Was over to the burg. Nothing of importance except the buffalo are coming onto the river and their rutting season is just commencing.

July 18. Very hot; (in) afternoon a black, heavy thunder shower came up with wind and a little rain; soon was over and nearly as hot as ever. A great many buffalo in sight up the Musselshell today.53 They keep up a terrible bellowing. Pete Koch was over to see us today. Sweeney began to work for me today, hunting nearly all the forenoon for the cattle. Found them in McGinnis' point after hunting through Well's point first.

July 19. Pleasant. J. Lee, Dean*, George Horn*, Charley Williams, and Mosser came down from Little Rocky. Bill Martin and party went up to Well's point to cut hay. The buffalo got a sudden fright today on the other side and disappeared suddenly; indicative of the presence of Indians. Cutting and hauling poles forenoon, splitting poles and fixing up the stockade.

July 20. Pleasant. Went over and worked all day in the shop for J. Lee, Dean, and Charley Williams. Three men came down in a skiff that belonged to J. Lee, who claimed it as soon as they landed. They said they had left a boat in place of it, just as good only a little smaller. They were broken or strapped, but gave a pistol in exchange rather than go back after their own at Little Rocky. They were probably deserters as they had but a needle gun between them.54

July 21. Quite warm. Looks like rain. Everything quiet. Old man Lee ------ with me last night. No buffalo to be seen today. Busy hauling logs for my shop.

July 22. Moderately warm; a small sprinkle of rain. Hauling logs for second story to house. No buffalo about today.

July 23. Cloudy, looks very much like rain. Watered the potatoes.

July 24. Sunday. Warm. My eye pained me considerable. Toward evening D. Denton and Joe Synix arrived from Little Rocky and just from Benton. Everything quiet and business very dull.

July 25. Moderately warm. Worked in the shop for Drew and Joe,

Ed, and Sweeney worked on the stockade.

July 26. Warm. A mackinaw from Benton with three men arrived . They were very anxious to get more men to go along with them. Sweeney, who has been working for me for some time, concluded he would quit and go as far as Fort Buford. A small boat also passed down with one man in it; he did not stop anywhere; a deserter probably from some post above. Three of us worked 1/2 day on my shop logs and I and Ed in the afternoon. No one but us two in the stockade now, but we have plenty of ammunition.

July 27. Quite warm today. Buffalo bellowing in the morning up Crooked Creek, apparently a great many. Finished hewing shop logs and tore down and hauled out the old stable. The hay party came down with their things from Well's point, done cutting hay, I suppose.

July 28. Very warm. Busy putting up the shop building. At sundown went over to Musselshell; everything quiet. P. Koch, Bill Martin, and Judd had gone up to the second point hunting; to be gone all night. The river is falling slowly lately.

July 29. Very warm. Felt a little unwell and did not work, either of us, until about sundown we worked a little. Judd and C. McKnight came over just before dark after a boat to go hunting with up the river in the morning.

July 30. Warm, but the mornings are nice and pleasant. Busy at work on the shop putting up logs. Looked very much like rain in the morning; smoky and hazy through the day. The hunting party started this afternoon from the other side.

July 31. Sunday. Hot from about 11 in the forenoon until nearly night. The days have been very warm for some time now. This morning, buffalo bellowing around a good deal, also this evening. Today some of the boys on the other side got after a lot of geese and killed 4 of them opposite here. I got one of them with the assistance of the dogs.

August 1. Warm. Worked in the forenoon on the shop. Early in the morning I was out and crippled a goose and a wolf but got neither. In the afternoon the hunting party returned on the other side.

August 2. Warm. Plenty of buffalo on the other side. The boys got after them. After breakfast we crossed the river and went up the river with Judd and killed a young bull and a cow. Gutted them and came back and got a yoke of cattle and swam them across and brought the meat in and brought a supply over for ourselves. Plenty of them on the Musselshell near the mouth of Crooked Creek. Put in a hard day's work today for the sake of a little meat. The river is falling lately again, only a small stream this side of the island; [can] almost jump it. French Joe is, or has been, quite sick lately but is able to be about at present.

August 3. Hot as hell as usual for the last week. Our garden is looking as if it had been brought up in an oven, notwithstanding we have been hauling water and pouring it upon it. I fear nothing will come to maturity on account of the drouth. No particular news. Put up and fitted one round on the shop and put up the two plate logs. Plenty of buffalo on the other side.

August 4. Not quite so hot and toward evening it blew up quite cool. I took a stroll over the hills. In the night last night I thought I heard a shot over toward town and Ed said he heard the same. Have seen no one today to learn yet what it might have been. Fitted down four logs today on the shop; put two of them up from the ground. The river is still falling slowly. I have not been to see but think the island channel is dry in places.

August 5. Quite cool last night; moderate today. One year ago today, Everett arrived from Capt. Cliffs party at the Black Butte, waiting for guides from this place. Everett was nearly dead for water; his horse the same. The weather is just as dry and hot now as it was then, but the dry weather set in later this season and there was more rain during this spring than there was last. Plenty of buffalo this evening in sight on the other side. I was busy chinking my shop building. Quite smoky today; for the last week or ten days it has been considerably so, but not so bad as today.

August 6. Quite cool today. Had some sport chasing a couple of old bulls from back on the ridge into the bottom and into the river at the wood yard where they both gave up the ghost. One floated off in the water.

August 7. Sunday. Quite cool again today; comfortable under a robe and blanket nights. In the afternoon a mackinaw with 3 men arrived on their way down the river. Had to go over to the shop to do some work on a Henry rifle for them. Got a letter from McNeal from Helena.

August 8. Moderate. Worked all day on the shop building. I forgot to mention at the proper time that [the] island channel of the river was dry in places one day last week so that a person could cross dry shod. The river is constantly falling.

August 9. A little warmer than for the last few days. Plenty of buffalo around yet. Pete Koch was over looking around to see about cutting and curing some willows for hay as the Col. had sent him orders to that effect.

August 10. Cold and a little rainy. Did nothing in the forenoon. In the afternoon took quite a hunt. J. and Ed tried to take the dogs by leading them but it was a failure. So Ed came home with the dogs and I went down to McGinnis' point and killed an old bull for bear bait. Got home after dark quite tired.

August 11. Cool. Last night was quite cool, froze ice 1/2 inch thick. Our potatoes look desperate. Rather early for ice, I think; I look for a hard winter. Went hunting in forenoon, crippled a bull and left him for dead up Wells Creek. Came back at noon and saw some Indians in town. After dinner I went over to see who it was and found a couple of Rappahoes and their squaws. One was the celebrated Natanee. He talks English fluently, has two squaws and four children. They want to come

This undated picture by photographer W. E. Hook Sr. shows Old Fort Clagett on the Missouri River. Courtesy Montana Historical Society Research Center, Photograph Archives, Helena, Montana)

over to this side and stop awhile, 'fraid other Indians will steal their horses. Charley McKnight was over to see us at sundown.

August 12. Moderate. Today Natanee moved over on this side and we put him and his family in the lower stockade. He talks of starting for Browning in the morning and that Judd and Charley Morrison are going with him.

August 13. Quite warm. Natanee and party started for Fort Browning. Charley Morrison went with them, going to go to Benton. I and Ed shouldered our guns and went up on the flat and killed three bulls, one of which was in very good order. Came back and got the team and brought a load of meat in for chickens and dogs. Left the other carcasses in the head of a coolie putting into McGinnis point. We shall poison them for wolves in a couple of weeks as their fur will be getting good then. I sent a letter to Baker of Benton and one to E.W. McNeal of Helena by Charley Morrison.

August 14. Sunday. Warm and windy. Stayed indoors all day. In the afternoon Charley McKnight came over with his violin. Cloudy and looks stormy this evening. Judd, Bill Martin, and Oleson started up the river a hunting yesterday afternoon, going as far as Hawley or farther and coming back on a raft.

August 15. Warm. I worked on the shop most all day. French Joe was over to see us and took dinner. He has been quite sick lately but is improving slowly now. In the afternoon, Ed went over to town with Joe. While Ed was gone I discovered 3 old bulls the other side of the timber in the foothills back of the stockade. Getting my gun and ammunition and locking the dogs in the stockade, I went after them and soon had all three Hors in combat; two dead on the ground and the other badly wounded, which I left for the purpose of trying to get on higher ground for the purpose of poisoning the carcass for wolves. Taking the two tongues I went home, got supper, and started back after the third one, Ed being with me, also the three dogs. After poisoning one of the dead carcasses, we soon found the other still alive. The dogs went for him and Old Steve, a bull dog, closed in on him and seizing him by the long hair on the head, was thrown in the air violently before we could get a shot into the bull. True grit to the last, Old Steve had hold of him when he fell from 3 or 4 shots we hastily poured into the bull. Waving his tail fiercely aloft the bull would charge for the dogs although one of his shoulders was broken. In one of his lunges he caught Old Steve on his horn and tore a gash in the hide of the dog on the left shoulder six or eight inches long exposing the flesh for a space nearly as large as a person's hand but without going in any deeper than the skin. So determined was he to hang onto the bull that he did not appear to know he was hurt until some time after the fight was all over. After getting home, Ed holding him, I sewed up the place as well as possible, although only skin deep still it is a severe wound.

August 16. Quite warm and windy as the devil. Went out to our bait this morning and while there discovered a couple bulls in the lower end of the point. Having the dogs with us, Ed stayed back to hold them while I got within a hundred yards of them and soon had both lying dead on the ground, not fifty yards from where they first stood. The tongues and a little fat was all we took of them.

August 17. Cool, afternoon the wind was very strong from the north; blew down a great many trees in the point. Windy, cold, and raining a little this evening. Just about sundown we saw J. Lee go into Musselshell on horseback.

August 18. Cold last night and all day. Rained a little in the morning. Crossed the river and worked in the shop there in the afternoon. A couple Arrapahoes and their squaws came down from Hawley with old man Lee yesterday. This afternoon they struck off again up the Musselshell going to the Rappahoe camp, I suppose. They say that the Cheyenne and Sioux are coming to fight us this fall and the Rappahoe are coming to trade. We tell them to come ahead, we have good guns and plenty of ammunition and like to fight or trade as they like.

August 19. Cool last night and today. Ed went over to town. I worked on the shop. Toward evening went to look after our bear bait. Found them all eaten up; nothing left worth watching after anymore.

August 20. Pleasant. Caught our first wolf today. Got up at daylight and went to see a bait in the lower end of the point, but saw no bear. Saw 3 or 4 wolves, one perfectly white. Afternoon Judd, D. Denton, Thompson, and Dean arrived from above. I received letters from S.J. Newhall, McNeal, and Bancroft Bros., San Francisco. The boys killed a few deer coming down but saw no elk.

August 21. Sunday. Warm. I and Ed killed three buffalo today, one at the lower end of McGinnis point, two near the upper end of long point. I shot 25 shots at them and a couple more that ran off wounded. Afternoon had to work in the shop for Thompson on his Henry rifle.

August 22. Warm. Judd and Denton came over while we were out looking at our wolf bait. They said they saw fresh Indian tracks yesterday up at the mouth of Crooked Creek. I intended to go below and draw a carcass into McGinnis' point with the oxen for bear bait, but was suspicious of the presence of Indians and did not go, merely drove up the cattle. About noon a party of 35 Rappahoes, 9 of them squaws, rode into Musselshell. We went over to see what was up. They say their camp is on the Yellowstone. As well as a person can learn from them, their object in coming here is to see what kind of a trade they can get here if their camp should come. One of them called Friday* is a fluent talker in English, better than Natanee was; one white man and a Spaniard with them. Just before night, we had a heavy thunder shower and some considerable rain. There appeared to be a heavy rain up the Musselshell, then came here and rained furiously here for 15 or 20 minutes.

August 23. Cool and cloudy, rained hard in the night; rained in the afternoon. During the day sawed up a log for puncheon and hauled it up. The Rappahoes still cross the river at Musselshell.

August 24. Cool and rained some. Toward evening went to McGinnis' point and Ed killed his first deer in this part of the country. The Rappahoe Indians left today going to Hawley most of them, some going back to their camp on the Yellowstone. They say they are coming here to trade this winter.

August 25. Warm. Busy forenoon putting mud on the roof of the shop. Afternoon crossed the river and worked in the shop.

August 26. Warm. Finished the shop roof. Ed and I were down to McG.'s point but got nothing. The bear all appear to have left for some other locality. I am awful tired tonight; shoveling is the cause of it.

August 27. Warm. Ed went over to town. I was busy all day hewing out puncheon for the shop floor. About noon Judd, Long, Bill Martin, and the Rappahoe stranger went down to long point to hunt, taking two horses and a mule with them. I saw some Indians go into Musselshell this evening.

August 28. Sunday. Cloudy and rainy this morning. Louis came up on the mule early this morning from long point, says he came up with four men that came from Peck. I soon went cross to Musselshell and learned they were only a party of hunters that have been hunting up the river. They said they had killed 8 elk this side of Peck besides a lot of deer. Old man Lee came down from Little Rocky on his little black mare which he says he has sold to Lohmire for $125.00. Also Lohmire has sold his interest in the Little Rocky wood yard to Joe Mosser. During those hard rains the other day, the buffalo disappeared from around here.

August 29. Warm but windy as the devil. I was busy fitting down sleepers and dressing out flooring in the shop. Ed sat in the house and read. Old man Lee went back again. Last evening the horseback party got back from below.

August 30. Warm, raining around in the afternoon, a little here, too. Ed cut a cord of wood for the first today. I was busy dressing out flooring. Toward evening we went down to McGinnis' point and only succeeded in wounding a blacktail doe. I shot her not over sixty yards standing looking straight at me, struck her in the shoulder. We are out of meat or I would have killed her dead in her tracks sure. No one ever saw it fail under such circumstances.

August 31. Moderate and cloudy; rained a little in the night. I got up very early this morning and went to Wells point. Saw 11 deer but did not get any, nor even got a good chance to shoot. I heard some shots down in long point, I suppose by the party hunting down there. Afternoon crossed the river to do a little work. Judd and Tom Hardenger came up from below. They killed an old bear and 3 cubs yesterday below Martin's point, but got no elk and but 3 deer. Bill Martin's party returned with three elk; Oleson killed two of them.

September 1. Warm and clear but rained a little in the morning early. I went up to Well's point at daylight. Shot a deer and lost it in the brush. Came back about 10 o'clock. I and Ed went back with the dogs. As we went out we heard a couple of shots down the river that sounded like a Henry rifle. We remarked it, but passed on and hunted the point without getting any deer then came back home and had been there but a short time when Bill Martin, Oleson, and French Joe came over from Musselshell and wanted to know if we had not seen the war party that was below the Musselshell and had been there for two or three hours shooting and shouting and burning up a small lot of hay that some of the boys had cut awhile ago. Of course we said no. The last they saw of the Indians they had separated, part going up the Musselshell and part going onto the bottom next to the Missouri below the Musselshell and none were in sight. When they left, one of the Indians came up behind a knoll on the other side of the Musselshell and bravely emptied his revolver in the air towards the town, while others "blowed" whistles, waved flags, and coup sticks nearly 3/4 of a mile distant. Four of us then proceeded up to Well's point and drove up the cattle and put them in the stockade. Saw nor heard anything more of the Indians. They will probably pay us a visit tomorrow if not tonight. French Joe is stopping with us tonight.

September 2. Pleasant, but looks a little like rain. Early this morning a mackinaw with 8 soldiers arrived; they ran all night. They passed 4 fires during the night between here and Hawley. They must be the Rappahoes returning or a party of the Sioux party that had crossed the river somewhere as the fires were on this side of the river. A part of the Sioux, at any rate, are in the point below the mouth of Musselshell as there was some shooting there this morning and nobody was out of our parties. Two or three of the boys came over and the cattle were stockaded again; at least our yoke and Bill Martin's. The soldier party stopped at Musselshell on account of the Indians, intending to run by in the night. I don't know whether they have gone or not. Nothing more has been seen or heard of the Indians since morning, that I have heard of yet. I was busy dressing out flooring. Ed who is getting very courageous cut wood part of the day between the two stockades. Our old cat kittened last night in one of the armchairs, had four nice little fellows this morning, a squirming and sucking away like all fury.

September 3. Quite warm and clear; this evening it looks like rain very much. Nothing has been seen or heard of the Indians today. Some of the boys on the other side were out hunting and killed a blacktail deer in the hills opposite us. Busy dressing out flooring.

September 4. Sunday. Quite warm. Nothing new of Indians today. Charley Morrison returned from Benton. Bill Martin and Pete Koch came with him in a small boat. The last two went from here yesterday to Hawley. French Joe came over this evening to commence hauling wood tomorrow if Ed wants to work.

September 5. Pleasant. Ed, French Joe, and I went to McGinnis' point this morning and got the cattle. I went to work dressing flooring while Ed and Joe went to hauling wood. A little before noon a war party of Crows came down the river and stopped at Musselshell. After dinner the boys were down after the first load when I saw a big smoke up in the hills on the other side which very much excited my apprehensions. I buckled on my ammunition and thought I would go down and hurry up the boys and bring them in as I was satisfied that there was something wrong somewhere. Before I went I thought I would go into the shop and take a look round. While there the movement on the other side attracted my attention and while looking at them I saw a couple of the white men come to the bank of the river and fire a couple of shots apiece and follow firing into the air. I knew that it meant danger on this side. I instantly turned to look back into the point and the first thing I saw was 3 or 4

Indians a horseback riding for the stock which happened to be within 3 or 4 yards of the stockade. I instantly opened fire on them at 4 or 5 yards distance and turned them away, but one had succeeded in getting to the horses and starting them, but they took the wrong direction for him and my shooting at the others frightened him so that he thought he had better leave. About this time Ed and Joe came in sight. When I called and hurried them into the stockade, leaving the team in good range, several Indians were in the timber opposite the stockade and above us. I fired a few shots at one a little below us and knocked him off his horse, but he mounted his horse again and rode off slowly. The cannon then opened on them from the other side toward the lower end of the point. Three men and a couple of Crows came over and drove up our team and all of them were put in the stockade. The Crow Indians now came over swimming the river with their horses and borrowed all the guns and pistols they could from the whites and then took out on the bluffs after the Sioux, one white man, well mounted, going with them. I, Judd, and Bill Martin went out as far as the point of the bluffs and listened to the fight for nearly an hour, as the two parties alternately ran each other back and forth on top of the hill. Learning from an Indian there were only some 25 or 30 Sioux, Judd, Charley Morrison, and I went on to the hill where the fight was going on. We only got within 4 or 500 yards of the Sioux and fired a few shots apiece. The Crows made a sally to get the Sioux to chase them back onto us in a coolie but the Sioux didn't bite and soon left. One Sioux horse lay dead on the ground and they thought there were several more horses and men hurt badly from the motions. Not a scratch on our side among whites or Indians. All hands returned home and the Crows crossed back to Musselshell.

September 6. Pleasant. The boys thought it best not to haul wood anymore and Joe went over home. I was busy on the floor of my shop. Afternoon Pete came in, said he had been on top of the hill back of us to see where a big smoke was that they could see way down the river. He was afraid it was down at his wood yard, but saw from the direction it was not. Says he has just got the first papers containing accounts of the war going on between France and Prussia. Toward evening French Joe came over and said their guard saw a couple of mounted Indians in the hill across and below the Musselshell, evidently watching around for these horses that are here now. Yesterday was the first time they ever ran a raid on this side and the first time any friendly Indians happened to be in at the time. Before it was always just before or after such parties were here. The Crow party left last evening after dark, taking with them Judd's glass, and today he started up to Hawley in hopes of finding them there.

September 7. Quite warm. A large party of Indians came in to Musselshell today: Grovents and Rappahoes. The same that were here a short time ago. They have been to the Grovent camp and persuaded a lot of the latter to go back to camp on the Yellowstone with them. They all say they will surely be here in about 3 moons. They arrived a little after noon and toward evening they moved in among the Col.'s building timber below his house and made themselves some barricades for themselves and horses. They have a Piegan squaw among [them] that the Grovents took prisoner a short time ago killing 7 bucks and taking 3 squaws prisoner at the time. The Indian called Friday that talks English so fluently says that the same party of Sioux that made the raid here took 5 horses from Louis Rumbar [Bompart]* at Hawley. Hawley is on the south side of the river but early in the morning he swam his horses cross for the purpose of taking them up the river. The Indians happened to be cached in the willows conveniently at the time and cooly drove them off as they came out of the water.

September 8. Quite warm. I slept in the shop at Musselshell last night for fear the Indians might try to break in. Worked for some of the boys during the forenoon. Afternoon commenced to move my things over to this side of the river. The Indians were packing up by sunrise and in a short time after, some of them began to roll out. All were gone by 8 o'clock. They have to go 30 miles to get water at a place where they have sunk a couple of holes. Charley Morrison traded for a big mule and a horse this morning and had them hobbled after the Indians left. At noon the mule broke her hobble and put out on the Indians' trail on the run. Charley saddled up his horse in hot haste and put out a line after her. I came from Musselshell at dark and he had not returned; more than possible that he might run into trouble and danger. Ed is busy putting up a coal pit for me close to the stockade as it is not safe to be out very far from shelter and assistance.

September 9. Quite warm. Busy most of the day moving tools and stuff over from the other side to this. As I went over this morning near 7 o'clock, Charley Morrison came in on his mule. He said the mule went straight to the Indians as fast as it could travel and that he followed as fast as he could on his horse, arriving at their camp just as they were building their fires. Some of the old men directed him to his mule which they had already caught before he arrived. Some of the young bucks did not want him to take it, said they caught it and it was theirs, but finally took his horse, pistol, part of his cartridges for his Henry, and his saddle, then let him take his mule. Some of those disposed to be friendly told him he had better leave as soon as he could as there were already five Sioux in camp that had joined them during the day; they didn't know what they might try to do. Charley took them at their word and lit out for home as fast as possible. Came back near half way and lay in a coolie until daylight, then came in, a sadder and a wiser man than before. Afternoon Oleson, D. Denton, George Horn, and Tom Hardinger started above. Oleson going to Benton, Tom going up the river hunting, the other two going to Little Rocky which they call their home.

September 10. Warm again. Still nearly all of the nights for a long time have been quite pleasant for sleeping and often cool enough for an extra blanket. Charley swam his mule to this side yesterday and keeps her tied up now to a picket rope. Finished shop floor, fixing bench and cleaning up a little. Ed fired the coal pit.

September 11. Sunday. Warm. Judd, Bill Martin, and Norris came down the river from Hawley. Ed went over and got half a deer of them.

September 12. Warm. Went over and moved the balance of my things today. At sundown a couple of fellows arrived from Buford; they came up on foot on this side of the river. They report the Indians below as not fighting the whites. Farwel is going to bring goods up to Little Rocky neighborhood or here.

September 13. Quite cool; sprinkled in the night last night and rained nearly all day today. The two strangers went to the other side after supper last night and are stopping at T.C.P. and Co.55 Charley M. here tonight.

September 14. Moderately cool and still raining most of the day. The boys on the other side killed an elk just above the graveyard on the bottom 5 or 600 yards distant from the houses in the afternoon. We went over and got a supply of meat. A very large buck with a big head of horns and fat as butter almost.

September 15. Still raining hard in the morning and all night nearly, and also nearly all day today. Afternoon Pete Koch was over to see us. Ed's coal pit is catching fits this rainy weather as it has been ready to draw the last two days. The sun shining toward night.

September 16. Moderate; sunshiny most of the day. Dried up the mud a good deal. I forgot to mention that the river rose 3 or 4 inches yesterday, and last night it rose all of two feet and still rising this morning, but began to fall toward noon and by night it had fallen 18 inches. Afternoon Judd and Pete came over and landed their boat where we go down to the river and when they got ready to go back their boat was a rod from the water. This morning Bill Martin, French Joe, Gus Tyler, and the two strangers from Buford went to Bill Martin's point with a boat to hunt elk and be gone 4 or 5 days. The river has been clear until today, showing the rise comes from rains above.

September 17. Moderately warm. Rained most of the day. Ed began to draw coal this morning, but soon had to quit on account of the rain. Several shots were fired this morning before it was light, what at we have not learned as no one has crossed the river today. Horribly muddy, was down to the lower end of the point barefooted hunting.

September 18. Sunday. Moderate; did not rain any but looked like it might at any moment almost. Pete and Louie were over in the afternoon. Pete said he was shooting at a skunk yesterday morning. The river is rising again this afternoon, nearly as high as it was a few days ago.

September 19. Warm; floating clouds. Went to work and made 50 adobois [adobe] and Ed went to drawing coal. Sundown heavy black clouds came up from the south with thunder and lightning. Had to carry my adobois under cover. The river is falling again rapidly.56

September 20. A little cooler, rained some last night and "blowed" considerable. Just before sundown a large mackinaw came down and stopped at Musselshell. Ten discharged soldiers on her going to Omaha. A couple of them came over to get a Lee's patent rifle mainspring; could not supply them as my forge is not yet up at this place.57

September 21. A little cool. Looked like rain in the forenoon. Pete, Judd, and Charley Morrison were all over. Judd was at work in the shop fixing an old Springfield rifle.

September 22. Quite cool; the first legitimate frost of the season, and quite a heavy one. Busy putting up my forge. Received a letter from I.G. Baker and one from McNeal. The latter from Helena, the first from Benton. The mail came in a small boat with a couple of men yesterday. Today they started on down again.

September 23. Cool. Heavy frost. Nothing unusual. Pete was over and said his word from the Col. was to the effect that he might be here in a week or ten days.

September 24. Heavy frost; quite windy during the afternoon. Pete was over [in] afternoon. Bill Martin, French Joe, Louey, and George went up the river hunting. Judd is busy shooting and working on some old Springfields. None of them shoot to suit him. Charley McKnight was over after dark and stayed awhile. Splendid aurora borealis this evening.

September 25. Sunday. Quite warm and pleasant.

September 26. Warm; no frost last night. The river down so the slough is crossable. Finished the forge or furnace.

September 27. Pleasant. Heard the wolves howling this morning back on the hills; quite a lot of them. Louey, George, Bill Martin, and French Joe got back; they killed 5 deer was all.

September 28. Pleasant and warm. The boys on the other side think there are Indians around. No wolfers have started out from here yet. It is time for them to be out now.

September 29. Same as yesterday. The cottonwood leaves are a bright yellow and have been for two days and falling off fast. Ed is chopping wood this week between the two stockades, chops about a cord a day. The news in the papers is very unfavorable to the French. The Prussians, it seems, have beaten them in several consecutive and important battles.

September 30. Nice and warm. Pete was over again today. Getting my shop pretty well finished except the daubing. Having considerable of gunsmithing along to do has made it a tedious job finishing.

October 1. Warm. The boys killed an old bull on the other side. Ed went over after some and is terribly hot, I think, by his look and actions, because I did not drop my work and start after it with him, and when I did arrive he treated and answered so shortly that I thought it would be the best thing I could do to keep out of his way and mind my own business. I finished Pete's gun today, a Spencer, and took it to him. It is fully a match for any of their Henrys for accurate shooting. D. Denton, Joe Synix, and George Horn came down from Little Rocky yesterday, going back tomorrow they say.

October 2. Quite pleasant. Went over to town and was over there most of the day. The boys went above, came on this side and got Hardinger's horse and went up about 11 o'clock. Judd, D. Denton, Joe Synix, George Horn, and Bill Norris. Ed is still grim as a bear with a sore head.

October 3. Pleasant. Helping Ed to build a hen house. Last night he had an eruption; a violent one. I can't see as he improves in temper or in charity toward those he has any dealings with.

October 4. Blustery and rained a little; quite cool and windy at dark.

Nothing of importance transpiring lately. Charley Morrison comes over regular everyday to tend to his mule that he keeps picketed close by. Hauling gravel this afternoon and putting in the sand.

October 5. Cool and cloudy. Putting gravel in the yard today; finished it. Engaged Charley Morrison to assist in hauling wood on to the bank.

October 6. Cloudy and cool. The boys hauled wood during the forenoon, when it began to rain and rained a couple of hours or more. I was hunting during the forenoon in the point below and in the hills. Saw a half dozen deer, but got [no] shots at them.

October 7. A heavy frost; moderate during the day. The boys hauling wood. I was to the lower point this morning saw 20 or 30 whitetail but got none; the grass awful wet. In the evening went to the point above; killed two wildcats was all. It is almost impossible apparently for me to kill a deer.

October 8. Moderate and pleasant afternoon. Started up the river on a hunt with Pete Koch and George taking a boat up with us. Went as far as Bill Martin's point and slept in the cabin there. Could shoot nothing on the way up but a goose that floated off down the river.

October 9. Sunday. Pleasant. Was out hunting at daybreak. Pete crossing the river, I and George hunted through the point; found nothing. Then took to the hills where I killed a large blacktail buck and George wounded another that ran off. We packed mine to the cabin, near two and 1/2 miles. As we started without breakfast we roasted some ribs right where I killed it and devoured with a hunter's keen relish. Afternoon started hunting down the river and arrived at Musselshell after dark. The weather looks very much like a storm. Bill Martin and Joe went out to Pouchette last Saturday and back again. Report plenty of water and game.

October 10. Pleasant. Stayed at Musselshell last night. This afternoon began to daub my shop with mud on the outside of the building. The boys are busy hauling wood.

October 11. Quite cool this morning. Nothing of importance.

October 12. Cool again, last night. The boys from Musselshell went below the mouth of the Musselshell and killed a bear, 3 buffalo, two deer, and a jackrabbit. Afternoon George Town* began to work for me cording wood below the lower stockade. The boys have been busy all week hauling wood.

October 13. Moderate. The boys banking wood. Toward evening

Ed broke the wagon and had to quit work. I dismissed Charley Morrison for a few days until I should be prepared for him again. George Town at work cording wood. Pete was over to see me. Looked very much like a storm all day.

October 14. Moderate. Rained considerable. Pete and Louey were hunting up Well's point but got no game. George Town worked about 2/3 of a day on account of the rain. Charley Morrison is fixing up to live in the lower stockade.

October 15. Quite cool. Building hen house yesterday and today. George Town worked enough today to call it two day's work. So far the weather looks very much like snowing. Town is going to live with Charley in the lower stockade.

October 16. Sunday. Quite cool. Some snow this morning visible on the other side of Crooked Creek; the first this fall. I did up a big washing today: 3 shirts, pair pants, 2 towels, 1 handkerchief, and 1 1/2 pair socks. Ed was hunting on the point below with the dogs and Charley and George, but got nothing. At sundown I was above with the same luck. Nothing of much interest except that Clendenin and Oleson have been expected for the last two weeks from Benton in a mackinaw and still they do not come. The snow today is just one day ahead of last year. Some flies still in the house, but they have not troubled meat outdoors for the last few days.

October 17. Monday; 18 – Tuesday.[sic]

October 19. Pleasant but still quite cool last night, froze considerable. Monday was quite warm, Tuesday was a little cool. Monday, I and Pete went down to Long point hunting. I killed a deer and Pete wounded a couple of buck elk. Just at dark when we got separated and had to go to our rendezvous in the point below where the boys have a cabin, before we found each other again. Tuesday we struck out again, hunted a little in the points and went out on to Hawley Flat where Pete killed an old bull and an antelope, and came home down Wells Creek, packing the antelope. Nearly tired to death, Oleson had arrived Monday after we left, but no word of Col. Clendenin. Tom Bogy is expected to come and take charge here. A war party of four Crows arrived from Peck yesterday. This morning they left for Hawley, Charley Williams going with them. Oleson brought down a half crazy man dressed in soldier clothes, also Bill Norris and Drew Denton. Fixing to go out onto the Pouchette in the morning after some buffalo meat with Bill Martin, Oleson, and French Joe. Also D. Denton, George Town, and Louey Larson with two yoke of oxen and wagon.

October 20. Moderate last night and rained some, also rained most of the forenoon. Quite cool in the evening.

October 21. Friday.

October 28. Friday. Last Friday I went to the Pochette in company with Bill Martin, French Joe, Oleson, Drew Denton, Louey Larson, and George Town. Toward evening it began to rain. Fortunately we were within a few miles of the Pochette, which we reached just at dark and camped. Rained all night and nearly all day Saturday. Saturday night and Sunday it snowed considerable. I and Louey killed three bulls Sunday. Monday a little warmer. Bill Martin and crowd putting up a cabin. Buffalo scarce; the storm appeared to have driven them away. When we came here there were plenty of them all around us. Tuesday I and Drew Denton killed a couple of buffalo cows; terribly muddy. Wednesday we started home, picking up the cows on the road. In the morning it was pleasant, but soon began to rain and get foggy so you could see nothing, and muddy terribly. Had to leave the wagon and team up at Well's point, and packing a little meat on our backs we got to my place at dark, but no one thought of stopping until they were where they could get something to put on their feet that was dry. George Town went down to the lower stockade where Charley Morrison had supper all ready prepared for him, he having heard us shooting at some geese in Well's point and concluded that we were coming. Ed had the gate barred when I arrived; he admitted me with a sullen silence that instantly quenched all feeling of sociability on my part. Not a word was passed between us during the evening, nor did he offer me the least civility. Although just coming in from a several day's absence, everything was in confusion and inconvenient for getting a hasty meal. Nor has a word passed between us up to this time, but his silence is preferable to his usual fault finding and bickering at least there is the semblance of peace and harmony. I did not feel like work today and in the afternoon after we got our meat down from the point above, I went over to town. George Boyd, it appears, has abandoned his place above and passed down the river on the 23rd stopping overnight. Old Louey Bombart is stopping at the post Boyd [George] built all alone, I understand. There will now probably not be any trading post at or near Little Rocky this winter. Tom Bogy is expected here everyday from Benton, in place of Clendenin. Yesterday was my birthday but very poorly celebrated, I assure you.

October 29. Pleasant, but freezes little nights and still muddy. The boys killed some more antelope today back in the hills. They killed 8 during the storm while we were out.

October 30. Sunday. Pleasant; mud nearly dried up. My eye paining me some today. Afternoon was down to see the boys below and took dinner with George Town. Ed is still dumby.

October 31. Pleasant. Pete Koch was over today. The boys think there are Indians around. The dogs made such a fuss last night. Concluded a bargain today with G.H. Town to cut 50 cords of wood.

November 1. Very windy. The boys out hunting today, killed a deer. Looks very much like storming ever since last evening; froze but little last night. The other side began to dig a landing in front of the store of T.C.P. and Co. Musselshell has but humble pretensions at present to being a town, only one building occupied beside the store of P. and Co., and averages about 6 inhabitants as a steady population. Flour is $12 per sack, poor quality of sugar .20 cts. per lb., coffee .50 cts., molasses $2.50 to $3.50 per gallon, beans .25 and .30 cts. per lb., dried apples .40 cts. per lb., green tea $2 per lb., boots $8 per pair. The present prices of furs is nearly as ------. Tanned robes $5 to $6 at the store, wolfskin $2.50 at the store, deerskins .20 cts. per lb. at the store pay, elkskins $4, red fox .75 cts. to $1, beaver .75 cts. per lb., other furs in proportion.

November 2. Nice and pleasant today. Snowed a very little last evening. George Town began to cut wood today on his 50 cord contract. Ed is still Dumby or Dummy. I am only afraid he will break the silence to jaw about something, that no one else would think of saying a word about but him.

November 3. Pleasant, but a little cooler than usual. Pete Koch was over today. He begins to talk like a Universalist[58] since reading several works on the subject that I had. I like to see it for he is a sensible young man and it confirms my own belief to see such believe as I do, especially when he was formerly a strong Orthodox. The boys were out hunting. Charley Morrison killed an elk, George killed a couple antelope. Raining this evening.

November 4. A little cool and trying to snow all day. Snowed enough last night to whiten the ground. No news from anybody or anywhere yet. Nearly everybody here is laying on their oars waiting for friendly Indians to come in to trade.

November 5. Some snow on the ground in the morning, but soon disappeared, except in shade, as the sun came out bright afternoon. Charley McKnight came over and he and I took a jaunt up Wells Creek.

Saw plenty of antelope but got none. Got back after dark; took supper at my house and went cross the river where I stayed overnight with them and am writing this Sunday evening.

November 6. Sunday. Froze considerable last night. Cloudy and threatening all day. Koch swam the T.C. Power cattle over to the other side today. Ed is as sullen as ever. It is like living with a wooden man; still it is infinitely preferable to his grumbling and fault finding heretofore. All I hope is that he will continue so for the next 8 months.

November 7. Snowed last night couple of inches. Cloudy all day, but not freezing. Ed went out today by himself and killed an old bull and an antelope. He will soon think he is an expert hunter. Gus Tyler was over today. He is an employee of the firm cross the river. They have several men employed there at present and all they have for them to do is sit around and play poker.

November 8. Quite cool. Froze a good deal last night, the first time I noticed meat being frosted through this morning. Today a big buck elk swam the river from the hills on the other side above town and came into the point between the two stockades. George Town was grinding an axe; he and Ed ran out, but George got ahead and commenced firing on it as it reached the road and soon got him down. It proved to be an old, poor one with one horn broken off. Bill Martin, Oleson, and Joe came in from the Pochette about sundown. They say buffalo are scarce out there now; a few old bulls is all. They came in for a fresh supply of grub. No news from above yet. Busy putting a window in the house today.

November 10. Nice and warm today and yesterday. After dinner yesterday, I thought I would go out and kill an antelope, as there was a band in sight on the hill back of the point. So I took a Spencer rifle that I had just finished for George Town and started. I succeeded in getting a fair shot and knocked two down in their tracks the first shot. One was still able to flounce around and almost get up as I came up to them. I lay down my gun and drew my knife; stepping up to it, I put my right hand on its back to throw it on its side in order to cut its throat. In its struggles it threw its head around and struck the point of my knife that I held in my left hand driving the knife back through my hand severely cutting me between the thumb and hand. Tying it up the best I could, I came back and crossed the river to get some sticking plaster, and left my antelope lay after shooting the one in the head that caused my mishap. After getting my hand tied up I concluded I would stop on that side all night, and stayed with D. Denton. This morning he and Pete Koch came over with me and we went up in the hills where we struck a band of antelope and killed five of them right there besides crippling a lot that succeeded in getting away. My hand, I am afraid, is going to lay me up entirely. Ed is still Dumby. Today he commenced putting up a smoke house in the stockade back of the dwelling house. George Town is very well pleased with his gun, a Spencer, that I put in a new barrel and double trigger.

November 11. Pleasant. Today I took a circuit up Well's point and over the hills. Saw plenty of buffalo on the Hawley flat and up Squaw Creek. I heard shooting up the river, and when I got back I found that Charley Williams, Judd, and Tom Hardwick had arrived at Musselshell with a boat and three horses from Little Rocky, but no news from Benton or Tom Bogy with his mackinaw load of goods. The boys, some of them, are going to Pochette in the morning.

November 12. Moderate. Rainy for awhile in the morning. George Town and myself went hunting. I killed a large 6-pronged blacktail buck. George killed two deer and an antelope, and together we killed two buffalo bulls in McGinnis' point. The rain this morning deterred the Pochette party from starting. D. Denton stayed all night with me last night. Ed is still on the Dumb order. I am afraid to say anything for fear of starting a quarrel and saying something I shall be sorry for, as I have lost all respect for him as a man of any sense or discretion. It is a moral impossibility for him to live and be on terms of confidence and friendship with anybody. He is a confirmed fault finder and grumbler, a monomaniac on a good many subjects and imagines himself imposed upon and an object of intrigue, when you are in reality trying your best to do fairly by him and favor him.

November 13. Sunday. Pleasant. Went out today, I and George Town, after the meat we killed yesterday and poisoned one of the old bulls in McGinnis' point. Tom Hardwick and Charley Morrison went over to Pochette this morning. Judd was over yesterday and today, both, waiting for me to return in order to do some work in the shop. Fully as tired tonight as last night and did not walk one-third as far.

November 14. Pleasant. Tom Bogy arrived last night after dark. Old Man Lee with him. Tom came down in a small boat without any goods, but Joe McKnight brought 6 tons down to Little Rocky, where he intends to be living to do business this winter having bought out the Lohmire and Mosser stockade. Judd was over all day and took dinner and supper with me. Late this evening there was some kind of an Indian excitement or raid on the other side but I have not heard the particulars. Ed went

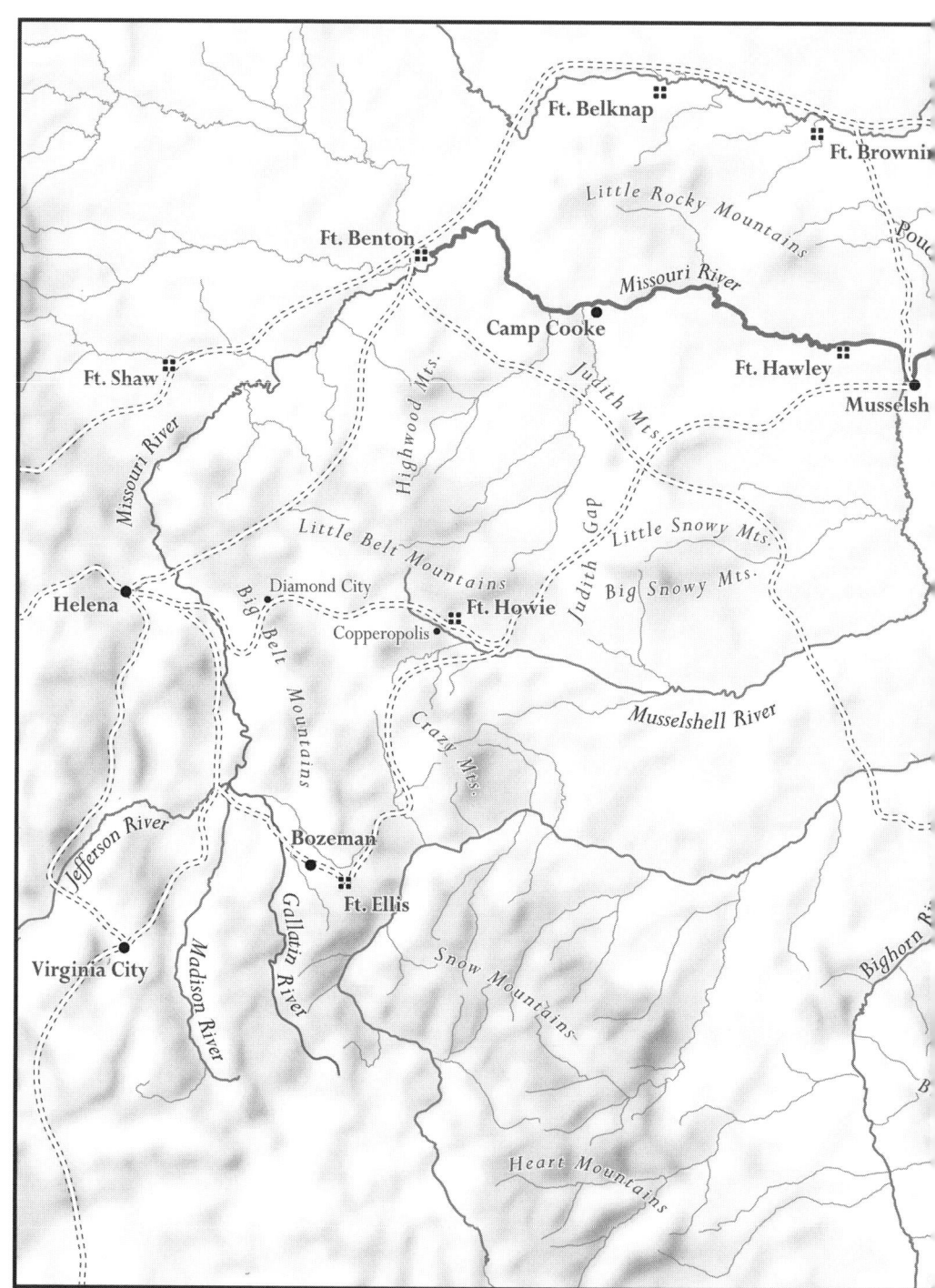

This medium scale map focuses on the geographic elements central to the Fort
Map courtesy

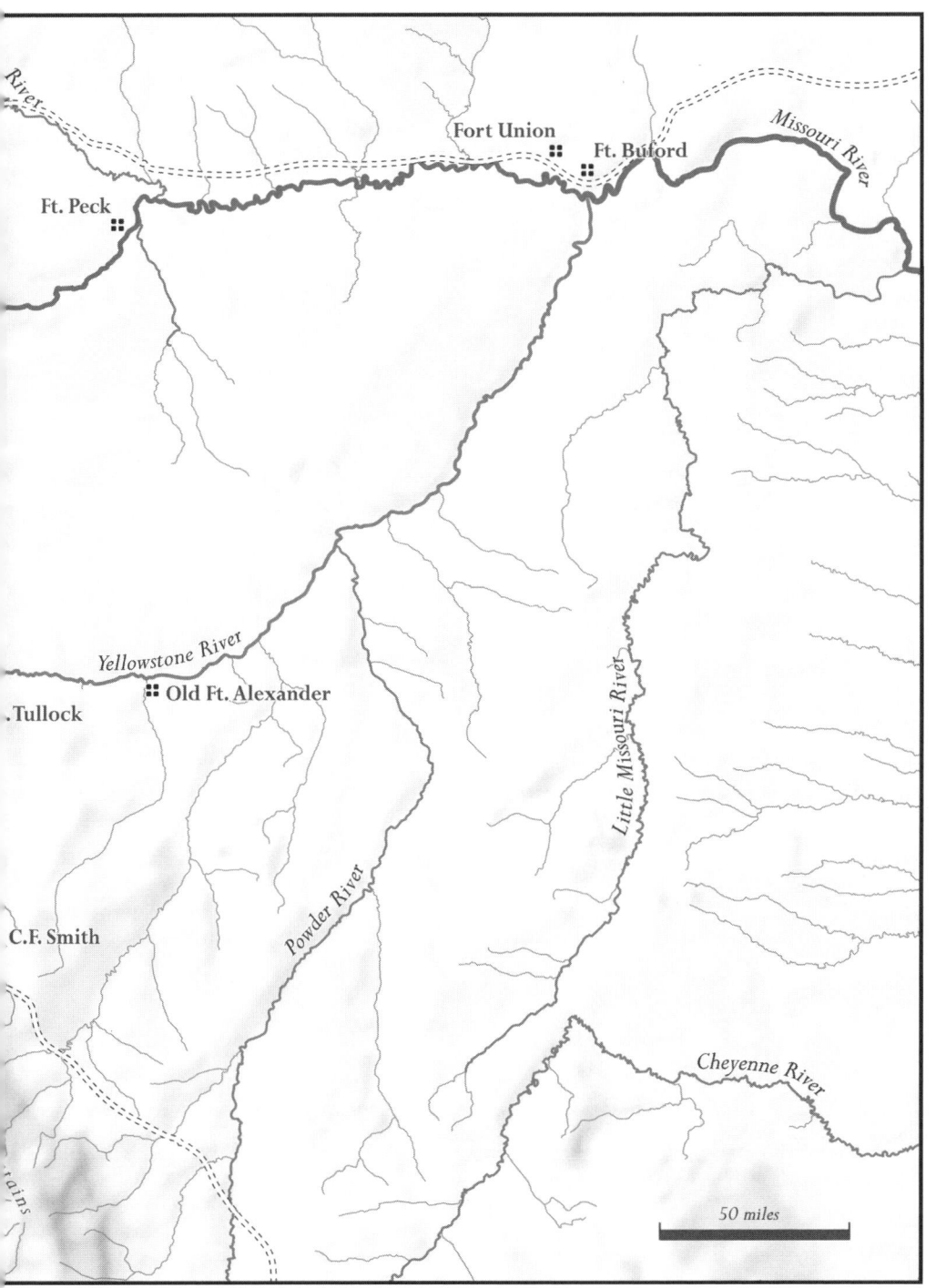

...ell story. All of these settlements figured in the story told in C.M. Lee's Journal. ...Hampton.

over but he is still mum, although there has been word sent to me by him still he will not even tell that. Thinks it would be doing me a favor, as he imagines himself a persecuted Jesus and that I am a Judas. I am afraid that if I speak to him that it will only be an introduction to some more of his quarreling and grumbling again and heaven forbid it.

November 15. Pleasant but cold last night. Was over the river and learned the particulars of the raid last evening. Just at dusk, it appears, a party of 20 or 30 Indians on foot and supposed to be Assinniboins, secreted themselves in the coolie and sagebrush 5 or 600 yards distant while a few of their number approached within 150 or 200 yards and fired on the boys. As they came up, some of the Indians called out that they were Crows. But seeing Indians, of course, everybody ran out with their gun. The Indians then opened the firing without coming any closer, as they might have come up and shaken hands before they would have been fired upon. Our Crow Indians are expected in everyday. Three horses belonging to Har[d]wick and Williams happened to be feeding next to the river. Tom ran out and secured one of his and led it to the house, under fire of the Indians. The dogs taking after the two loose ones, ran them up the river, the Indians apparently soon following them, but by this time it was dark; further operations were suspended 'till this morning when a party of four men went up the river to see what had become of the horses. They found them in the first point. One of them had an arrow sticking in the root of his tail, while the ground in the point showed that the Indians had tried hard to catch them, but being on foot, the horses were too wild for them. The boys were very glad to get their horses again, Williams especially, as he had just bought his off Hardwick* and paid 50 dollars in greenbacks for him. All hands were preparing to go up the river early this morning and had just swam the horses across a short time before. About noon the party got ready and started, consisting of Judd, Bill Norris, Joseph Lee, Charley Williams, and Tom Hardwick. I sent letters to W. Jenkenson, one to Mother, one to John Fattig, and one to I.G. Baker, also sent five dollars in money with Joe Lee for potatoes and $25 to get cartridges.

November 16. Moderate. Nothing of importance except a lot of the boys were over today. Tom Bogy has taken charge of the house cross the river and discharged Pete Koch and Gus Tyler. The Col., I understand, is expected here in ten days. Bogy is prepared to sell him all the property belonging to T.C. Power, provided the Col. has the cash to pay down. Rumor says that the Col. intends then to move the goods out to the Basins; if the sale is not made, Tom Bogy expects to stay here this winter.

November 17. Nice and pleasant, could work in the shop without a fire. Ed and Charley Morrison were hauling wood today. Tom Bogy is busy putting up some of the houses they pulled down last summer. What his object is in putting them up I do not know, if he is going to sell to the Col.

November 18. Pleasant. Today the boys, that is, Ed and Charley Morrison, finished hauling wood of the old stack, and finished the sixty cords at the lower stockade. I went down and measured it and took memoranda. Ed is still mum. I have to ask all my questions of Charley, but am careful to ask important ones in Ed's presence. Charley also told me that he and George Town had hardly spoken for a day or so. It is the greatest country for quarrelsome and disagreeable men I ever struck. Looks very much like a storm this evening.

November 19. Saturday; Sunday and Monday 21. The last three days have been quite pleasant. Saturday I went hunting on the Long point with Pete Koch in the afternoon. We killed six old bulls and cut out their tongues except one, getting so dark we could not find him. If it had been a little earlier we might have got two or three more, as they ran off badly wounded. There was a dozen of them all together. I crossed the river with Pete and stayed all night and until afternoon Sunday. In the evening I was so busy reading that I forgot all about writing up my journal. Early this morning Charley Morrison and I went to McGinnis' point where we expected to find a bear at a bait I and George killed some time ago. George and Charley found one yesterday morning and thought there was another near. We found no bear, but signs that he had been at the bait again last night, but had eaten most of his meal of his kind, the dead bear which the boys had skinned and imperfectly poisoned. I put another bottle of poison in it, then proceeded to Long point to poison one of the six killed Saturday, while Charley returned home. We killed a couple of antelopes in the point as we started out in the morning. George and Ed, I see, are chopping in the green wood at the lower end of the point this afternoon. Ed is still mum although I spoke to him when making memo of the wood Friday last.

November 22. Quite pleasant and warm although it looked very much like a storm last evening. Today cut up and salted down a lot of buffalo meat for the purpose of canning it for spring use.

November 23. Nice and warm, froze a little last night. I have

Bridge Street in Helena, Montana Territory, in 1865. No. 954-177. Courtesy Montana Historical Society Research Center, Photograph Archives, Helena, Montana.)

been busy daubing up the house for cold weather. Ed is still sullen and silent.

November 24. Warm but very windy during the afternoon. Busy in the forenoon cleaning the yard and burning chips. Oleson and French Joe came in yesterday and left again this morning for the Pochette. They say they have caught a hundred [wolves].

November 25. Pleasant and warm. Busy in the shop. Charley Morrison and George Town divided their mess today as they could not agree. It is hard to tell who is to blame.

November 26. Quite warm but a little cloudy and threatening to storm. Busy in the shop. Nothing of importance except the local disturbance between Charley Morrison and George Town.

November 27. Sunday. Nice and warm, a little cloudy. The boys on the other side killed some buffalo on the other side up Crooked Creek, just at dusk. I heard that Tom Bogy offered Gus Tyler $100 to go to the Grovent Camp and get White Eagle to come in with them. This I heard privately from George Town whom Gus wants to go with him.

November 28. Moderate but a little cooler. A band of antelope ran close to the stockade today. I emptied an old patent Henry among them and got four of them. Three of them within 75 yards of the stockade. Ed and George and I heard firing at them but they only got one apiece. The trip to the Grovent camp will fail on account of the parties having no horses to ride and hunting up an Indian camp on foot is an uphill business, besides the danger of running into hostile war parties of Sioux or Blackfeet.

November 29. Nothing of importance, but pleasant as usual of late.

November 30. Last day of fall. Moderate and cloudy. Events of importance are casting a shadow over the country now. Yesterday a messenger started for the Grovent on horseback to try, if possible, to persuade them to come here to trade. The messenger was Charley Morrison. Last evening after dark, the Col. arrived at Musselshell. He came across the country on horseback, four men with him, Ross, Everett, and two strangers. One of them, I understand, is the agent for a man of the name of Black* that commands a capital of $300,000, who talks of opening the road from here to Bozeman and intends to send a train here as soon as possible in the spring. The program for the meantime I am not apprised of. The Col., I believe, has bought out Powers' interest in the goods and store in Musselshell. I am busy today working on their guns.

December 1. First day of winter. The old whiteheaded villain showed his authority this morning by the first floating ice in the river, but pleasant during the day. Afternoon I crossed the river to see the new arrivals. Mr. Harlowe speaks very favorably of the route across the country to Fort Ellis, the most natural road in the territory. The Col. is sanguine of freight being shipped through here next summer.

December 2. Nice and pleasant during the day, but cold nights. The river was full of ice. No crossing the river today. Busy in the shop. Ed is still mum. A greater saint, in his own opinion, God never created; but a more unreasonable, suspicious, ignoramus I never saw nor wish to have any dealings with.

December 3. The river still full of ice. Nice and pleasant through the day. Yank and Samy started up the river night before last. Their business was a secret it appears.

December 4. Sunday. Snowing this morning but soon quit and partly cleared up. I and George Town were down in the next point hunting. I got a wolf at a bait there and also had considerable sport shooting at whitetails as George ran them out of the brush. I knocked three of them down but two got up and ran off again. Thought I saw Indians and concluded we would go no farther and returned.

December 5. The Pochette boys came in today. Last night was the coldest night of the season. Ice running thick. Was over to town with Oleson and Joe who came back again on this side fearing the river would be impossible in the morning, as they wish to start back. Quite moderate this evening about 8 o'clock.

December 6. Quite cold last night, froze hard, ice running thick. The boys started back with team to bring their skins in from the Pochette. George Town went out with them. Ed found a nest with several eggs in it today. Ed and I had the first talk we have had since before I went out on the Pochette after meat. I spoke once before but he never spoke back until today. Heard a good deal of shooting up Crooked Creek. I expect it was someone after buffalo, probably from Musselshell. The place on this side has been christened Leesburg, I believe, by some of the boys and is likely to go by that name after this altogether.

December 7. The same as yesterday. The Col. is setting his men to hauling some pinewood he has, I see today. The river is chuck full of ice, while the strip along the edge keeps getting wider except where the current strikes the shore and there the constant friction of the running ice has worn the bank way under, in some places as much as 3 or 4 feet.

December 8. Same as yesterday. The river still full of ice, but running. Col., Pete, and Louey were over today. The Col. was making out hopes for his hay that the Indians burnt on Wells point this last summer. Also the boys got back from the Pochette. Geese are thick, the boys say, on the prairie.

December 9. Quite cool last night; snowed in the night a little, gone on the south side of the hills. Was over the river. Judd and Bill Norris arrived last evening, got froze up in a boat near Hawley. Had to leave their boat and stuff which they cached in the willows, had 2,000 cartridges aboard for me, that Old Man Lee got in Benton. Started for Pete Koch's wood today. The Col. sent men and horses after his stuff to the boat but refused to allow them to bring mine.

December 10. Moderate today; snowing and raining a little nearly all day. Kind of slush ice running in the river. The Col.'s men got back with the stuff that Judd and Norris cached above. They say the river is open above and below there. Plenty of buffalo on Crooked Creek; the boys killed 8 or 10 this morning. I took some mail over to send to Benton. I am sending two letters to Dimick, 1 to McNeal, 1 to 1.6.

Baker, 1 to Mother, 1 to Sallie J. Newhall, 1 to L.M. Rogers. Some of the boys are getting scared about their caches as the report is that there is a man on the way down here to investigate such matters; hope not though.

December 11. Sunday. Snowing and cold this morning. Snowed nearly all day. Early in the morning I and George Town started down the river hunting. Saw a good many deer on McGinnis' point and upper end of Long point. Found 13 wolves at my bait there where I and Pete Koch killed six old bulls. Went down in the lower end of the point where I killed a blacktail deer and together we killed a couple of old bulls and poisoned one of them, then returned and arrived back just at dusk. [Spilled ink makes the rest of the page illegible.]

December 13. [Part spoiled by ink.] About noon George Town crossed on the ice in front of the stockade. He has not returned yet – ten o'clock at night. I guess he thinks the ice not very safe. I hauled up some firewood this afternoon on the sled.

December 14. Bitter cold last night and today; 10 degrees below zero. The river safe to cross anywhere almost. The Col. and party left day before yesterday. Today Charley Morrison, Tom Hardwick, and a few Indians – one Crow and four Grovents – came in, or rather, late last night. They think the Grovent camp, or part of it, will be here in 8 or 10 days with plenty of robes. Was hunting; cold as hell; killed 3 antelope.

December 15. Very cold last night, the first time it has froze in the shop; a little moderate during the day. The Indians left today. Antelope by the 1000 acres today on the hills. George Town killed 14 of them. I have been busy all day making a pair [of] cowskin pants. I spilt this ink tonight and it has made me so mad I can hardly write anything. I have to damn the thing everytime I think of it. [Refers to ink spilled on previous page.]

December 19. The weather has been moderate since last Thursday. Friday I was out antelope hunting on the hills. A great many of them all the time, coming into the river for water and in particular cold, stormy weather. Ed has already killed over 50 of them and G. Town about the same. Saturday I fixed some shoes for Charley's mule. Sunday I put them on. Last evening Johnny Cochran and Jimmy Boyd came down from Little Rocky, walked down in one day. This is about 8 o'clock in the forenoon. I and Charley Morrison are going to start up the river today with a sled and his mule after my cartridges that Judd and Bill Norris cached along the river near Hawley. Getting cold fast today.

December 23. Got back from up the river yesterday about two o'clock. Been cold as the devil all the time we were gone. Yesterday the thermometer stood at 28 degrees below zero and day before at 12 below. We reached Hawley on that day and Johnny Cochran and Charley Morrison both broke through the ice on that day a few miles this side of Hawley, but both got out all right. The next day we went up to where my things were and returned and came back as far as the third point above Musselshell, while Johnny Cochran and Jimmy Boyd went on up to Little Rocky where they live. Yesterday we stopped in the cabin until 10 or 11 o'clock it was so bitter cold, then came home. Today has been a little more moderate. I was out and killed 10 antelope and brought in 9 of their skins. Ed got 7 of them; in the evening Charley McKnight was over to see us and tell his funny yarns.

December 24. Cold. Nothing of importance but antelope hunting; nearly everybody out after them. I killed four [in the] afternoon and this evening it is blustering and snowing. Christmas bids fair to be dull and dry.

December 25. Sunday. Christmas today. Cold and clear. Stayed in the house 'till most night, then went over to town where I was just in time to help them eat their Christmas dinner or supper as it was about dark.

December 26. Moderate and pleasant; thawed considerable. I killed four antelope back of the stockade.

December 27. Moderate, took off a good deal of the snow. Went down to Long point today and killed a couple of elk. On the way down killed an antelope on the hill. The elk were not fat. Saw 20 or 30 of them. Bill Martin, Joe, Oleson, and Drew Denton all went down to the next point below Long point to stay a few days and take an elk hunt. I did not see them.

December 28. Moderate, thawed but little. A strong suspicion of Indians being around, but I hardly think so and still would not say there might not be as they are more than liable to be around.

December 29. Thawed a good deal, quite muddy. Windy this evening. Nothing of importance.

December 30. Moderate. Snowed all day, snow 3 or 4 inches deep. Was out nearly all day down to McGinnis' point twice. I and Ed skinned some wolves there and brought them up. Snowing still this evening.

December 31. Moderate and clear. I and Ed went down to Long point and brought up a load of dead wolves from the lower end of the point, 18 in all up the hill and two more after we got on top of the hill making twenty. Got home at dusk.

1871

January 1, 1871. Moderate and snowing through the day a good deal of the time. Judd, C. McKnight, and Ross were in today.

January 2. Cold today but clear. In the evening put the wolves in the shop and heated the room up warm and nice to thaw them out to skin them. Went over to town after dark; nothing new under the sun.

January 3. Cold. Ed was out and killed 3 antelope. I was out and got nothing at all. Ed carried the horns over to town and got 65 cts. a pair for them.

January 4. Warm. Thawed a good deal. Skinned first of the wolves we had in the shop. Terrible hard things to thaw out. They began to put up ice cross the river today. In the evening I was over and learned that there was strong suspicion of Indians being around as firing was heard near the mouth of Squaw Creek[59] by Bill Martin and party this morning while they were at the cabin on the third point below here, but they saw nothing as they came up. No one was out hunting in that direction today which makes it suspicious. Town, Tyler, and Long went up the Musselshell this morning. Snowed like the devil for a short time this evening.

January 5. Cool. Thawed but very little. No news or excitement whatever. Skinned a few more wolves today. The nights are very bright and moonlight now.

January 6. Cold in the morning, soon moderated and thawed; after dark was raining. No Indians have shown themselves around here yet.

January 7. Moderate; thawed. Last evening Tom Hardwick and Charley Williams arrived from Little Rocky. They say the Crows and Grovents are all up at Camp Cook trading. Afternoon Tom Bogy was over, said he looked for the Grovents here yet, that Louis Bompart had gone from Little Rocky to try and bring them from Camp Cook, that they were trading but very little there. The Crows are trading the most. [He] is not sure that the Col. will be back here at all this winter. Bill Martin and party went down to bank wood. Drew Denton and Louis going down to hunt.

January 8. Sunday. Thawed. Charley Williams, Charley Morrison, and Tom Hardwick started up the river this afternoon, the two latter having rigged up a two mule sled and took up their truck with them.

January 9. Thawed. I and Ed went with team out on Hawley flat and brought in a ton of wolves. Got back a little before night. Looks like a storm.

January 10. Cold and snowing all day; this evening quite hard. We got up this morning here two hours before day, had breakfast and were sitting by the fire at daylight when Judd and Bill Norris knocked at the gate. When they came in they said that Louey Larsen came up last night from Long point about 10 o'clock in the night and said that they had a small Indian fight yesterday afternoon and that Joe Gerard [Girard]* got wounded in the shoulder by a ball and that they wanted some help and that they and George Town and Long are going down. Just at dark this evening they returned. Bill Norris stopped in and said they found the boys all sitting in the house waiting for them, but no Indians were to be seen or heard. From all accounts and appearances one Indian was either killed or badly wounded. Their trail was down the river again. It appears that D. Denton and L. Larsen were out in the hills after some elk opposite the middle of the point below Bill Martin's and heard the Indians hollering at their horses. Returning [to] the house they reported it and the boys stopped hauling wood and went to the cabin. After staying awhile they went out onto the river bank to see and were fired upon, wounding Joe. The boys returned the fire, they thought killing one of the devils, then retreated into the cabin. In trying to get up hill at the foot of Well's point, which was very slippery, they took the cattle off and hitched to the end of the tongue. When nearly up the hill the fastening gave way and the wagon went down the hill and turned a complete somersault end over end with Joe and a lot of guns in the wagon. Fortunately no one was hurt. They then ran the wagon down by hand on the ice, as Bill Martin would not allow his cattle to go on the ice. Poor Joe began to think his time had come surely.

January 13. Cold. The weather has been very cold. Wednesday I sat in the house all day doing nothing but keep fires. Near noon on Wednesday Ross and Charley McKnight stopped in and chatted for near an hour, on their way to some of the coolies back of the point to get a stick of ash for a wagon bolster, and tried to get Ed to go with them, but he thought it was too cold and directed them where to go. We saw no more of them during the day but wondered [why] they did not stop in to warm as they went back. Thursday morning early, Tom Bogy,

Judd, Norris, Town, Tyler, and Larry came over and said that Ross and Charley had not returned. Hastily preparing myself, the seven of us all well armed with breech loaders, started on the boys' trail in the snow which is near six inches deep. On the hill just out of sight from here we struck the trails of Indians on horseback and on foot. We followed the boys' trail into the second coolie where their axe stood up against a tree and where they evidently first became aware of Indians being after them, as they left their axe and started out of the coolie, then returned and ran down it, the Indians on both sides on foot and horseback. A couple of hundred yards or more down the gulch we found Ross's body scalped, lying on his back with an arrow in his forehead. Besides being stabbed, his hat and overcoat, a citizen's coat, gun, revolver, and ammunition [were] all gone. His butcher knife they left. The body was frozen stiff. Carrying the body part way down the coolie we left it and followed the trails on down to the mouth and into the sagebrush where we found Charley's body lying on his face, several arrows sticking in his back and sides, stabbed in several places and the butcher knife still remaining in him. He had evidently run as long as he was able to. All his arms and ammunition were gone and a couple of pieces of his scalp were cut off and left lying on the ground beside him. A broken bow was also lying by him. He was sandy haired which was probably the reason they did not take his scalp. Charley's arms were a new patent Henry rifle, a Smith and Wesson cartridge pistol, and knife, and a belt full of cartridges for his gun. Ross had a Spencer rifle and a Colt's Navy revolver. The rifle was one that I had lately rebarreled. Their two guns were as good as any on the river. He also had a belt full of ammunition. Leaving the bodies lay, we came back and found that 12 or 15 of the Indians had come into the lower end of this point, coming up along the willows next to the willows, the island in the river in front of Musselshell hiding them from view. Some of them came through the willows and went down the road. Our oxen, that I supposed were down there, I could see no trace of and could not tell whether the Indians got them or not. Going up into Jenk's point we found the cattle of the Col. all right and drove them down. We also saw Bill Martin's cattle. Hitching up a yoke of cattle, we went down the river on the ice to opposite where the bodies lay, carried the bodies to the wagon and returned, getting home after dark. This morning Ed went over to assist in preparing for their burial. I returned from town a short time ago since writing the above, and saw the bodies stripped. They are shot and cut more than we thought at first. Both of them had their right arms broken. Ross's right in the elbow, a ball in his left leg, one in his breast and his left thigh. Charley's arm was broken near the shoulder, a ball through his right leg, one in the left hip, and a horrible gash on his back just below the left shoulder blade 6 inches long standing open nearly two inches wide exposing his lungs. Thomas Bogy is the only one now at the store, but 11 hands united in assisting to dig the grave and prepare the bodies for burial tomorrow morning. From all appearances, I judge, there must have been at least as many as thirty Indians in the party and as many as 12 or 15 after the boys. By some unfortunate coincidence their right arms must have been broken early in the fight thus rendering their own rifles useless to them. No evidence could be found of their having fired a shot. All Ross's wounds appeared to be in front while Charley's were in the back and right side. Evidently he must have suffered severely before death relieved him of his murderers.

January 14. Cold. Went over the river about 11 o'clock to assist in burying the boys. They both were washed and decently dressed and placed in separate boxes and buried side by side in the same hole on the bench west of town. Each box was marked with their names. Charley McKnight on the side towards town with their heads towards the south. Nine of us accompanied the bodies to the grave, leaving two sound men and one wounded one in the place, while our side was entirely deserted.

January 15, Sunday. Cold as usual. Early this morning Bill Norris started for Camp Cook on horseback, being sent by Tom Bogy with a message to Joe McKnight at that place. Been snowing nearly all day.

January 16. Cold as the devil. The snow is 8 or 9 inches deep. Nothing of importance except everybody keeps close to home.

January 17. Clear and cold. Tried to shoot some antelope this morning, but the dog got after them. The lower end of the point was full of them. George Town got out after them and killed several. In the afternoon a big band tried to cross the river just above the stockade. Larsen, Town, Ed, and I went out after them but only got two of them.

January 18. A little moderate. Plenty of antelope around. Some of the boys ventured up into the hills after them. In ten days they will probably all be over their scare again. Bill Martin and crowd drawing firewood cross the river today. I am working in the shop this week.

January 19. Same as yesterday. Some of the boys said they heard shooting on Squaw Creek yesterday; more than likely they did.

January 20. Warm and pleasant; snow settled fast.

January 21. Moderate. Today Ed and I went to McGinnis' point to look after our cattle. Bill, Judd, Bill Martin, Louis Larsen, and George Town going with us. Could find no sign of them. Found a pouch of Henry cartridges that belonged to Charley McKnight that the Indians lost. After we came back Ed, Bill Martin, Gus Tyler, and Oleson sent up to Well's point, but still no signs of them. We are certain now that they were taken by the Indians the day they killed Ross and Charley.

January 22. Sunday. Nice and warm. Bill Martin, Oleson, Louis Larsen, Gus Tyler, and George Town started out to the Pochette with ox teams. Snow melting very fast.

January 23. Thawing some. Only four men on the other side of the river now; I and Ed on this side.

January 24. Snowed a little last night; thawed during the day a little; looks stormy yet. Ed is sitting round the house and I am at work in the shop fixing up a couple of Needle guns.

January 25. Cool; thawed a little in the sun. Old Steve got a hold of some strychnia somewhere today about noon; lived for an hour or so but finally gave up the ghost. He got his dose, I think, at Ed's bait above the house only 3 or 400 yards. The owls were screeching around terribly last night.

January 26. Cool. Everything quiet as far as heard from.

January 27. Cold; good winter weather. Nothing new yet that I have heard up to 8 or 9 o'clock this evening.

January 28. Cool. Judd was over this afternoon. Nothing of importance on the other side. Bogy is looking anxiously for the return of Bill Norris from Camp Cook.

January 29. Sunday. Cool. The Pochette party got in that left here last Sunday. They found 100 wolves; hauled most of them to their cabin and left them.

January 30. Thawed a little. Judd and Bogy were over. No news of importance. Everything quiet on the Potomac.

January 31. Thawed a little. I was cross the river in the afternoon. The boys hauling wood cross the river for the store with two yoke of cattle.

February 1. Same as yesterday. Fixing to try and get out some ice.

February 2. Thawed. George Town stayed with us last night. Suspicious of Indians this morning partly on account of the actions of the dog last night and partly because Ed dreamed of Indians three times in succession last night.

February 3. Warm. Hauled wood. Went over to town. George Town moved up into the house with us.

February 4. Warm. Boys playing poker.

February 5. Sunday. Cold and raw; thawed a very little in spots. Yesterday arrangements were made to go up Squaw Creek with Martin's team after some wolves for Larson and Gus Tyler. This morning I and George Town got up early and crossed the river and learned that Bill Norris and George Horn arrived last night. Brought no news of importance except of a fight between two Crow Indians and Tom Hardwick. See tomorrow's journal. As soon as the boys were ready we struck out, seven of us, down the river on the ice, then up Squaw Creek about 3 miles and found where the Indians camped near the boy's bait in a little grove of small trees. [They] built a lodge of dry poles and had killed Old Red, one of our oxen; they had shot him in the forehead. From the size of the lodge there could not have been over 25 Indians at the most. We loaded up near 40 wolves for the boys and returned; could find no trace of Stag the other ox. I began to entertain serious hopes that he was down in the point at the mouth of the creek, for as we went up we saw tracks that I and Martin pronounced to be ox tracks. On our return we kept a close watch and found him as we expected, but terrible wild. In trying to head him off, I narrowly escaped a toss on his horns as he rushed at me and into the thickest patch of willows he could find. We then drove the other oxen to him and succeeded in getting him up as far as McGinnis' point where we left him. He appeared to be terribly frightened and to have a slight wound in his left shoulder. Arrived at Musselshell about sundown.

February 6. Cold. Went down to McGinnis' point, five of us, and two loose oxen, and drove up the Old Stag. The two Crow Indians killed at Little Rocky were Lone Tree and his brother, or rather, only one was killed while Lone Tree himself was severely wounded in both arms. It appears that the fight originated from whiskey trading; both Indians were drunk at the time on whiskey got from Tom Hardwick and Charley Morrison. The Indians got into a quarrel with Tom and wanted to kill him. They bursted open a door to get at him, when he shot them with his Henry rifle, killing one dead, [?] barely missing Morrison's head. This occurred last Friday night. The next morning Tom and Charley left for parts unknown.

February 7. Cold and snowing. Wrote a letter last night to Dimick.

Stayed in town last night and today; slight Indian scare; false report.

February 8. Cold. Boys playing poker all day. Drew and Long over. George Horn started back to Little Rocky today.

February 9. Cold. Everybody sitting round their fires.

February 10. Cold and snowing a little all day. Nothing of importance.

February 11. Cold. Nothing going on. The boys talking of going out to the Pochette. I am at work in the shop.

February 12. Sunday. A little moderate. Drew, Louis Larson, Bill Martin, and Oleson went out to Pochette on foot without a team.

February 13. Moderate but does not thaw any. Nothing of importance except that I killed Old Tom and Richard, a couple of Tom cats that had become a nuisance.

February 14. Moderate and warm and sunshiny all day; thawed. The ground hog, I am afraid, saw his shadow today.

February 15. A little cooler than yesterday. The boys [are] fixing to go up the Musselshell tomorrow. Ed and George went over the river so as to be all ready at once and start early in the morning. Tom Bogy and Judd were over during the afternoon. Just at night, I went over to get some antelope skins of Bill Norris and returned by myself.

February 16. Quite cold and spitting snow nearly all day. Part of the time you could hardly see across the river. The boys, I suppose, started early this morning. Bill Norris was to start up to Little Rocky this morning, but I see his pony back in the point yet although he took it cross the river last night when I went over. Four men on that side now and myself all alone on this side, with the dog Nig to stand guard, my Henry rifle and plenty of cartridges.

February 17. Moderate. The boys only went up the Musselshell to the first crossing, 5 miles distant and returned. The traveling being so slippery that it was almost impossible for the oxen to travel. George and Ed came over the river late in the evening, talking of going down the river on the ice tomorrow after some wolves for me and some skins for some of the others.

February 18. Warm. Rained a little in the morning early. After it quit I and George Town went over the river and all hands concluded to start about 9 o'clock. After we had got below McGinnis' point it began to rain again and all hands concluded the best thing we could do was to go into Long point and get what wolves I had there and return the same day. Accordingly we did so, getting 25 wolves at my bait and 5 more on our return at McGinnis' that Ed has an interest in. It kept raining or snowing nearly all day. The snow was nearly all gone from the ice when we reached home an hour before sundown and the water was pouring onto the ice from every little gulch. The Musselshell was evidently rapidly rising, having already broken up the ice in the Missouri half way cross the river at its mouth. Everybody was cold and wet. I treated to a bottle of whiskey at Oleson's that was speedily devoured among seven men.

February 19. Sunday. Warm; snowed a little last night, cloudy all day, and raining tonight.

February 20. Warm. Muddy as the devil. A lot of the boys went up Squaw Creek to some baits to the right of the creek. Found 16 wolves, skinned part of them. They also killed a bull or two toward the mouth of Squaw Creek when they went out. Judd and Bill Norris were over today shooting away a lot of cartridges.

February 21. Warm; freezes little at night; muddy as hell during the day. Ed, Drew, Oleson, Martin, Tyler, and Long went down the river to see some baits. Judd fixing the sight on his Henry.

February 22. Warm and cloudy; froze very little last night. The river is rising considerably. The boys returned yesterday afternoon, but Ed stayed in town until this morning. Found 3 wolves at Drew's bait and 5 at mine and Ed's. Found Ross' hat in McGinnis' point; there was a ball hole through it.60 Long was over today and he and Town crossed back to town about noon. By the middle of the afternoon the river was so high that it was impossible to cross. My wolves that I brought up the other day were still on the sled at the foot of the bank as you come up from the river. I had to go to work and pack them up the bank to keep the water from them. This evening it is about as high as it was any time last summer. The ice still holds firm in the middle of the river yet but it will have to go soon if the weather keeps this way, as the snow is not all gone yet quite except in the most exposed places. Town crossed the river for the purpose of going up the Musselshell tomorrow.

February 23. Moderate. Froze hard last night. This afternoon the river is falling some 5 or 6 inches. Busy after dinner stretching skins and skinning wolves. The boys, I think, started up Musselshell this morning. This evening I have written several letters in answer to advertisements in Harper's Monthly.

February 24. Thawed but little. The boys returned from up the Musselshell this forenoon. We could see them come in. No crossing of the river as it about holds its own. The ice still holds in the main channel.

February 25. Moderate. The river falls slowly. Skinned a few more wolves [this] afternoon. No communication with the other side since the river has been up. Fiddling tonight, the first for a long time.

February 26. Sunday. Warm; thawed a good deal, the river falling slowly, water running in from the coolies fast today though. Everybody stays close to home, I think, from appearances on the other side. The river, I think, will certainly break up in a few days if the weather continues as has been for the last week. Playing again tonight. Makes my fingers sore in a short time.

February 27. Moderate but windy as the devil. This evening it is blowing great guns and is getting colder every moment. I cut a piece out of the end of my thumb today skinning wolves. It makes writing tolerably awkward awkard, I don't remember which. Can't cross the river yet.

February 28. Moderate; froze hard last night. Town and Bill Norris came up on the ice to opposite the stockade but could not get off on this side. The last day of winter. This evening is quite moderate. I am afraid March is coming in like a lamb and going out like a lion.

March 1. Moderate but windy after ten o'clock. The morning was nice and calm. Has looked like storming for the last week. Skinned 6 wolves this afternoon and stretched 9.

March 2. Moderate. Considerable of wind. This forenoon Town came over on the ice in front of the stockade and wanted to get across. We put Oleson's boat into the river and brought him over in a short time. Bill Norris came over and took his horse on to the other side. The river holds its own very well. I begin to think it will break up without freezing up again this spring.

March 3. Pleasant; sun rose nice and clear. The boys came afternoon to prepare to go out to the Pochette. Quite windy afternoon and "blowed" up quite a little spurt of snow, or rather a soft hail, but soon passed over. Joe and Long stayed while the others went home again. Settled up with Ed today. He is just as ready to quarrel with me as ever and accuses me of things that I never thought of nor no sensible man would think of.

March 4. Moderate but cloudy and windy. The boys all started for the Pochette. There are only Tom Bogy, Bill, Judd, and Bill Norris on the other side and none but myself on this side. The boys expect to be gone 4 or 5 days. There are eight of them well armed.

March 5. Sunday. Pleasant but windy. Sat in the house most all day.

In the evening Nig gave me a scare by barking furiously ... where he was tied and as I went out to see what the matter was, I thought I heard something run back of the stockade.

March 6. Warm and calm in the morning but the wind rose as usual before noon. The ice in the river has broken up this morning in a couple of places, I see, a little above here. I see them moving around and hear them shooting cross the river. I suppose they are all right over there so far.

March 7. Moderate. Rained a little last night, very heavy wind nearly all day with a sprinkle of snow toward evening. Just at dusk the boys got back from the Pochette; 154 wolfskins on the wagon. The road was very heavy, the team nearly played out. The ice is open clear cross the river opposite the woodyard. The boys are all stopping here tonight. The boys saw some geese and ducks.

March 8. Moderate and nice in the morning but windy as usual after while. This morning Bill Martin, Louey, D. Denton, George Town, Gus Tyler, Ed, and myself started over the hills to hunt up wolves. We had a few baits on the hills and in Long point; we had skinned 14 on our way and got within 400 yards of the bait at the lower end of Long point when we discovered an Indian who appeared to be skinning wolves at our bait. He discovered us at the same time and darted up a convenient coolie. In a few moments we saw him pass over the ridge at the head of the coolie, going down the river. Concluding discretion the better part of valor, we returned following the trail up through the willows part way, then taking a straight course over the hills picking up our skins on the way, arriving home without any trouble. Gus Tyler and Louey crossed the river on the ice; the other boys stayed to stretch their skins.

March 9. Moderate. Last night about midnight, George Boyd arrived on horseback. Said he came from the Santee Sioux camp on the mouth of the Pochette. He has been with their camp all winter; also Harry [Charley?] Woodward* and Hunter, two other white men. Boyd was anxious to cross the river but was persuaded to wait until daylight. His object in coming willing to smoke. 125 lodges of the Santees; at the Round Buttes there are 2 or 300 Yankton and Yanktonais lodges, they prefer to fight than smoke. About sundown Boyd crossed the river back again with about a hundred pounds of stuff to take with him. He evidently has a party of Indians along with him as he has been making signals several times today, but he neither acknowledges or denies it positively; he laughs it off, says they are friendly and is taking a plug of tobacco to camp from every man in the place. Tom Bogy offered him $500 if he would bring the camp in here to trade but he wants to run the trade himself. He says he will be back in 4 or 5 days, that it was the Tetons that killed Charley and Ross, that 700 lodges of them are camped on the head of Dry Fork two day's travel from here, that they are at war with everything that trades with the whites. A half breed that was in their camp saw two scalps that were killed at this place. Major Reed, it appears, is in bad luck as everything he had has been confiscated at Browning. Buford he says, has 300 citizens and the whole country staked off in town lots as the N.P.R.R. proposes to cross the river there and go up the Yellowstone. From St. Louis the news is that 25 boats are advertised for this upper county. This is about the substance of what he has to say, but he is not reputed to be the most reliable authority in the county where talk is cheap. This evening Oleson is quite sick which will keep the boys from starting up the Musselshell tonight as they intended.

March 10. Snowed a little last night; cold and cloudy this morning.

March 15. Pleasant. Returned yesterday afternoon from up the Musselshell with the party of wolfers. We started Sunday morning about two o'clock. We were 25 miles up the Musselshell. Went to six baits, skinned and stretched 150 odd wolves. Camped out two nights; we carried a pair of blankets and grub with us on our backs. The weather was cold and disagreeable Monday and Tuesday. Sunday night it snowed and rained on us, but we worried through a couple of most miserable nights. We had just been at Musselshell long enough yesterday to take a drink, eat, and smoke, when we saw a lot of buffalo on this, the north side of the river coming on the full run down into the lower end of the point. While watching the buffalo, I saw a party of Indians stop at the stockade, and some white men with them. Someone of them fired a couple of shots to let folks know they were around. I immediately started cross the river a lot of the boys going with me, and soon found George Boyd, a man named Hunter, and a Frenchman called Half Breed Joe, with a party of Santee Indians, 18 bucks and 3 squaws, who had come in to talk and smoke with the whites. They soon crossed the river and I followed, staying overnight with Oleson. The Indians say they want to come here and trade or have goods come to their camp, but Tom Bogy tells them he can't send goods to camp and for them to come here and trade, that they will be well treated as long as they behave, and a good deal more that was necessary to ally their suspicious natures. Several of them who came in had relatives that were killed here the 8th of May 1869. They went out there and picked up a lot of bones and took them off to camp today. They were all apparently well pleased with the treatment and presents they received but one of them, but his ill will apparently amounts to but little with the balance, as they all talk against him. They are about as good on the bum as the Crow Indians for all I can see of them. So far here they succeeded in stealing a hatchet, hammer, and a couple of shirts, with a few minor things that amounted to nothing. They started for camp this morning about 9 o'clock, where they will have to talk with the balance of camps before they can decide what to do. Joe, the interpreter, says if all is right he will be back in four days. If he apprehends trouble he will be back in two days, to let us know in time to prepare for them. The ice is still crossable in the Missouri River.

March 16. Cloudy and raining. The ice is getting quite poor. The river is all open from here up to the woodyard. The boys came over this morning on the ice but are afraid to venture back this evening. They wore out hunting the cattle today but could not find them in Well's point where they expected them to be. The Indians might have driven them off. Last night, late, George Town and Louey Larson started for Little Rocky on foot after a horse to bring in their wolfskins.

March 17. Nice and pleasant. The boys went down to McGinnis' point this morning but found no trace of the cattle there. Came back and went to Well's point again and found them in the lower end of the point. They brought them down and we hauled a couple of loads of wood and put it in the stockade. The boys crossed the river in the boat by going up a little. Once today it was entirely clear in front of us, but in a short time a few big cakes came down and blocked it up again for a short distance. The ice is getting quite rotten and is bulging up nearly down to town. St. Patrick's Day this has been. What whiskey, no doubt has been drunk today by St. Patrick's disciples.

March 18. Snowed all day from early in the morning, fast as it could fall almost until noon when it slackened up a little and melted nearly as fast as it fell. Tonight it is all of 5 inches deep. We put the cattle in the stockade last night to swim them across to Jenk's point today, but it is most too bad a day to put them into the water.

March 19. Sunday. Pleasant. Snow melted a good deal. George Town and Louey Larson got back from Little Rocky about noon, stayed at Hawley last night. They brought no news of any kind, no one having come down from above.

March 20. Moderate; cold during the night. A few buffalo in the lower end of the point. Some of the boys came over and went after them, but got none. A little after noon Tom Bogy hollered across the river that there were Indians on the hill. We shut up the stockade and drove up the cattle, just as a horseman rode up that proved to be Harry Woodward from the Santee Camp. He said that there were 50 or 60 Indians and squaws back a short distance that would soon be in and that they had sent him in ahead. He went right on cross the river. The ice in the river is breaking up a good deal today. About noon it was entirely clear in front and for two hundred yards below us. During the afternoon considerable ice came down the river. The Indians soon arrived and among them was Standing Buffalo*, the head chief of the camp. He is a large and powerful Indian. He was well dressed for an Indian, but nothing flashy or gaudy about him; everything was intended for service. He had a keen black eye that at first appeared as though he was a little cross-eyed, Roman nose, slightly hawk bill shape. His skin, where not constantly exposed to the weather was near enough white for him to be a half breed. They were all very civil and quiet. Tom Bogy came over and took the chiefs across the river and set George Town to putting the balance across the river in Oleson's boat, 6 or 8 at a time. He got the last over just at dusk. Bill Martin and party were over here when the Indians came. They watched their wolfskins awhile then went to work pulling them up and brought them in. This evening about dark it began to rain. I think the ice will be running good tomorrow. Hope so, as it will soon be over, so near rotten now it will not last long.

March 21. Moderate and muddy. Rained but little last night. The Indians crossed back today and started for camp as fast as they got over. They picked up all the loose things they could pack off. Five or six of them stayed back and got drunk on whiskey that Drew Denton gave them. Boyd's father-in-law got mad because I would not let him in the shop and fired his gun off in the stockade. No one paid any attention to him. About 3 o'clock, just after they had all got crossed, the ice began to run pretty thick and broke up and moved down some distance in front of Musselshell, but soon stopped running and blocked up again leaving it clear in front of us still.

March 22. Pleasant; froze hard last night. Went over to town this morning with George Town. Louis Larson and Harry Woodward came back with us.

March 23. Pleasant but froze hard last night. I was up this

morning a few moments after sunrise and found the ice running thick and fast. No doubt now but what she has completely broken up. Toward evening it began to get a good deal thinner and less in quantity. About noon it jammed below somewhere and raised a couple of feet but soon broke loose.

March 24. Moderate but freezes nights. Very little ice running this morning. The boys crossed in the boat just after breakfast. Nothing of importance during the day except George Town hired out to Tom Bogy to work and Harry Woodward will stop for the present with us on this side of the river.

March 25. Moderate; very foggy this morning with a fine mist. Cleared off soon and was pleasant.

March 26. Sunday. Pleasant. Ed stayed over the river last night. The boys all came cross today and drove the cattle across the river into Jenk's point above. They were talking of going up the Musselshell after their wolfskins but postponed it as Indians are expected in every day from the Santee camp.

March 27. Pleasant. The mornings lately have been cloudy and chilly, then clears off and is pleasant. The ice lodged along the shore is melting very fast. Geese and ducks are flying around.

March 28. Pleasant. Tom Bogy and Town came over yesterday after one of their oxen that swam the river. Nothing of importance.

March 29. Pleasant. Rained a little last evening. All hands staying close round home lately.

March 30. Pleasant. Tom Bogy with four men took their mackinaw up to Well's point this morning after some grass for their ice house. I am looking very anxiously every day for a small boat down the river with news from the outside world and letters.

March 31. Pleasant but windy. Louis Larson came over and says the boys want to go up the Musselshell tomorrow after their wolf skins. Ed and Harry Woodward will go with them and I shall stop on the other side until they come back as they intend to be gone out one night, and the Santees, I think, have concluded not to come back here to trade anymore as their time is up in which they were to come back in.

April 3. Pleasant and warm. I went over the river Friday evening and the boys all went up the Musselshell after their wolf skins, early Saturday morning taking a wagon and two yoke of cattle. They returned Sunday all right. Got their skins and killed 7 buffalo bulls. The meat begins to be tainted with wild onions. Saturday afternoon 11 Indians, Boyd, Hunter, and Indian Joe came in from the Santee camp to trade. They brought about 40 robes. They stayed all night on the other side with Tom and let their horses run loose on this side. Sunday morning they started back saying there would be a big party in today. I did not return to this side until late yesterday. Gus Tyler came over with me. Ed stayed on that side to play poker. Gus returned this morning. I have just had my dinner and no Indians yet and no one from the other side. The grass begins to show itself now considerably. Still no word from the outside world. Ed and Harry came over this evening; Harry pretty full, Ed slightly so. Bill Norris arrived on a raft early this morning before day from Little Rocky. Brought some mail for Tom Bogy only. Says there is a government train on the way here from Ellis and is due here now. Col. Clendenin is at Helena. The Crows are out in the Basin, also the Grovents. The former are determined to kill somebody for the Crows killed at Little Rocky by Tom Hardwick. Fort Hawley has lately been burned down. The news of the death of Charley and Ross is in all the eastern papers; also the killing of the Crow Indian. No Santees in today.

April 4. Nice and warm. It appears that the Crows sent word to Johnny Cochran and Dean to leave the river or they would kill them as the Crows think they are to blame for the killing at Little Rocky. George Horn and a man named Gordon* are missing now; they started from Camp Cook to Little Rocky as near as I can learn and have not been seen yet, but Norris says they did not appear to feel much alarmed for their safety at Little Rocky. It is also reported that the Assiniboins killed two or three men lately on the Marias. The Blackfeet are also reported to be stealing horses around Benton. The next thing they will be killing somebody also. A band of buffalo [was] in the point today.

April 5. Nice and warm. Cleaned up around the stockade today. Towards evening I discovered Old Man Lee and Charley Williams cross the river as I was looking with the glass. We all went over in hopes of getting some mail, but were disappointed as they had been out hunting their horses that strayed from Little Rocky. They followed them out towards Black Butte then gave up the pursuit and came in here late last evening. Several of the boys were on a drunk. Uncle Joe Lee came over with me and stayed all night. No Santee Indians today.

April 6. A little cool and cloudy. Uncle Joe returned to the other side today.

April 7. Raining last night after dark. This morning the ground was covered with snow and snowed quite hard part of the forenoon.

April 8. Cold. Froze last night and snowed some more; stormy and cold today. George Town and Louey Larson were over. Uncle Joe and Charley Williams are still over there. The latter drunk most of the time. Harry Woodward is quite sick; something like the bloody flux. The effects of bad whiskey and the onion buffalo meat I think.

April 9. Sunday. Clear during the forenoon but cold all day. This morning the river is rising for the first time since the ice went out. Last year it began to raise on the 23 of this month.

April 10. Moderating. Some of the boys were over from the other side. I was over there for a short time to send some letters up the county by Lee and Williams when they go.

April 11. Moderate; rained a little this morning about ten o'clock. George Boyd arrived from the Santee camp, said that the Santees had a fight on Crooked Creek and with a small party of Crows and had killed all of them, 11 in number; 4 of the Santees got wounded; 20 of them all together. The Crows offered to smoke and said they were fighting the whites. The Santees answered back they were not fighting the whites. The Crows then opened the fight by firing a revolver. In the afternoon he returned to camp saying he was going to the Assiniboins camp on the Dry Fork before he came in again. Plenty of buffalo yet where the Santee camp is. As long as that is the case they will probably remain where they are. At least they do not talk of leaving, Boyd says.

April 12. Pleasant. The river still rising. Raised near two feet, I think. Ed and Harry Woodward went over the river this morning and are there yet. 'Tis after dark now. The river fell a very little this afternoon. Cloudy and windy this evening.

April 13. Cold and cloudy. The boys came back and Gus Tyler came over with them. The river is falling a little.

April 14. Pleasant. This morning we discovered a couple of wagons across the river in front of the store. We all crossed over to see what was up and found it was only an outfit of Clendenin's that had come by the Crow Camp and got a lot of robes and brought them here to get a new supply of goods. Lohmire came in with the outfit. They left Fort Ellis sometime in February and brought very little news.

April 15. Pleasant. The river is about on a standstill. Lohmire is stopping with me and everything is quiet on the Potomac. I forgot to mention the teams narrowly escaped a war party as they came in 20 miles from here. They saw where 40 odd Indians crossed the road, they heard a shot and saw game [buffalo] running. They evidently had passed but a few hours ahead of them.

April 16. Sunday. A little cool. Had to work in the shop. Was over the river [in the] afternoon. Harry and Lohmire both staying over there.

April 17. Snowing and raining this morning. Saw a two horse team drive up to the store on the other side. This morning after breakfast I and Ed went over and found the Col. and a man named Seaton, also a 7 footer called Howard. The party left Helena [the] 30th of March and stopped several days in the Crow camp. While there, three Crow Indians came in who escaped from the Santees in the fight up Crooked Creek, and told their story. Such a crying and going on for the dead, the Col. says he never heard in all his life. The news in regard to steamboats is still unfavorable. Col. says there are but ten advertised for the upper Missouri. The boys are all very much discouraged in regard to the wood business. A couple of hours after the Col., the Negro Andrew Jackson and a young white man arrived, also belonging to the Col.'s party.

April 18. Still cold and drizzling all day but the sun set clear this evening.

April 19. Cloudy and dull. Was over to town part of the day. Tom Bogy and Bill Norris started out after the Grovent camp, I believe.

April 20. Snowed a little this morning; very windy all day, blowing downstream. The Col.'s wagon started back up Crooked Creek this morning for the Crow camp and Fort Ellis.

April 21. Clear but a little chilly. The river seems lately to be on a standstill. Still there is steamboat water in the channel. It appears that the man Seaton is the Chief Clerk of Col. Viall, the Superintendent of Indian's Affairs in this territory and it is imagined that his business here is to find out what he can in regard to whiskey traders throughout the country in general. From all accounts above, the poor devils have got fits from all quarters. Maj. Reed, the agent for the Grovents who has had the reputation of being a chief among such traders, has been thoroughly ventilated and all of his clique scattered in every direction. It appears that Col. Viall is determined to stop the business if possible. These efforts will only make it the more profitable for those that will engage in it next winter.

April 30. Sunday. Pleasant and nice. On the 22nd Bill Martin, Oleson, Joe Gerard, Ed Scharf, Harry Woodward, myself, and a half-breed Crow called Frank went down to Bill Martin's point below to bank wood and returned last Friday evening a little after dark. We banked near 200 cords of wood. We kept two men on guard all the time. The weather was a little cool and rainy most all the time with a couple of heavy frosts. When we returned we found Tom Bogy, Bill Norris, and a Rappahoe Indian called Nutany. Tom and Bill could not succeed in getting any Indian camp to come in here and trade. The acting agent at Browning threatening to send soldiers after the Grovents if they did not stay on their reservation. George Boyd and the Santee camp were over on Milk River also the Yanktonais and Assiniboins. George Boyd was trying to get an outfit to trade, but the agent told him to keep his hostile Indians away from there as he did not want them about there. Charley Morrisson and Hardwick were at Browning. This afternoon Bill Norris and Nutany started back for Browning.

May 1. Cold and disagreeable.

May 2. Warm and pleasant. The river began to rise today. Hauling and cording wood today into the upper yard. Judd and Gus Tyler were over to go a hunting but did not go as we were all tired. Bill Martin, Oleson, and Joe Gerard are helping us. Strong suspicions of Indians being round; a shot was heard up the Mussel this morning and the dogs keep up a terrible barking nights.

May 3. Warm and pleasant. Went down to the lower yard to cord wood there with Oleson on guard. He thought he heard something like Indians singing down in McGinnis' point. As the Medicine of all hands was weak we concluded to play it as Indians anyway and returned home and laid over. The river still rising slowly.

May 4. Hot as hell today; green flies terrible thick. Hauling wood to the upper yard. While at work I discovered 3 antelope in the hills back of the point. I went up and killed all 3 of them. Came back and went after them with the team; three buck antelope neither fat nor poor but it is the first fresh meat we have had since Lohmire was here. The river is getting muddy as the devil.

May 5. Cold this morning. The river on a stand. Finished cording wood today.

May 6. Warm. Toward evening Bill Norris and George Houk* arrived from Browning. They left there last night; brought a horse for Judd to ride back. Jim Wells, they say, should have been here some time ago from Benton. The Santee camp is over at Browning trading, the Assiniboin and a lot of Yanktons and Yanktonais. The report now is that it was the Yanktons that killed Charley and Ross and that they don't deny it. There are 5 or 600 Sioux lodges on the Milk River now near Browning. The Grovents have had to leave there on account of the Sioux fighting them. There are several large war parties out now; where bound for, they do not know.

May 7. Sunday. Warm; rained some last night. The river rising again slowly.

May 8. Warm; rained last [evening], considerable thunder and lightning also. The river rose near 3 feet during the night and is still rising. Yesterday I crossed what we call the slough by taking off my pants and wading. This morning a steamboat can run through there. The boys on the other side brought over George Seaton's buggy this afternoon. They intend to start for Browning tomorrow morning. A very heavy rain toward evening with thunder and lightning.

May 9. Rain and chilly. Last night about ten o'clock James Wells, Charley Williams, W.A. Thompson, John Cochran, Drew Denton, George Palmer, Bob Little, and two Grovent squaws, the property of Wells and Cochran, arrived in a mackinaw. Most of the party belong at Little Rocky. Old Man Lee was killed by the Indians on the 12th of last month. The particulars of the fight I will record some other day. The party were almost expecting to find this place cleaned out. They landed in front of the stockade and had to shout and hollar before they could get us out. They intend to stay here until boats run. Stayed overnight with us, then crossed to the other side. I received two letters.

May 10. Trying to clear up; the river fell a little yesterday but is higher than ever this morning. Splendid steamboat water now. Ten more days will certainly bring a boat. I wrote the first in the morning. Afternoon I crossed over the river and had been there but a few moments when a steamboat whistled down the river and soon hove in sight: the *Ida Reese No. 2*, Durfee and Peck's boat. They report only 3 or 4 boats coming up. Col. Clendenin offered them wood at 4 dollars. They only took 3 or 4 cords. Bogy, Denton, Thompson, and Williams went up on her. I and Oleson went up to the third point and sold her 15 cords [of] wood. Got back in a small boat at dark. The boys are all discouraged at the poor prospect of selling wood. Wolf skins sell readily at $2.50 cash to Farwell and others on the boat. The worst thing today was that George Seaton started cross the country to Browning in his buggy with Bill Norris, Judd, George Houk, and the Crow half-breed, Frank, who came down with [the] Col. They could not have been more than ten miles from here when the boat arrived. Seaton was very anxious to go up on a boat, but was afraid one would not arrive for some time yet. The boat also says the Indians were at Peck that fought the boys and killed Old Man Lee. They were Santees, Yanktons, and Yanktonais. They acknowledged 11 killed and one fatally wounded, while several were severely wounded.

May 11. Cloudy but warm; the river still rising. The grass this spring is unusually good and thick but trees are slow in getting leaved out on account of the heavy frosts we had that killed their buds two or three times, but they are beginning to look green now. Jim Wells and some of the boys were over today. I gave the former a note I had in my possession given by John McDonald.

May 12. Quite cool; river rising slowly. Was over to town and made arrangements with the Col. and Bill Martin and party by which they gave me their entire control of the sale of the wood in the three yards; each yard furnishing 350 cords of wood on the bank from which to make a dividend. If one or two yards are closed out they are to have a proportionate interest in the others that may be left. The arrangements apparently give entire satisfaction to all parties.

May 13. Still a little cool.

May 14. Sunday. Pleasant. Went to McGinnis' point to measure some wood of the Col's., six of us altogether.

May 14. Pleasant. A large party of Crow Indians came in today to trade. Louis Bumbar and Mich Boyer with them, also the darkey Andrew Jackson. The wagons that left here some time ago went to Bozeman, as the men with it would not come back with it. Those Crows have a good deal to say about us allowing the Sioux to come in here some time ago. The squaws are all nearly covered with blood where they have hacked themselves in mourning for those killed up on Crooked Creek by the Santees this spring.

May 18. Rainy today and chilly. Day before yesterday we had quite a hailstorm. The river was up higher than it was any time last year. Now it is falling a little. The Indians are still cross the river. They are very anxious to trade for breech loaders to fight the Sioux with. They talk of bringing their whole camp down this way.

May 19. Tolerably pleasant. The Indians still at Musselshell. Steamer *Ida Stockdale*[61] today. Jim Wells and John Cochran went away on her.

May 21. Sunday. Chilly and disagreeable. *Ida Reese* passed down. Tom Bogy came back on her. Some of the boys from Little Rocky on her.

May 24. Been same as Sunday with a little rain. Bought Oleson's cooking stove yesterday. Can't brag much on the prospect for boats yet. Ed went to work for the Col. Monday morning last.

May 26. Nice and warm yesterday and today. The river falling slowly. The Col. is busy putting up his new arrangements for Indians by the sound of his men at work. I and Harry stopping alone over here. Think I shall move on the other side.

May 30. Cold and raining; been so for the last 3 days. Steamer *Nellie Peck*62 arrived at dark, lay at the upper end of the point. Grant Marsh,* Captain. The river rising rapidly; 12 or 15 inches last night.

June 2. Pleasant yesterday and today; the river keeps rising and falling, yesterday the upper end of the island was entirely under water clear into the willows.

June 3. Pleasant. J.S. Brewer and Major Reed arrived at Musselshell from Deep Creek. Their business is to see that a delegate to the Democratic Convention is sent from this place.

June 4. Sunday. The river is rising rapidly, 6 inches an hour, clear on top of the first bank where the willows are.

June 7. Pleasant. Monday evening 4 or 5 Democrats held a meeting at Musselshell and Gus Tyler was appointed delegate to the Democratic Convention. His proxy, I think, is Brewer. Brewer and Reed started last night on their return. Yesterday the Steamer *Far West*63 passed down. Bob Gordon, George Horn, and Hammond got off at Musselshell to wait for another boat. The river has fallen 2 1/2 or 3 feet in the last few days. Wilkinson of the Gazette is the proxy.

May [June?] 9. Pleasant; looks like rain; a heavy shower south of us yesterday. Some buffalo in the point yesterday.

June 10. Pleasant weather. The river falling slowly all the time. The Col. is fixing his stockade very well at Musselshell. The first time he has ever had it in decent shape.

June 14. Hot and dry lately. Yesterday morning at sunrise Steamer *Nellie Peck* passed down the river without stopping at all. Nine or 10 o'clock Hunter came in from the Santee camp. Says their camp is on the Pochette 20 or 25 miles from here at the head of Well's Creek. He says he had a brush with 40 or 50 Tetons and Cut Head Indians mostly on foot. They fired a volley at him just as he saw 75 or a hundred yards distant. He was riding a very excitable little mare and the motion he made to seize his Winchester and turn, and turn her, that her motions were so rapid and uneven that their shots all missed him. He promptly returned their fire off his horse, they all dodging behind their cover. He retreated a couple of hundred yards to the brow of the hills toward the river and dismounted and fired 30 or 40 shots at their heads, finally mounted and rode away and came in. The Indians asked him where he was going. He told them; they said they were coming, too. He asked who they were. At first they said Grovents but finally said Tetons and Cut Heads. As he came away he saw them start up the river. The river is still high but falling slowly, while everything is horribly dull about the place. The prospect for Indians round here next winter is good; for wolfing in consequence is very poor and exceedingly dangerous.

June 16. Hot. Yesterday Steamer *Peninah* passed up [in the] afternoon. Dave Winner was aboard with a stock of goods. Says there is but one more boat coming up the river; that is the *Flirt*64, will be along m a week. Joe Butcher* from Peck got off at Musselshell, says Farwell has been superseded at that place. Joe is going cross the country with the boys, Drew Denton, George Horn, George Hammond, Bob Gordon, and Thompson all went up on the *Peninah*. None of them will hardly be back here again before next season if then. Harry tight and fell in the river.

June 18. Sunday. Warm. The river a little on the rise. Yesterday Harry was over in town and got drunk and lost his knife, thought Mich Boyer stole it. In the evening he went back again to make him give it up but did not succeed. In returning after dark still tight, one of his oar locks gave way, he says, when near the middle of the river. Then he had to paddle the boat with an oar. He reached the bank at the drift pile below the lower stockade where the boat capsized, dumped him and his gun into the river, and the boat [went] on down the river, while he succeeded in reaching the bank by cooning a log in the drift. Joe Mosser, Courtney,* and Charley Williams came down in a boat.

June 20. Warm; river stationary. Yesterday afternoon Col. and five men went to Well's point to cut hay.

June 22. Warm. Been busy putting my things in boxes and my tools in shape so I can use them if I want to and still lock them up and be ready to move there at short notice. Also taking invoice of everything I have on hand. A couple of Grovent Indians and squaws came down the river Monday evening in a boat they stole. They want to wait for the Rappahoes to come here.

June 23. Pleasant. Col. brought down a raft of hay from Well's point. Steamer *Peninah* passed down; landed in part of the stockade here.

June 24. Rained last night. Steamer *Flirt* passed up. The Little Rocky boys all went up on her, the Grovent Indians also.

June 27. Warm; last two nights cool but the days are hot. Moved most of my things; crossed to the other side again yesterday into Oleson's building; fraid to stay here by myself.

June 29. Warm. Laying in the house yesterday and today doing nothing at all.

June 30. Thermometer 109 in the shade.

July 1. A little cooler today. Still on the north side of the river waiting for the boys to start cross the country, to live in Oleson's building cross the river. Killed a buffalo cow in front of the stockade as she came out of the water; plenty of them around.

July 3. Warm, but cool nights. Steamer *Flirt* came down just at night.

July 4. Warm. The *Flirt* lay here all night. Today I moved the balance of my things over into Oleson's building. Am now living in the city of Musselshell. Five men came down in a small boat today.

July 8. Sunday. Moderate. Twenty odd men here lately, most of them at work for the Col., all wood hawks nearly.

July 14. Hot as Hell; 120 degrees in the shade. On the 12th Steamer *Silver Lake No. 4*65 arrived and discharged 3100 sacks flour for Sims, Fort Browning agent, then left for Benton yesterday morning. Hundreds of buffalo all round. The passengers and the boys here killed 12 or 15 on the point at the mouth of the Musselshell.

July 16. Sunday. Warm; a slight sprinkle. Steamer *Miner*66 passed this morning. I and Harry went over to the stockade last night and stayed. Killed a fat cow at sunrise on the potato ground.

July 20. Hot as the devil. The boys moved into the lower stockade yesterday, Ed, Bill Martin, Hunter, and Joe Butcher. Let them have the ox yoke. Lots of buffalo bellowing around.

July 23. Sunday. Hot as usual, trying to rain the last three or four days. Mostly along the river between here and Squaw Creek the boys in the lower stockade have been making hay and a hayrack. No steamboats down yet. The *Silver Lake* and *Miner* still above yet, and the river still on the fall but running through the slough yet. Toward evening *Silver Lake* arrived; lay at Musselshell, only went as high as Cow Island.

July 27. Hot as usual. Toward noon quite a thundershower and some rain last evening. Yesterday I killed a cow and calf or yearling and this morning a cow and a bull buffalo all in point. Two or three hundred in the point this morning. They make an awful noise mornings and evenings with their bellowing. At a distance it puts me in mind of prairie chicken in the States in the spring of the year. The river is getting down very low.

July 28. Pleasant. A very heavy wind and some rain last evening at dusk. During the afternoon a fellow called Slim Jim* arrived from Browning. Says the Santee camp is way the other side of Milk River and that a camp of a hundred and fifty lodges of Yanktons and Yanktonais are camped on the Dry Fork of Pochette between here and Milk River.

July 29. Pleasant. The river raised 6 or 8 inches last night and took off the boat here. With 3 of the boys from the lower stockade, I followed down the river to Long Point where we found it on the other side of the river where the wind had stuck it on a sandbar for a short time. Joe Butcher swam over and got it. The boat that Harry lost we found, in a drift a little lower down on this side bottom side up, with ease. When I returned, I found I had 14 more young chickens that just made their debut. While eating dinner, Oleson and Drew Denton arrived on foot, said they came from Benton on a raft which they left a short distance above, probably with contraband articles of trade aboard. They brought me a letter from Mother, the contents of which surprised and distressed me beyond measure. Their nature I do not wish to record. Last night shot a buffalo that came in ten feet of the gate, but he got up and ran off

July 30. Sunday. Pleasant.

July 31. Awful hot. Went down to McGinnis' point after Oleson's boat with team. I came home sick with headache during the afternoon; had high fever and vomited a considerable.

August 1. Feel a little better. Quite warm. Steamer *Andrew Ackley*[67] arrived near noon. During the forenoon Oleson and Bill Martin came up and broke up the wood arrangement because I wanted my share of the money from that yard and would pay over to them one-third of all the money I received, as if I owned no wood in that yard. I had considerable fever during the afternoon. Drew Denton went up on the boat.

August 4. Moderate; quite cool last night. The Col. has torn down all the buildings on the other side but Oleson's. Afternoon the *Miner* passed down without stopping at all. The Col. also found a yoke of cattle that strayed away last spring. They came back into Jenk's point.

August 5. Moderate. A young fellow named Smythe came over today, said the *Miner* landed on the point above and put off Dexter and his horses, and Oleson's up there. This Smythe is connected with the election next Monday, sent here as one of the Judges by some Court Commissions. Smoky today. Letter from George Town.

August 6. Sunday. Warm. Steamer *Andrew Ackley* passed down

during forenoon. Drew Denton came down on her and brought his things into my stockade this afternoon. I brought over some provisions that I bought off the *Silver Lake* and put in Oleson's house. On going after them, I found Oleson had double locked the door and nailed up the window to keep me from getting them. The house had been left in my hands and I deliberately drew the staple and took my stuff out, nobody saying a word to me.

August 7. Cloudy; tried hard to rain last night, thunder and lightning a plenty. Had election today. In the evening Smythe, Brooks, Hunter, and Mich Boyer started for Browning horseback. The Col. is trying to get matters compromised in the wood arrangement, don't know whether he will succeed or not. Sent letter to Town. The cannon was fired a couple of times.

August 8. Nice and warm forenoon; hot as hell afternoon. Some shots have been heard lately that makes the boys think Indians are hanging around after horseflesh, which they have a great penchant for. The boys saw a big smoke down the river on the other side.

August 9. Cool and cloudy. Drew and the other boys up to Well's point haying. Began to rain about one o'clock.

August 10. Cool. Rained very hard last night; poured down for awhile.

August 11. Hot. Everybody cutting hay in Well's point.

August 12. Cool and cloudy. Hunter, Mich Boyer, and Slim Jim returned this morning.

August 13. Sunday. Pleasant. Went over to town according to agreement yesterday, to leave the dispute between me and Bill Martin's wood party to arbitrators. Charley Williams was appointed by them, Dexter by me. They chose Harry Woodward as referee. I presented my statement in writing; their reply was nothing but a few insinuations. The arbitrator soon decided in my favor, which left the party owing me $47.50 instead of my owing them. In the midst of the business, Gus Tyler came running in saying there was Indians down in the point. Everybody rushed out with their guns just in time to see 15 or 20 Indians on horseback driving off three horses that belonged to Col. and Dexter, while a lot more Indians were visible cross the Musselshell River on the hills. The Col. refused to fire a shell [at] them at first until he heard them shooting down in the point and he thought they were killing a yoke of cattle that were in the point. Then he commenced and fired 8 or 10 cross the Musselshell. The Indians disappeared down the river. A party then went down to look for the cattle; could not find them. There were no doubt, from appearances, from 40 to 60 Indians in the party. In the evening the cattle were found, one of them wounded in the shoulder. They fired some 10 or a dozen shots down there at something.

August 14. Cool; begins to look and feel like fall was coming on. The boys are building a stable below.

August 15. Cool this morning. Steamer *Nellie Peck* passed up during the forenoon without stopping, only to let a man jump ashore on the other side. Farwell and Reed were on her.

August 16. Moderate; cool nights. Harry went with Bill Martin and party to the second point above, hunting. To be gone all night.

August 17. Moderate and clear; hot toward noon. The boys returned about noon with 3 deer and a fawn. Joe Butcher killed the 3 while Bill Martin killed the fawn. Hunter killed a wolf and a beaver, while Harry only wounded a doe that ran away.

August 18. Windy as the devil. My eye pained me last night and this morning. Lay abed until 9 or 10 o'clock.

August 19. Warm. Fixed up the stockade in front of the door of the house.

August 20. Sunday. Warm. A year ago today I and Ed caught the first wolf. Mich Boyer came up here in the night last night drunk, called Drew out to treat him. This morning I learned that he and Gus Tyler were both drunk down at the lower stockade. Drew found Mich's gallon [he] keeps out by the stockade this morning with near a quart in it of whiskey. It is a great wonder to Drew where the whiskey came from, didn't know as there was any about.

August 24. The days are quite hot and about every other night is cold and chilly. Busy this week fixing up the bastion. Tuesday evening the first buffalo for some time were heard bellowing on the hill. The next morning, the boys in the lower stockade went out and killed three. We went down and got some of the meat at the lower end of the point. Today they are all gone again out of sight and hearing. Forenoon the steamer *Nellie Peck* passed down; stopped and took on a lot of flour at the Col.'s. Col. Peck and Farwell aboard.

August 25. Moderate, cool nights and mornings. Slim Jim and some others started up the river. Killed three bulls in the point above the house; poisoned one.

August 26. Rained some today. The boys busy fixing to go out to Black Butte country hunting and wolfing.

August 27. Sunday. Pleasant during the day. The boys took their cattle and wagon cross the river to the other side. They feel very hostile towards me on account of the trouble concerning my interest in the lower wood yard.

August 28. Pleasant. When I got up this morning a little after sunrise, I could see no sign of the boys or their wagon on the other side. I suppose they have shoved out for the hunting ground. I and Harry Woodward are alone on this side in the upper stockade, while the Col. with four other men are all that are on that side. Eight men left with the team, two going through to Bozeman. Mich Boyer and Gus Tyler, the latter being the Col.'s clerk, says he expects to bring a few loads of Indian goods back for the Col. There are no buildings standing on the other side now but the Col.'s, the others all are torn down. The Col.'s are all enclosed in his stockade so that he has that side entirely under his control. The men he has in his employ now are Dexter, Charley Williams, Joe Gerrard, and a Pilgrim named ------.

August 30. Warm and pleasant during the day, nights a little cool. Good many buffalo round. Yesterday one came within two hundred yards of the stockade, when he mistrusted something and turned off. We fired at him from the door of the shop as he was running off, but failed to drop him though severely wounded. The other side turned out quickly at one rapid firing of 5 shots, 3 with the Henry and 2 with Spencer by Harry. In the evening the upper end of the point was full of them. We went up to the wood pile and fired a shot a piece into an old bull. He ran a short distance and fell and was perfectly dead when we reached him. The others ran out onto the foothill and stopped. This morning they were bellowing at a great rate on the hill.

August 31. Pleasant. The Col. was over today, had a long talk with [me] in regard to little misunderstandings between us. He has too many of the little foibles of human nature to be a successful public man.

September 1. Moderate and a little smoky. Toward night a boat arrived from above with four men. They landed on the island and camped. They said they were photographers, had followed the Missouri from Gallatin down.

September 2. Moderate and smoky; night quite pleasant lately. This morning Smith arrived from Peck with two horses to stop in this country somewhere. He was here with Town last year, says Durfee and Peck are going to put up 5 new posts this fall. Fort Peck is to be headquarters. Thum* is General.

September 3. Sunday. Moderate; rained a little last night. Smith went cross with his horses to the Col.'s to stop. Wolves howling last night considerable. The Col. is looking for a train from Browning in a few days, after some of this flour that the *Silver Lake* left here.

September 4. Pleasant. Cold last night. Smith started cross the country this morning to Bozeman and the Crow Agency for the Col. Wolves appear to be plenty around here now. Have not been able to find any at our bait yet. Smith said he saw one dead one on the hill as he came in.

September 5. Moderate. My eye sore today. No buffalo; lots of wolves round.

September 6. Cold night. Wolves come right up to the stockade after old pieces of meat. This morning I saw a band of buffalo on the hill. A boat came down during the afternoon and stopped on the other side. A lot of bulls in sight, we started out as the Col. and Dexter sailed up the river for the same purpose. We succeeded in getting one that I crippled. Dexter knocking it down as it passed him. Got back just after sundown.

September 7. Warm night and day; smoky. The new arrivals were over today with a little gunsmithing to do. Finished the bastion by the house; put in the door.

September 8. A little cool, rained a little afternoon. In the morning we saw some buffalo on the hills, thought we must have a bait. Went up and killed a bull and dragged the hams down and poisoned them, leaving one on the foothills and the other on the bar at the woodyard. Just as we shot the bull, Dexter and Tom appeared behind us. They had brought the cattle to drag their meat down but we spoiled their fun. Tired this evening.

September 9. Moderate during the day; the first frost of the season last night, quite heavy. No wolves this morning.

September 10. Sunday. Cool but no frost. Caught 3 wolves on the sandbar near the woodyard. Toward evening a small train arrived from Browning after flour, sugar, and coffee for Indians over in that county. There were six double wagons with six yoke of oxen to each, with an escort of 18 soldiers under Lieut. Kendrick.* The soldiers had two four-mule teams. They camped close to the stockade on the Garden Patch. Bill Norris was the only country man in the crowd. Got letter from Judd; lots of Indians over in that country and will be all winter.

September 11. Moderate. The train moved onto the island and

began to get their loading cross the river.

September 12. Moderate; cool nights; no frost. The train still crossing and loading. A party of wolfers started up the Musselshell today, the Col. taking them up with his team. They intend to put up a cabin.

September 13. Quite moderate, but smoky. The train on the bar still this morning. Their cattle ran loose day and night in the point, a herder with them. Was over to other side today. Toward evening the train pulled up to the stockade and camped.

September 14. Moderate. The train left today. Smoky as the devil.

September 15. Moderate; still smoky and looks like rain. Wrote 6 letters yesterday and sent them off today by Bill Norris who stopped today with the Col. for the train. In the evening I and Harry went to Jenk's point. Saw several deer but got none.

September 16. Quite moderate but very smoky, can hardly see the tops of the bluffs around. This evening killed and poisoned a cow at the head of the point in a coolie, badly wounded another; quite a herd of cows and calves.

September 17. Sunday. Pleasant. Killed a young bull at the head of the point, right at the water's edge.

September 18. Nothing of importance except the smoke has blown away and it is clear as a crystal now.

September 19. Moderate. The wolves appear to have left; have caught but three yet. Afternoon Harry was cross the river and returned the Col.'s newspapers.

September 21. Moderate.

September 22. Moderate but windy downstream. Yesterday I, Harry, and Billy somebody started up the river with the boat hunting. I locked up everything and left them alone. We went up to the second point on the other side and killed an elk and three deer. Slept in the willows. This morning we crossed the river and killed two more deer. Got home about noon, tolerably hungry.

September 23. Moderate, that is, warm as usual during the day. This evening we heard 4 or 5 shots up the river somewhere. Busy rigging up mast and sail in the small boat.

September 24. Sunday. Moderate. Was cross the river and learned that Dexter was shooting up the river last evening. We were trying the new sail; concluded to alter it to what is called a fore and after, as less liable to upset in squalls.

September 25. Moderate. Altered the sail and made a trial trip up the river; worked well. Near our bait at the head of this point we found lying in the edge of the water three wolves and a bear. The wolves we loaded right into the boat; the bear we skinned and went on to the second point where I killed a wolf just at dark. Then returned home by the light of a full moon.

September 26. Same as usual. Nights a little cool and the middle of the days quite hot. Think of starting up the river [this] afternoon to be gone a few days.

September 29. Pleasant. Tuesday afternoon started up the river in the boat, the wind being good for sailing. We had our blankets and grub with us. Killed a bear at the head of the second point, then sailed up the third point after dark and lay down. Took a hunt the next morning; killed nothing, then sailed up to fourth point, the wind being pretty high, we went flying. Killed an elk in each of the fourth points. The wind having fallen, on the 28th we returned having 2 elk, 1 bear, and 2 deer. Arriving home we found the wolfing party returned to the lower stockade, having returned the same day we left, bringing in some 226 wolves, 2 bears, and a few other skins. They used up 65 bottles of strychina. Being 6 men, the shares are comparatively small. They were not very well satisfied with their trip. Today the Col. arrived from Browning saying that the train would be in this evening as he left it on the Pochette. I took him and his horse cross the river and went down to the point and found Gus Tyler and Little McDonald there. They arrived yesterday afternoon; brought me a letter from Mother, one from Dimick and some gun caps for Needle gun, also a book from Harper Bros, called <u>Sketches of Creation</u>.68 Toward evening the train arrived all right. The Col. and a Spaniard and his squaw reported hearing and seeing Indians in Jenk's point. The same escort came with the train. The wagon boss brought me a letter from Judd with order for the Howitzer at the Col.'s of the Skin and Grease.

September 30. Was over the river. The train crossed their flour over.

October 1. Snnday. Pleasant as usual during the day; rained a little last night. Today was over and got the cannon cross the river. The Lieut, said he would haul it up for me.

October 2. Pleasant. The train started this morning. The Lieut, left the gun at the door. In the afternoon, Courtney, Bill Ivey, and Dave Congden* came up afoot from the mouth of the Pochette, after a team to haul the timber to build their post at that place.

October 3. Pleasant. The flies still blow meat so that it will not keep but a short time. The Col. and Dexter started cross the county this morning for the Gallatin. The Col. expects to build a post in the basin.

October 4. Windy as the devil. Courtney started back about noon. His [He] got drunk at the lower stockade. He got thrown from his mule and slept all the afternoon then started just before night while the other followed on after the wagon. Drew and the other boys got drunk below and Drew and Hunter had a sort of a fight in their drunken foolishness during the morning. Hunter and Joe Butcher then started down the river in a small boat for the Pochette or lower as per circumstances.

October 5. A little cool. This morning Drew and his crowd found some wolves at our bait. We went out [in the] afternoon and got six at the head of the point. Nothing of importance likely to occur for some time now. Three men at each stockade on this side and 6 men in the Col.'s stockade.

October 6. Moderate. The Spaniard started for the Yankton camp this morning. Put the stove up in the shop.

October 7. A little cool. Trying the range of the Needle gun today, shoots to the lower end of Jenk's point. Drew and his outfit went to Long point to their bait; got no wolves but killed a couple of deer. In the evening it began to rain.

October 8. Sunday. Rained all night and still at it this morning and a little all day.

October 9. Clear and bright; cold and heavy frost last night. Tuned up my fiddle yesterday; the first time since last July. Froze quite hard last night.

October 10. Cool. Trying to get all hands to go up the river after meat. Toward night we went to the point below the Musselshell, Bill Martin and Ed going with us. I killed a whitetail; got back just after dark. As we went we stopped at the Col.'s place, and found the Spaniard had got back and reported that he had been run by a party of 100 Blackfeet Sioux down near the Round Butte. His horse was all that saved him. They were all on foot but three who chased him for 10 miles, he says, to the mouth of the Pochette. He also reports a party of 35 Yanktonais three points below here, all on this side of the river. Like all Mexicans he has the name of being such a liar that no one knows whether to believe him or not.

October 11. Cool and cloudy.

October 12. Cool, sprinkling and spitting snow. Bill Lehr stayed with Drew last night. The boys were all ready to start up the Musselshell this morning but were afraid of the weather.

October 13. Quite cold last night; heavy frost and froze still water near 1/2 inch. Big band of buffalo cross the river this morning. The boys there killed two or three right opposite to us on the side hill.

October 14. Moderate. Harry went to long point; the other boys to their bait. They saw the first antelope near here on the hill and killed a couple of them.

October 15. Sunday. Moderate. Last evening after dark, Dave Congden, Bill Berry* and a stranger arrived from the Pochette with the boy's cattle that Courtney hired. Berry stopped with us. No news of importance except they are busy putting up their post there. Berry, who is the interpreter there, thinks they will only have Santees to trade with this winter, that Sitting Bull of the Yellowstone Sioux was in at Peck not long ago and said he was not going to fight traders and citizens anymore, only soldiers. He wants to trade this winter all he can at all of these posts along the river near here. The post that they are building is a branch of Fort Peck under Durfee and Peck, who are building several branch posts this fall.

October 16. Moderate. The boys below moved cross the river to go out wolfing again; up the Musselshell, I believe, this time.

October 17. Quite pleasant. Harry and Billy Thompson began to wolf together today. They went up Crooked Creek and put out a bait on an old bull. Billy has a couple baits on that side and Harry the same here that the other boys gave him. Saw a big band of antelope in sight this evening for the first time this fall.

October 18. Pleasant. Harry and Billy were down to Long point, got no wolves but killed 4 antelope.

October 19. Pleasant and warm. Killed the old grey rooster this morning.

October 20. Pleasant. Lots of antelope in the point this [morning] about sunrise. I was up and shot at an old bull cross the river at the woodyard but he ran in behind the willows. After breakfast went with the boys to their bait on the hill. Together we killed 4 antelope. A little before sundown the lower outfit got back on the other side, I saw, and drove their cattle cross. Something unusual must have brought them back as they were to be gone a month. Today was the first time I have been clear up on the hill since the 12th of last January to hunt the bodies of Charley and Ross. I noticed quite a lot of prairie dogs that have settled there this summer.

October 21. Pleasant. The trouble up the Musselshell was there was no wolf sign nor feed for cattle, so they came back again.

October 22. Sunday. Pleasant. Last evening between 8 and 9 o'clock we, that is I and Harry, were considerably startled by the reports of 10 or a dozen shots fired apparently in the stockade of Col. Clendenin's cross the river. At the first shots we ran out and up into the shop building to listen to the firing which lasted some 10 minutes, accompanied with shouting and crying as though someone was hurt badly. In the course of half an hour Billy Thompson and Jack Mail* came over and said Bill Lehr was killed, didn't know but supposed that Tom Walling was the one that killed him as there were two or three doing the shooting. They wanted us to go over. We went over and found the whole community collected there. Tom they had locked up in the hen yard back of the kitchen where he had retreated at the close of the shooting. Lehr was dead with a ball through his left temple and out at the back of his head, which he must have received at a distance not over 10 or 12 feet from the muzzle of Tom's Henry rifle, as he stood in the door of the hen yard. It appeared that they were both shooting but the truth exactly it was impossible to learn as no one appeared to know or would tell. Both parties were drunk, also several others that had no hand whatever in the shooting. Charlie Williams and D. Denton were both pretty tight and sitting in the kitchen and thought they were being shot at. James Brooks was crazy drunk and out in the yard where the shooting occurred. After asking Gus Tyler, the person in charge there, if we could be of any assistance to him or be of any benefit and receiving a negative reply, we returned home. Today we went over again. Gus is lifeless in the matter and will do nothing. Lehr was buried at the graveyard during the forenoon, Tom Walling assisting in doing it. A short time after we left, he got out of his lockup and went to bed. In the morning he said he was not going away as he did the killing in self-defense, that Lehr fired the first shot. He told me that the trouble started from card playing, when or where he did not say. Today Lehr was found to be shot in the right shoulder also, the ball lodging in his body.

October 23. Pleasant. Today afternoon, I understand, Tom W. has gone down the river. I also learn from two that were out in the yard at the time of the shooting and saw most of it, what puts a different color on the matter entirely. Instead of Lehr doing the first firing, Tom began to shoot before Lehr had a gun in his hand and probably received his wound then, before he got hold of a gun, a Spencer rifle used by a Spaniard, Antoine.

[Remming] If all this was the case, I am sorry he was not detained at all hazards.

October 24. Pleasant and cloudy. Today D.H. Denton sold off his provision and skins on hand and says he is going to Benton.

October 25. A little cool. Drew left this morning on a horse he bought of Oleson, going up the river on this side. Afternoon I and Harry packed up a lot of wood.

October 26. Moderate. Only 3 men now at the lower stockade, Ed, Bill Martin, and Oleson, who are all talking of going to the Basin. Harry goes out nearly every day with Billy Thompson to their baits, while I am doing but very little besides the necessary work of living comfortably, once in awhile a small job in the shop, or making butcher knives.

October 27. Moderate. Today is my 38th birthday. All the celebration it received was I went out on the hill with Harry and there got after some buffalo bulls, where we wounded one of them and by following him up with a little shooting and a good deal of running got him down in 300 yards of the stockade, then went to work and butchered him and skinned him, and packed part of the meat into the stockade.

October 28. Moderate last night, but cold and cloudy this morning and commenced snowing; the first snow of the season.

October 29. Sunday. Froze a little last night, but muddy today. Brooks, Hunter, and Jack Mail got back from the mouth of Pochette today. They left here Thursday last, brought three strangers with them, stayed at Bill Martin's cabin last night, came in muddy and hungry. A couple of them, I believe, are from Buford. They say there is a post on the Yellowstone now that left Fort Rice some time ago, 6 companies of soldiers, 75 or 100 citizens besides 50 scouts who are half-breeds, Indians and white hunters and trappers. One of them was at Browning just before they came up here and said that Simmons* and Charley Hard* were at Browning and waiting for a squad of 300 soldiers to start for Fort Peck to bring old Sitting Bull to terms if possible, as he is now close to that place. Strychnia is worth $16 an oz. at Browning. The three new men just replace the 3 lately left here, D. Denton, Walling, and Lehr.

October 30. Quite cold last night, thaws days.

October 31. A little colder last night; freezes meat the last two nights for the first.

November 1. Quite pleasant. Harry came back again this morning from an Indian camp and says there are 30 lodges [of] Assiniboin and

20 of Yanktonais within 30 miles of here and coming in 8 or 10 days and want the boys to burn their baits on this side of the river to save the Indian dogs. Also says there are 700 lodges of Tetons at Peck and 300 near Round Butte, who all say they only want to fight soldiers. One of the clerks at Peck got frightened and left for Browning in the night. Also all the Assiniboin squaws that were staying there have left for safer quarters, as they say there are but 4 or 5 white men at that place. The report also is that the Grovents are hostile now; have told Farwell to leave Clear Creek, that they intend to fight. They have been friendly for a long time, they say, now the whites have driven them away from their country and are giving it to the Sioux.

November 2. Moderate; everything quiet.

November 3. Worked in the shop. Harry and Billy went on the hill.

November 4. Pleasant. Felt quite unwell all day; eat scarcely anything. Some of the boys heard shooting not accounted for yet and think it must be Indians. Just at dark the train from Browning arrived, after their third and last load, they say, which goes to the Black Foot Agency[69]. Received letter from Judd, also my letter returned from Benton to the Deputy Collector saying Gunsmith Lycense was abolished.

November 5. Sunday. Cool and cloudy. A new guard of soldiers with the train this time. A company of soldiers are at Browning they say and talk of going for the half-breeds for whiskey trading.

November 6. Cloudy and snowy. The train loaded up and pulled up to the stockade.

November 7. Still cloudy and stormy. The train lay here all day, the Lt. Bordent* of the guard, stopped with us in the house.

November 8. Cleared up. The train started this morning. Smith and a man named Patterson* arrived from Bozeman on the 6th with 3 horses and 3 mules, traded off a horse and mule yesterday, then left saying they were going to Bear Mountain to wolf. James Brooks left with them, slipping off to escape being seen; what he owes yet I have not learned. This Smith has the name of being a horse thief. He is the same man that passed through here this fall and sold a horse to the Col. The supposition is that these they have with them are stolen. The news by them from above is that the Col. will not be here under six weeks. I have been busy in the shop although my eye has pained a little.

November 9. Cool and windy. The talk is now that Smith told cross the river that their horses and mules were stolen from near Bozeman. Slim Jim also took several different articles off with him that belonged to different ones.

November 10. Moderate. All quiet as far as Paris.

November 11. Today a party of Sioux Indians came in on the other side, they appeared in sight cross the Musselshell. Billy Thompson was sent out to talk with them and bring them in which he did. All hands were frightened and undecided whether to let them in or not, but finally let them into the stockade where they behaved very well for Indians, only picking up little things they could carry off easily. Had a big talk with Gus Tyler, the man in charge. The Indians were all soldiers from a camp they say is down the river on the other side somewhere, but no one could find out exactly from their description. There were Assiniboins, Yanktons, and Tetons in the party and say they want to trade here this winter. They do not like the trader at Fort Peck now and say they won't trade there. They came in one or two o'clock and said they started this morning so they cannot be very far. At first they said there were 400 lodges of them, but finally there were only 200 of them, and they had any amount of robes at camp; they had but few with them. Came in to get acquainted and see if the whites' hearts were good to them.

Saturday, November 11. Snowed last night and today considerable. Last night just at dark 65 of the sons of bitches came here and we were fools enough to let them in, when they concluded to stop all night with us. There was no help for it, we had to submit gracefully and give them coffee and hard tack. They offered no violence, and I must say with the exception of an Indian's instinctive propensity to stealing, they behaved with remarkable goodwill towards us, leaving in the morning just at daybreak, taking with them various little articles as momentoes probably of our good regards such as knives, blankets, strychnia, cartridges, clothing, axes etc. to the amount of near 75 dollars and leaving the house and yard generally upside down. [The above dates are as entered in the journal.]

November 12. Sunday. Snows everyday, near 3 inches deep. Was over the river today. Jack Mail, Hunter, and two strangers went up the Musselshell a few days ago to be back in two or three days and were due yesterday and still are absent. I fear they have been murdered by the devils. The boys are, some of them, talking of leaving if Gus does not do differently than he did last time with the Indians. The situation is by no means enviable at present in this vicinity. This evening the Spaniard, Tony [Antoine Remming], returned from the mouth of Pochette with a stranger; had not seen or heard of an Indian at that place or on the road. The Indians came in here on the day he left, that was Friday last. Ed, Bill Martin, and Oleson started up Well's Creek that morning and discovered a war party and beat a hasty retreat but were not followed as they could see. I must state here that during the last month I have got in a day too much but since last Saturday, the 11th, the dates are correct.

November 13. Cold as the devil. Yesterday morning was the first running ice in the river. Last year it was not until the first of December. Snowing some tonight.

November 14. Cool, but not quite as much ice as yesterday. Saw nor heard no one today. I fear those four men up the Musselshell are no more as they would certainly give me a visit as soon [as] they made their appearance.

November 15. Moderate. W. Thompson was over, said the party up Musselshell were in Monday and were all right. Also there were 7 more Indians in on Monday, and went away with a very favorable impression the good hearts the whites have at this place.

November 16. Cold as the devil. The river full of ice. Snowed some more last night.

November 17. Cold. Lots of antelope in the point. Was out and killed 7 of them and packed them in to the stockade. As we were out the last time, we met Skelly [Skelton] who started from here for the mouth of the Pochette on the 15th and got lost and laid out two nights without blankets or grub but fortunately a fire. Froze his feet a very little. When we met him, he thought he was getting into Pochette, no idea where he was.

November 18. Cold this morning but no ice running. I think the river is over a little ways above. Joe Butcher came in this morning, came from Pochette yesterday, stopped at the lower stockade, came up to get his gun fixed. Says the river has been frozen over for three days down there. No Indians round there, they have got the post nearly completed. A lot of the boys from the other side were [over], among them was Jack Mail after his Spencer. Antelope shooting in every direction. This evening I see a lot of horses on the other side, some Indians, I suppose, from the Yankton camp.

November 19. Sunday. Moderately cold. Skelly and Joe Butcher went down to the Pochette. Antelope round thick. I struck out after them and succeeded in getting 11 of them. Harry got only one. There is firing going on from morning til night all over the point and the foothills. Still the antelope keep coming down, wanting to cross the river. When fired upon they run back over the hill; after a few moments quiet, here they come again as though nothing had happened.

November 20. Thawed considerably. The river is frozen over at Well's point down to the head of this one. It closed probably on the 18th. Was out today and made a big antelope killing. Killed 39 myself, 7 of them with a Needles gun. Then thinking that was too slow, I came in and got my Henry and caught a band on the bar just above the house, and got close to where they had to come to get up the bank. As they made a circle or two on the bar and went by me, I fired 50 shots and got 32 antelope. Billy Thompson came along as I was hunting them up and helped me to skin them. There was an unusual number of antelope in the point today. The firing in every direction was almost incessant. Harry was out to the foothills and succeeded in getting 11 of them.

November 21. Cold. Killed one antelope; shot it from the top of the house. There were 110 killed in the point yesterday.

November 22. Moderate; snowed two inches last night and some during the day. I killed 8 antelope; shot them from the top of the house while the other boys were firing at them in the back of the point. Harry killed 5, Bill Martin killed an elk. Just at dusk 23 of [the] red friends of the other night returned and wanted to stop with us, but we couldn't see it. Gave three of them a little to eat and told them it was good to go and stop with the trader on the other side and turned them out into the storm. Saw no Crows.

November 23. Moderate. Hunting antelope today and killed 36 of them in the point. W. Thompson moved over into the stockade with us.

November 25. Cold as the devil. Everything froze solid in the house. Finished skinning the 24 antelope of yesterday and I killed 5 more. The point literally covered with them, but too cold to go out after [them]. Harry froze the tips of his fingers trying to skin one. Been skinning in the house all day.

November 26. Sunday. A little moderate. I was busy making moccasins. Last night was horrible cold, closed the river up in front of the post up to the head of the island. Harry killed 11 antelope.

November 27. Thermometer 30 degrees below zero. Saturday it was 40 degrees and the mercury froze. The river channel is still open in front of us. I killed 4 antelope from the top of the house.

November 28. Four degrees below zero this morning. Harry and Bill busy taking their hams cross the river. In the evening they came home from the lower stockade, Harry drunk as a fool and Billy slightly so.

November 29. Cold but the sunshine nice.

November 30. Twenty degrees below zero this morning, but sunshiny. But few antelope around now; most of them have crossed the river, I think, which is still open in front of us yet along the other side. Harry was down below and came back in the evening and said those fellows were disposed to be friendly with me if I would meet them half way, of course I was glad to do so. Our trouble started from the wood business last summer.

December 1. Warm last night and part of the day, but turned cold again. Killed one antelope.

December 2. Cold as the devil. Killed 3 antelope. Just at night a party of Sioux came up from below Pochette where their camp is. Two of them stopped with us.

December 3. Sunday. Cold. Indians still round and damn nuisance.

December 4. Cold. The Indians left today.

December 5. Quite pleasant. Thawed a good deal. Last evening Bill Norris and some Indians arrived from Pochette and Browning at least Norris was, says the Santee camp is at the Pochette.

December 6. Quite warm; thawed a good deal. Bill Norris was over to see us. He dropped quite a suspicious letter that Harry picked up.

December 7. Thawed but little. No Indians round. Hunter started for Browning. Rumors of whiskey around here that occasion a good deal of talk. The Indians told at the Pochette that they got liquor up here somewhere, but would not tell who the parties were.

December 8. Moderately cold. Worked in the shop yesterday and today. Harry is getting drunk everyday on a little liquor. He has and is making an ass of himself generally.

December 9. Moderate. Worked in the shop.

December 10. Sunday. Moderate. Harry started for the Pochette this morning on horseback. I killed 13 antelope; Billy 8.

December 11. Moderate; 6 or 8 inches water on the ice. In the morning a stranger arrived from Pochette on foot, been at work there; is a Norwegian, I think.

December 12. Moderate. Hunter returned from Browning with the mail. Billy was over and brought my mail, said the Col. was there and arrived yesterday evening, a Jew with him. Major Reed and Dexter were on the road with two teams.

December 13. Moderate. Two Yankton Indians came in this evening;

sent them cross the river.

December 14. A little cooler. Hunter was over today; everything quiet at Browning.

December 15. A little cool. Tony returned from the Pochette and said that Boyd threatened to have him put in irons if he went to the Yankton camp. The Col. started him again this morning. Bill Norris also went down.

December 16. Just good winter weather.

December 17. Sunday. Turned cold last night; 10 below zero. French Joe was over to see us.

December 18. Cold and snowing a little all day. Bill Norris, Bill Benwar* [Benoir], Bill Ivy, and a stranger came up from Pochette, also about 100 Santee Indians. Stopped at the Col.'s. Can hear nothing of Harry since he left. Benwar brought me a letter from Courtney.

December 19. Tuesday. Cold. The Indians don't bother us any here today. Half-Breed Joe came up with them, says Boyd went over to Browning. There are so many hostile Indians around Peck that they are afraid to send goods up to Pochette. The chances are they will have none. They are here after flour now. Have been living on flour and meat now for some time. Sitting Bull with the Ung ka pa pas [Hunkpapa] is round Peck and we hear is only restrained from fighting that place by the presence of the Mandans and Rees who are friendly. The Yankton camp is at or near Round Butte. Everyone of them they say that can raise a gun has gone down to Peck leaving only old men and boys with the squaws at camp. What their object is no one knows.

December 20. Cold but sunny. The party returned to Pochette today, Indians and whites. Was up in Jenk's point hunting; saw nothing. A good deal of snow and ice on the ground.

December 21. Cold; snowed a little last night. Sat in the house.

December 22. Cold. Sat in the house. Do nothing but get firewood, I and Billy Thompson.

December 23. Cold. Snowed considerable last night. Sat in the house, got wood, fed the chickens and dog. Boxer.

December 24. Sunday. Cold. This evening some Assiniboin Indians came in from the fort of the Little Rocky Mountain about 50 miles distant. Among them was the Long Sioux and Tah chong kipy Yanktonais. They say their camp is coming here to trade.

December 25. Christmas. Killed 2 antelope, skinned only one of them. Two more men came up from the Pochette yesterday, stopping at the Col.'s. Twenty-two degrees below zero last night.

December 26. Cold as the devil; 40 degrees below zero last night. During the day a little moderate about zero, I believe.

December 27. Cold.

December 28. Cold.

December 29. A little moderate. The Assiniboins returned to camp. Think their camp will be here in a month. We have had no word yet from Harry since he left. He has not been seen by Indians or whites. He has gone to Cow Island or Fort Browning, or else run into a party of hostile Indians and been killed.70

December 30. Cold as the devil. Killed 5 antelope from the top of the shop in front of the stockade. Nothing new.

December 31. Sunday. Moderate. French Joe was over to see us.

1872

January 1, 1872. New Year's. Snowed a good deal. Worked in the shop. Nothing new. Valentine* the Spaniard, was over to see me to get his gun sighted.

January 2. A little moderate. Worked in the shop. The cats in a wearing way today. The snow is about a foot deep.

January 3. Thawed a good deal. Jack Bowers was in, he bursted his Needle gun the other day. He is wolfing up the Musselshell, also Tom Rose, and Eugene ------. Billy said he got some slight hints favorably for trade today on the other side.

January 4. Thawed. Killed 3 antelope; Billy got 4. Tony returned from the Assiniboin camp. Haven't heard any news yet. Saw some buffalo in Jenk's point. The snow, I find by traveling around a little, is from 10 inches to two feet deep.

January 5. Thawed. Oleson thought he heard a cannon down the river. A Yankton was in and said their camp was this side of the Pochette.

January 6. Moderate. Making knives.

January 7. Sunday. Moderate but does not thaw much. Bill Norris and Big Hunter that went out to meet Reed and the Col.'s wagons came in last night. They went as far as Arnell's Creek; saw nothing of Reed or the wagons. One of their horses froze to death during the cold, stormy weather. While they laid by the fire and lived on meat staight. Little Hunter and Santee Joe also came up from Pochette, say there are 300 lodges of Indians at Pochette, Mandans, Rees, Yankton, Santees, and Unk a pa paws.

January 8. Moderate. This evening a few Indians came in and crossed the river.

January 9. This morning 3 Assiniboins came over on their way back to the Pochette. They came up after grub for the post there. They had a note for me from Higbee, the boss there. They say there are 500 lodges of Indians round that place. Tepu (Lelak Otah), Bill Norris was over afternoon. He is in the employ of the Col. at present. Quite warm today and thawed a good deal. I met Bill Marin today right in front of the gate and made it my business to stop and speak to him. I can hardly [tell] whether he wants to be sociable or not.

January 10. Moderate. Nothing of importance.

January 11. About freezing point. Bill Thompson, Valentine, Frank Hunter, and Charley ------ started early this morning for Pochette on foot to be gone three days. I am all alone except the cats, chickens, and Boxer.

January 13. A little colder last night. Been all alone since the boys went to Pochette. Everything appears to be quiet; no Indians, traders, or bummers have made their appearance lately.

January 14. Sunday. Moderate but windy. Thompson and the boys got back last evening. Joe Butcher and three Indians came up with them. Terrible hard walking they say. 200 or 300 lodges of Indians round there, hard to tell how many. Most of them camped in the second point above the Pochette. On the 12th, Old Man Courtney got shot by one of them. He was out a couple of hundred yards from the post after wood when one of them came up to him and jerked his knife out of his belt, then wanted to trade a finger ring for his belt. Seeing he was bent on mischief and being without weapons, Courtney traded with him and shouldered his log and started in with it, the Indian right behind him. As he was going down the bank of the creek the Indian fired, the ball entering just below the point of the hip behind and coming out on the inside of the left leg half way down to the knee, making a wound a foot long. He dropped his log and wheeled throwing up his axe and made for the Indian who stood with the other barrel of his gun, a double shotgun loaded with trade balls, cocked, but instead of shooting again he turned and ran off. The wound proved to be only a flesh wound. The post is destitute of surgical skill or medicine. He will undoubtedly suffer a great deal with it. The other Indians made a great show of hunting him up to punish him and finally they said found him and gave him a severe whipping with their bows; maybe so and maybe not so. The post got a sled load of goods a short time ago.

January 15. Moderate; thawed. Joe Butcher was up today. Billy was out after buffalo but got none.

January 16. Moderate. Eugene ------ was over today with Billy.

January 17. Moderate. Some Assiniboin Indians came in today after dark and said their camp was close. They stopped and took coffee with us.

January 18. Moderate. Worked in the shop.

January 19. Moderate. The Col. was over today; very sociable. More Assiniboins in today.

January 20. Moderate. Billy hauled in 5 wolves. Red Stone, chief of the Assiniboins, was in to see me today. Bill Norris with him. Red Stone wanted to see the man that fixed guns, had a Henry rifle to repair.

January 21. Sunday. Moderate. Old Long Sioux stayed with us last night. Thawed a good deal.

January 22. A little cool. Worked in the shop. Some of the Assiniboin lodges have got down to Well's point; I believe 7 or 8. Several were in today with their squaws. Charley Williams and Gus Tyler have squaws they traded for a few days ago. Yesterday the Col. traded for one, a young girl. In the evening after retiring to the nuptial couch the bride became alarmed and concluded not to stop. The Col. became indignant and took the goods back and turned her out, when she returned to camp the same night with a couple of bucks.

January 23. Windy and snowing. Five or six of the boys were here last night from the other side. I had to play for them awhile.

January 24. Cold as the devil last night and today. The Assiniboins all came to Weller's point. Old Long Sioux and another buck had some fun here today with the Col.'s squaw, also Billy. A Yankton's dogs got poisoned in Well's point. Raised a blank this evening, I and Billy.

January 25. Thawed a little. Long Sioux and his lodges moved down and camped [with]in 75 yards of the stockade. Tah chunk ape was in, called Billy a fool, who ordered him out of the house when he said he did not mean it. Lots of Indians cross the river from Well's point. Toward night 250 or 300 Yanktons came in to trade; more than could get in the Col.'s stockade.

January 26. Moderate; snowed last night; Indians everywhere. Long Sioux tries to show that he is our friend by keeping the others from crowding into the stockade. Billy traded for a Yankton squaw tonight.

January 27. Cold; snowed last night. This evening Billy's squaw ran off and left him in the lurch. After dark 5 of the boys from the other side came over to serenade him.

January 28. Sunday. Cold as the devil last night. This evening Billy's squaw's daddy brought her back. She froze her feet and legs going to camp last night. Nothing else of importance.

January 29. Cold as the devil. Get wood and cook and sit around the fire all day. Long Sioux was in telling who was trading whiskey.

January 30. Cold as the devil.

January 31. Same as yesterday. The Col. was [over] yesterday and today to see about baits as 15 dogs have got poisoned and the Indians feel hot about it. Long Sioux got mad cause we kept him out; said he was not coming again. Told him that was good. In the evening he was in same as ever. They are trying to find out who was in that fight 8th of May, 1869. Long Sioux's brother was killed then.

February 1. Warmer. Lots of squaws round. Jack Mail was over. Indians say Boyd is back to Pochette, also that Bill Martin's, Oleson's, and Joe Gerard's wood and cabin is burned on the third point below here. Considerable stink about whiskey trading; everybody laying it on someone else.

February 2. Cold. Ellinger and Bill Norris started for Browning. Five Indian camps between here and Spread Eagle, the Indians say. Also Mabbot will be here tomorrow and Thumb at Pochette.

February 3. Cold. The Indians say Simmons is going to take every wolfer out of the country in irons. Red Stone, chief of the Assiniboin camp, was in today and wanted to trade me one of his female relatives for a gallon of whiskey. Anything they have they will trade for it, if they can find anyone that will trade with them and swear never to tell about it.

February 4. Sunday. Cold as the devil. The Indians say there is lots of snow above 3 and 5 feet deep; that the river will wash everybody away in the spring.

February 5. Cold and snowing; lots of snow, knee deep or more. Jim Mabbot and George Boyd, Little Hunter, and Santee Joe came in last evening. Boyd was over today; brought me some mail; letter from Mother. Everybody is suspicious of Mabbot's business, Deputy Marshall they say. Trading party of Yankton and Lower Grovents up today.

February 6. Not so cold. Worked in the shop. George Powell came up from Pochette. Billy sent his squaw to camp yesterday.

February 7. Warm; thawed a good deal. Mabbot was over. Boyd went back to Pochette. I stayed alone last night.

February 8. Warm; thawed.

February 9. Cold. Part of the Yankton camp talk of coming up here. Jack Mail was here and brought the Indian, Tah chunk ape, with him. Of his operations W.R. Thompson is a witness.

February 10. Cold.

February 11. Sunday. Cold.

February 12. Cold as the devil.

February 13. Cold. Bill Norris got back from Browning last night. Snowing this morning. The Col., I understand, has got up a certificate signed by a few of the men there that there has been no liquor sold about his stockade. He is not stout enough to do so; as righteous as the devil.

February 14. Warm and sunny. Yanktons moving up.

February 15. Warm; thawed fast. Some Yanktons moved into the lower end of the point.

February 16. Thawed; water running. Lots of Indians round. Mabbot was over. In the evening Phillip the Spaniard [Philip Alvarez] was over and had a good deal to say of the way he has been treated.

February 17. Thawing; Musselshell bank full. The Indians are skinning up the boys' wolves for the meat to eat as buffalo meat is scarce with them. My hens laid their first egg today since last fall. The water is pouring out of the Musselshell furiously this evening. I heard this evening that 40 cords of my wood is burned at the farther end of the point by the Yanktons.February 18. Sunday. Warm. The river raised up to the bank on this side 3 or 4 feet.

February 19. Warm; river rising. Indians shot into the stockade today, just bluffing. Winter was over, also Jack Mail.

February 20. Warm; rising yet. A lot of the boys over. I got one day ahead the 10th or 11th; this is right now. The Indians are camped on the hill back of us. The river has raised 6 feet; the ice is solid in the channel.

February 21. Warm; river is breaking up a little.

February 22. Warm. Jack and Hunter stayed here last night. River fell 3 or 4 feet. Mabbot was over.

February 25. Sunday. Warm. Indian camp left yesterday; went up the river; some of them round today. Jack and Hunter went to camp last night. Gus was over today.

February 27. Thawed but little. Bill and Charley Wood went to Pochette last night. The river is dangerous to cross. The ice is very rotten. Lot [of] dogs got drowned yesterday.

February 28. A little stormy. Bill Berry came up last evening and went cross the river. This forenoon the ice moved down a little in front leaving the channel clear for a short distance.

February 29. Cool and cloudy. River clear in front clear down to Pochette, Berry says. He went home today. An Indian came in late last night and stayed with me. ------ Courtney is up and about.

March 1. This evening Thompson and ------ returned. Higbie also came up with 5 men; going [to] raft some flour down to Pochette from the Col.'s. Everything quiet on the Potomac.

March 3 – Sunday. Cool. Yesterday the Col. made a raft to take his flour down. [Saw] the first duck of the season.

March 4. About sunrise the ice started for good; been running thick all day. Higbie was just ready to start out with his raft at the Pochette. It went out on the 23rd of February, a month sooner than usual.

March 5. Warm. The ice slackened up last night. After breakfast it began to come thick again. Higbie started this morning, Billy Thompson going with him on the raft.

March 6. Moderate. All alone. Ed has concluded to give up the wood and leave on the first boats.

March 7. Chilly. All alone. Mail and ------.

March 8. Chilly. The river is down again; ice all gone but some crowded onto the banks.

March 9. Moderate. Phillip and Jack Mail were over. Jack saw Indian signs on the Musselshell early this morning. Then Tony, [and] Phillips, the Yankton Indian, went down to see about it and discovered a party of Tetons, 4 or 5 of them. Waded cross the Musselshell pretending to be friendly. One of them wanted to look at Phillips' gun, a Henry. No loads in it he let him take it. Stepping back a few steps he snapped it twice at Phillips, then the fight began. Tony got an arrow in his hip while the Yankton put an arrow into a Teton and caught one in his legging. Phillips by good dodging escaped unhurt. The Tetons retreated. Tony walked part way in then had to be carried. Phillips is out a gun.

March 10. Sunday. Moderate. The Col. and a lot of the boys were over with their squaws to the other stockade.

March 11. Moderate. Thought there were Indians round the stockade last night.

March 12. Cold and snowing. Rained last night.

March 13. Cold; snowed and froze last night. Tom, Frank, Tom Rose and Powell were over yesterday.

March 14. Cool; froze ice 1/2 inch thick last night. Hunter and the Yankton Indian went to the Assiniboin camp this morning; swam horses cross the river. Powell and Bowers were over today.

March 15. Cool; ice running in the river; quit before night.

March 16. Cool. Hens want to set. Today in place of yesterday, the ice was running, also trying to snow all day. Phillips' horses are in the point yet, I saw today.

March 17. Sunday. St. Patrick's Day be Gad. Chilly and windy. River full of running ice; snow all gone again. Alone by myself; sit and read, cook and eat, feed the chickens and the dog.

March 18. Cool. Hunter and the Indian got back last evening after dark. No ice running today. The Yankton was in today telling about shooting the Teton when Tony got shot; considers he is a tried friend of the whites now.

March 19. Chilly and windy. The Col., Mabbot, and a lot of the boys and the squaws were over to hear some fiddling. Phillips and his boy and girl came over to start for Browning tomorrow, also G. Tyler's squaw and her mother. Wrote a letter to Mother and one to Baker at Benton.

March 20. Clear and windy. The party got off for Browning. The Col. and a lot of the boys came riding by today and called for me on returning. They asked me to take my violin over and stay all night, which I did. In the evening had quite a dance, the Col.'s and Mail's squaws attending.

March 21. Clear; windy. Downstream, river raising a little. Stayed over all day. In the evening had another dance.

March 22. Cool and windy. Came home this morning. Everything all right; Boxer glad to see me.

March 23. Cool and windy. Took physic last night. On the sick list today. All alone since coming home from the Colonel's.

March 24. Sunday. Cool and windy. Tried to snow this morning. Took more medicine last night. Feel better today.

March 25. Cool and windy. Last evening the Col. and party came over after me to have another dance. I went over and came back this morning. Everything quiet, except Ed was in today and always has something he would like to quarrel about. Wants me to keep his wood now.

March 26. A little cool and windy as usual; the mornings and evenings are calm and nice. Went up the river a way with the boys to hunt, but the wind changed on us and the mast broke loose and we returned. Got home at noon.

March 27. Pleasant and nice. Bill Martin was up today and had a pleasant talk. He was a little tight.

March 28. Cloudy and chilly. Plenty of geese around. Cleared off.

March 29. A little cool. Col. and party over today. Mabbot stopped with me.

March 30. Cool; snowed last night about an inch.

March 31 – Sunday. 200 eggs laid.

April 1. All Fool's Day. Pleasant. Saturday afternoon I crossed the river; the boys wanted to dance. Snow all gone. I got back today, Monday. George Powell came over with me to stop awhile. The hens have laid 215 eggs to date. Got 14 oncoming hens.

April 2. Moderate. Nothing of importance.

April 3. Pleasant. George Powell and Bill Martin were to McGinnis' point.

April 4. Warm. My eye hurts some.

April 5. Warm. Tom Ferd was over, says the wolfing party are all right at Rock Springs 31 miles out. Oleson's dog, Prince, got poisoned yesterday. George was cross the river while today.

April 6. Moderate and cloudy. Making a pair of pants out of a couple of seamless bags. The river began to rise a little yesterday, last year it was on the 9th.

April 7. Sunday. Moderate. George went cross the river. Mabbot, Norris, and Eugene were over a short time. The river is an inch a day.

April 8. Moderate. George came back and said Bill Norris was on a hell of a drunk yesterday afternoon.

April 9. Moderate. Mabbot and Norris were over. The river rising slowly.

April 10. Cold and spit snow.

April 11. Cold. Went cross the river last evening for them to dance. They had a big time. Joe and Gene got a squaw of Jack Mail's. Charley Williams got quite drunk over it. I got back this afternoon. George stayed there. I stopped into the lower stockade; quite sociable. My hens have laid 275 eggs to date, April 11.

April 12. Cool; froze quite hard last night. The lower stockade boys were up today selling their cattle to Oleson. Lying Bill Martin pretty tight; stopped to dinner.

April 13. Cool and windy. The river on a standstill; raised altogether about 6 inches this spring. George Powell came over again today, this evening. Forenoon Mabbot and Charley Williams stopped in, they were taking a gun.

April 14 – Sunday. Cold and snowed all day. Everybody drunk, I understand, from George Powell who went down to the other stockade.

April 15. Cool; snow went off by noon. Toward evening it rained some. Began to build a boat to cross the river. The river is falling slightly. The weather this spring has been moderate, but too cool to start the snow in the mountains yet to raise the river.

April 16. Pleasant. Gus Tyler was over today. George went cross with him.

April 17. Warm. Bill Norris was over and said the Col. was going to start a boat to Buford tomorrow; anxious to sell cord wood, I suppose. My hens have laid 312 eggs up to this evening.

April 18. Nice and warm but windy. Gus Tyler and Norris started for Buford in a small boat at noon today taking a lot of antelope hams to sell. F. Hunter and Valentine went to Pochette horseback. Bill Martin was up and said they heard shooting this morning up the river on this side. Indians round.

April 19. Cool and windy. Mabbot was over. Hunter returned, says the Assiniboins are at Round Butte below going to Fort Peck, and the Yanktons are above on the river. The report by the Indians is that Joe Senix, Bob Gordon and George Horn and two squaws are killed; they were living at Cow Island.[71]

Author's Note: *Lee's diary ends with this last entry. As indicated in the Introduction, he evidently used all of his ink early in December. The entries from December 12 to April 19 are in pencil. He also ran out of journal. The March and April entries are on the Journal's back and front covers. Subsequent Lee journals detailing his later years may surface in the future; I hope they do, and if so, I can only apologize for not having found them.*

Some of the biographical information on Lee is contradictory. In Montana, he adopted the name of Cornelius. Elsewhere, he is noted as Corwin. Born November October 27, 1833, (one source says 1843, but is incorrect) to Fernando H. Lee (described as prominent settler, local *politician and county judge) and Martha Newhall Lee in Williamsburg, Indiana. The family moved to Iowa City in 1840, and after the death of his father, Lee and his mother relocated to Sioux City, Iowa. There, Lee operated a gunsmith shop on Pearl Street. In 1861 he enlisted in the Sioux City Cavalry commanded by Captain Andrew Milllard who was aided by 1st. Lieutenant James Sawyer. Two years later his unit became Company I, 7th Iowa Volunteer Cavalry and assigned to guard General Sully's headquarters. The unit traveled north into Dakota Territory, constructing forts (Forts Sully and Rice) and experienced several encounters with renegade Sioux. Returning to Sioux City, the unit was mustered out November 23, 1864. His obituary described him as having been a good citizen and a kind neighbor. Union Star, Eldora, Iowa (clipping, no date). Census Returns, Iowa, 1860, Woodbury County; Missouri River, 1870, Dawson County; Official Roster of Soldiers in the State of Iowa in the War of Rebellion, 1861-1866, Akron, Ohio: Werner Printing Lithograph; Roster of Sioux City Volunteers, IAGenWeb, Iowa Soldiers in the War of Rebellion. Susan B. Doyle, in her Journeys to the Land of the Gold, Helena: Montana Historical Society Press, 2000, relies upon the LDS Ancestral File for her Lee information.*

The famous sterograph of Fort Musselshell (listed as Muscleshell, lower left) discovered by Dr. James S. Brust at an antique photography show in Los Angeles, California, in 1996. Photo Courtesy Dr. James S. Brust.

THE STORY OF THE FORT MUSSELSHELL PHOTOGRAPH
By James S. Brust

I purchased the "Muscelshell" stereograph at an antique photography show in Los Angeles in January 1996. Neither I, nor the dealer I bought it from, were aware of its full significance at the time, but I thought it worth acquiring simply as an early Montana view and potential research project. I quickly began to make inquiries about it, first to my good friend and research colleague Mike Cowdrey of San Luis Obispo, California, and then to the staff of the Montana Historical Society, especially Lory Morrow, the Photo Archives Supervisor.

As it became apparent that I might have located an important image, I decided to turn to the highly-regarded Montana historian, John Popovich, who I had met briefly a couple of times, but who barely knew me. His prompt and enthusiastic reply, dated Feb. 14, 1996, left no doubt about the significance of this photograph. "When I opened your letter and saw the stereo photo of Muscleshell, it was the most exciting thing that has happened to me in years," he began, and then after a scholarly discourse about Fort Musselshell, he ended with the words: "I hope you realize what a treasure you have."

Anxious to share this photograph with other interested historians,

I submitted it to *Montana The Magazine of Western History* where it appeared with an accompanying letter to the editor in the Autumn 1996 issue (vol. 46, no. 3, p. 92). I had hoped that this would lead to more information, the location of other images of Fort Musselshell, another vintage print of this one, or perhaps a better idea of who the photographer might have been (a question that the best research efforts of John Popovich, Mike Cowdrey, myself and others had failed to reveal). But such was not to be the case. Some one hundred and forty years after it was taken, and fifteen years after it first surfaced, this remains the only known print of the only known photograph of Fort Musselshell, made by an unknown hand.

The image close-up. The photograph was most likely taken from the deck of the steamboat whose railing is shown at the lower right. The majority of the individuals shown, given the presence of several women and children, were most likely passengers from the steamboat. Note the cordwood stacked in the foreground, which was sold to the passing steamboats, and the high cut bank of the Missouri River where the boat would have been tied up for its stop at Musselshell.

Biographical Sketches

Andrews, Ray W.

Referred to with the honorific "Captain," Andrews was apparently a man of many talents. One newspaper item described him as: "Captain Andrews, the ubiquitous, is practicing law, medicine, surgery and dentistry, whacking bulls, poisoning wolves, chopping wood, killing buffalo, building houses, and making himself generally useful."

He was also insensitive. Following the battle that took place May 9, 1869, on the Musselshell, Andrews "cut the heads off the dead Indians, removed the flesh and brains by boiling, labeled the skulls with awe-inspiring names, and started on a lecturing tour throughout the states ..." or so reported Henry McDonald a few years later in 1888.

He ultimately made his home in Olathe, Kansas. *Helena Weekly Herald*, February 25, 1869, May 21, 1868; *Forest and Stream*, August 23, 1888; Eleanor Banks, *Wandersong*, 97; *Montana Post* (Virginia City), November 11, 1865; John S. Gray, "The Northern Overland Express," *Montana, The Magazine of Western History*, 16 (4) 66.

Armstrong, Adam

A trader and wolfer, Armstrong, with William Cochran, 0. B. Nevins, and John Dillon, constructed a stockade and trading post in 1865 on Rock Creek in the Little Rockies. The site was approximately one mile east of the present-day town of Landusky. Cochran describes Armstrong's death – killed by Indians – in Noyes, *In the Land of Chinook*, 85.

Baker, Isaac Gilbert

I. G. Baker was a Connecticut-born (1819, New Haven) trader. He came to Montana in 1864 to serve as chief clerk for the Pierre Choteau, Jr. fur company at Fort Benton. A year later, when Choteau sold his trading company to the Northwestern Company, Baker organized his own company in partnership with his brother George. The I. G. Baker and Company and the T. C. Power and Brother Company became the dominant trading powers on the Upper Missouri and southwest Canada. In 1874, George Baker sold his shares in the company to the Conrad brothers, William and John, and I. G. returned to St. Louis where, as a senior partner, he continued to direct the trading company. He died in 1904. Paul Sharp, *Whoop-Up Country*, 213.

Barker, E. A. "Buck"

Barker had taken part in the California gold rush and later, in 1879, made the first discovery of minerals in the Little Belt Mountains. The resulting mining district was known as the Barker district; Barker sold his claims, returned to his former home in Odessa, Missouri, and there purchased a farm. He died in 1886, "poor and almost helpless." *The River Press* (Fort Benton), December 8, 1886; Muriel Wolle, *Montana Paydirt*, 326.

Bennett, Frank

A miner turned wolfer, Bennett had earlier mined at Deep Creek and Copperopolis. In 1867, he and 22 other men left Helena for an extended buffalo-hunting trip down the Musselshell. Contemporary newspapers carry no mention of his untimely death. Lee's *Journal,* February 16, 1868, entry; Leeson, 14.

Benwar, Bill

This surname is variously spelled Benair, Benoist, Benware, and (most probably correct) Benoir. Whatever the spelling, Bill acted as a scout for the party sent to build Ft. Pouchette in late 1870. He was also a regular visitor to Ft. Browning in the spring and fall of 1872. James Stuart assumed that he had close contacts with the Assiniboine. University of Montana Clipping File, article on Ft. Pouchette, no date; Diary of James Stuart at Ft. Browning, *Collections* Montana State Historical Society, 1, 58.

Berry, Bill

The United States Census, 1870, "Below Ft. Benton, Choteau County," lists a William Berry, age 34, employed in a woodyard. Another account indicates that a William Berry was killed by Blood Indians on the Elbow River, southwestern Canada, in 1874. Leeson, 179.

Black, Leander M.

A successful merchant/trader who operated his expanding business from his headquarters in Bozeman, Montana. By 1872, he had become president of the First National Bank there, and two years later he was a partner in the National Park Wagon Road and Hotel Co. His family occasionally spent their winters in St. Joseph, Missouri. At least one person thought Black's mercantile success was due to less than honest contract manipulations. See letter, M. M. McCauley, Agent for the Blackfeet, to E. S. Parker, Commissioner Indian Affairs, Feb. 13, 1871, in *House Exec Doc*. No. 15, 42d Cong., 1st Sess., 2, Serial 1471, *Helena Weekly Herald*, February 1, 2, March 5, 1870; *Helena Daily Herald*, November 6, 1872, May 7, 1874

Blossom, Charles

"Charley the Negro" worked as a cook, and, according to the 1870 Census, Dawson County, Missouri River District, he was living with Joe Mosser, S. Dean, and Fountain Dennis.

Bogy, Thomas

Born in St. Louis in 1845 to a family prominent in steamboating and river trade on both the Missouri and the Mississippi, Thomas came to Montana in 1865 and worked as a clerk for his uncle, Joseph H. McKnight, a trader and business associate of T. C. Power at Fort Benton.

He moved down river to the Musselshell and there clerked for George Clendenin, taking charge of the trading establishment in Clendenin's absence (Koch, *Contributions*, Historical Society of Montana, 2, 299). He later established his own trading post at Fort Clagett and from there moved to Fort Belknap. His diary from the years at Belknap (1874-1879) is located at the Montana Historical Society. He died sometime before 1913 (Sanders, *History of Montana*, 1157).

Bompart, Louis

Various spellings of this name appear in the literature: Le Bompard, Bonfort, Rumbar, Bombard. Born in 1791, he entered the fur trade as a young man. He came up the Missouri River in 1822 with the Missouri Fur Company and, in 1829, joined with seven other partners in forming the short-lived French Fur Company. He is listed among the men of the Upper Missouri Outfit in 1855 and remained on the upper river, trapping and trading for the rest of his life. He died at the age of 81 at Fort Clagett, January 1, 1872.

Borden, Lieutenant George Pennington

Borden served in the Civil War as a private in the New York infantry from July 1862 until October 1863. Gaining an appointment at the United States Military Academy, he was commissioned a 2nd Lieutenant with the Fifth Infantry on October 1, 1866, and promoted to 1st Lieutenant twelve years later. He saw action against both the Sioux and the Nez Perce while serving in Montana and gained the rank of Lieutenant Colonel before his retirement in 1902. Heitman, *Historical Register*, 231; *Contributions,* Montana Historical Society, 2, 286.

Bouyer, Minton ("Mitch")

Bouyer was a much admired French/Sioux scout who died with Custer at the Little Big Horn. Married to a Crow Indian, Bouyer learned the West under the tutelage of Jim Bridger, and many considered him second only to his fabled teacher in ability. He served as a guide on the Bozeman Trail and worked for the Army as a dispatch rider from Fort C. F. Smith. In 1873 he assisted Lieutenant Gustavus C. Doane in a survey of the Judith Basin. Three years later he was in charge of Colonel John Gibbon's detachment of Crow scouts, and it was Gibbon who loaned Bouyer to Custer's 7th Calvary. With Custer, Bouyer is credited with first sighting the Sioux village. His badly mutilated body was found near the Little Big Horn River. W. H. Banfill, *Hardin Tribune* May 5, 1931; Stewart*, Custer's Luck*, 27, 105; Brown, *Plainsman of The Yellowstone* 142.

Boyd, George W.

Boyd was a noted trader and scout in central Montana in the 1860s and 1870s. Born in New York, he arrived in Montana in 1862 at the age of 22. He worked out of Fort Hawley until that post was abandoned in 1868 and then divided his time between Fort Browning and the small settlement at the mouth of the Musselshell. An item in the *Salt Lake Herald,* reprinted in the *Helena Daily Herald*, December 4, 1873, contained the following: "Nature played a freak with him /Boyd/ at his birth, and turned him out from his laboratory deformed in feet and hands, yet has endowed him with a fine physique and a manly spirit ..." George Boyd died at Fort Assinniboine in January 1880. His younger brother, Jim, was also a well-known scout and interpreter. John Grey. George W. Boyd, Montana Frontiersman, Chicago Westerner's *Brand Book 22 (1965) 33-40.*

Boyd, Jim

Younger brother of George, Jim was born in New York in 1848 and came to Montana at the age of 16. He spent his first three years in Montana at Virginia City, then, in 1868, he moved north to Fort Benton and worked first for the Northwestern Fur Company and then for Durfee and Peck until 1875. Boyd spent the next 20 years along the Missouri River, working as a guide and interpreter before turning to ranching. *Progressive Men of Montana,* 1499-1500.

Brewer, James Scott

Born in Virginia in 1830, Brewer was lured west in 1861 by the reports of gold in Colorado. The dream of a big strike led him to the goldfields in Idaho, Nevada, and finally, in 1864, to Montana. A year later, Brewer and "Captain" Ray Andrews led a group of 22 men to the mouth of the Musselshell with the hope of securing freight business from that point to Helena. In the succeeding two years, Brewer led others to the Musselshell and in 1868 constructed a warehouse and laid out a town site on the south bank of the Missouri. Previously, Brewer had discovered the hot springs that were first called "Brewers Hot Springs," and in 1870 he preempted a quarter section there and later, aided by a partner, Major R. C. Walker, established the town of White Sulphur Springs. Brewer died near Lewistown, Montana on August 17, 1914. Brewer Autobiography, Montana Historical Society; Leeson, 806; *Contributions,* Montana Historical Society. 8, 346.

Brown, John

Jack Brown typifies the early Missouri River resident. He was relatively young (28), a hunter and woodcutter married to a Crow woman, and was killed by Indians before his thirtieth birthday. Leeson, 117; U.S. Census, 1870, Missouri River, Choteau County; Noyes, 82.

Burdick, James

The 1870 Census, Dawson County, Missouri River, lists a John Burdick, age 33, born in New York, following the occupation of woodcutter.

Bushaway, Joe

Various spellings of his last name appear in the literature. Peter Koch and Henry McDonald agree upon Bushaway; J. J. Healy tried both Beeshway and Bushway; Lee occasionally spells it Bushaney. Eleanor Banks (*Wandersong*) speculated that Bushway may have been his real name, or a local corruption of the French Bourgeois, the term for local agents of the large fur companies. Henry McDonald first met Joe in March 1869 and described him as the "gigantic Frenchman, as gallant and brave a man as ever fired a rifle ..." They became partners in putting up ice and cutting wood and when they constructed their cabin – just below the mouth of the Pouchette – they used the smokestack of a wrecked steamboat for chimney and fireplace. Koch, *Contributions,*Historical Society of Montana 2, 295; Healy, Interviews; McDonald, *Forest and Stream*, August 2, 1888; Banks, Wandersong,

Butcher, Joe

Also known as Joe Butch, his actual surname was Chamberlin. He emigrated to the United States from England where he had been born in 1846. He served in the Union Army (1863-1964), was discharged, then reenlisted. Transferred to Fort Yates, Dakota Territory, he deserted and headed up the Missouri as a deckhand on the steamboat Trevor (Trover?). When the boat sunk (near present-day Frazer, Montana), he and five companions established a wood yard in an attempt to make money to finance further travels. During an Indian raid, one comrade was killed, the other four separated and fled. (One of the four was A. B. Hammond, who later established a timber dynasty; he contacted Butcher in the late 1920s.) Butcher continued to follow the life of a woodcutter and plainsman, married an Indian woman named "Steps on Joe," and raised two daughters. Fearing discovery as a deserter, he assumed the name Joe Butch or Joe Butcher. He died at the age of 92 in March 1931. *Great Falls Tribune*, March 24, 1931; U.S. Census, Dawson County, 1870.

Cameron, Alexander

Listed in the U.S. Census, 1870, Missouri River, Dawson County as a miner from Missouri, age 24

Canfield, Lieutenant Andrew N.

Canfield was born in Pennsylvania, joined the Union Army in Iowa, served as a Sergeant Major, 1861-1864, commissioned as Lieutenant in 1866, and resigned in

1869. Both the Lieutenant and his wife kept brief diaries during their stay in Montana Territory. The diaries are on deposit at the Montana Historical Society. Heitman Historical Register 1, 280.

Chamberlin, John (See Butcher, Joe)

Charley, Mountain

The name "Mountain Charley," or occasionally "Rocky Mountain Charley," was apparently claimed by (or given to) several women who traveled the West dressed in men's clothes. In 1885, George West published the autobiography of one "Mountain Charley," – Mrs. E. J. Guerin – who was still alive at that time and had been married for 18 years to a man she met in Colorado. Another candidate, and probably the one Lee refers to, appears in a newspaper column under the heading "Suicide of Old Mountain Character"; [In Clarkstown, Utah Territory] .. last week, a woman from Montana committed suicide ... [she] formerly resided in Helena. Upon inquiry, we learn that she is the same woman who years ago figured in Colorado, in male costume, under the name Mountain Charley, and who will be remembered ... as a dashing, devil-may-care sort of person ... who always appeared ... well-armed, and always ready for a fight. It appears that after many queer episodes in life, she brought up in Helena, where she married a drayman ... by the name of Symmons, who removed with her to Utah last fall; and now comes the news from Clarkstown that she blew her brains out in that village the other day with a revolver." Guerin, E. J. *Mountain Charley* (Norman: University of Oklahoma Press, 1968) *Rocky Mountain Weekly Gazette* (Helena), August 20, 1873.

Clendenin, George (occasionally spelled: Clenndenin)

Described by one contemporary as being about 5' 10" tall, slim, weighing about 160 pounds, light complexioned and good-natured, and by another as being "a likeable man who understood the Indian character better than most," Clendenin had been born in New York City in 1838. He entered the Union Army from Rhode Island, received three breveted commissions (Major, Lt. Colonel, Colonel) for gallantry in action before being mustered out at the end of the Civil War. He arrived in Montana Territory in 1866, and a year later focused his attention on the area around the mouth of the Musselshell. Believing that the location was a promising one for trading as a freight terminal, he established a post there in 1868, just a few months after the rival Montana Hide and Fur Company of Helena had located there. Clendenin's hopes for the Musselshell never materialized; population and trade dwindled after 1870 and in 1874 he moved his operation to Carroll (located some 25 miles upriver from the Musselshell) where he traded until 1878. Later, he became interested in the Barker Mining District (southeast Cascade County), and in partnership with T. C. Powers and others he constructed a smelter there in 1881. A year later he was killed in a cave-in while inspecting his mine, the Clendenin Lode. Skelton, William, *Reminiscences* Archives, Vertical File, *Kalispell Times*, March 14, 1935; Heitman, *Historical Register* (Washington, Government Printing Office, 1903) 310; Stout, Tom, ed. *Montana, Its Story and Biography* 1, (Chicago: American Historical Society) 305; *River Press* (.Ft. Benton), February 15, 1882; *Helena Daily Independent*, July 22, 1874; U.S. Census, 18 70, Dawson County, Missouri River.

Clendenin, Richard H.

"Doc" Clendenin, brother to George, was originally a partner in the Musselshell trading venture but moved his family from Carroll to the forks of the Musselshell where the town of Martinsdale grew up around his general store and blacksmith shop. He was one of the earlier individuals who established sheep ranching in this area. Skelton, *Reminiscences*, p. 7; Leeson, Michael, ed., History of Montana 1739-1885 (Chicago: Warner, Beers and Company, 1885) 507, 816, 1085; Stearns, Harold, *A History of the Upper Musselshell Valley of Montana, to 1920* (Harlowtown: Time-Clarion, 1966) 35-37.

Clift, Captain Emory W.

Emory White Clift was born in New York in 1832, enlisted in the Union Army in 1861 from Michigan, attained the rank of Captain during the Civil War, and was assigned to Fort Ellis, Montana Territory, in 1868. Two years later, Major General Hancock directed him to explore the area between Fort Ellis and the mouth of the Musselshell, seeking a suitable route for a road connecting the Gallatin Valley, Helena, and the Missouri River. He retired in 1885 and died two years later. Heitman, 1, 310; *Helena Weekly Herald*, June 11 and 18, 1868; U.S. Census, 1870, Meagher County.

Cochran, John

A 23-year-old woodcutter from Ireland. In 1870 he was working with George Grinnell and later owned his own woodyard upriver at the new settlement of Carroll. His brother, Billy, figured prominently in the events of the 1860s and 1870s in central Montana. U.S. Census, 1870, Dawson County, Missouri River; Montana Historical Society *Contributions* 1 58; Banks, *Wandersong* (Caldwell: Caxton Printers, 1950)160; Noyes, *In the Land of the Chinook; The Story of Blaine County* (Helena: Montana State Publishing Company, 1917) 82; *Helena Daily Independent*, June 23, 1874.

Congden, Dave

Age 28, laborer, born in Wisconsin according to the U.S. Census, 1870, Dawson County, Missouri River.

Cook, James

A private in Company E, 13th Infantry. Lt. Canfield diary (5/24/68) states: "Indians attacked about noon and killed the two herders Pvts. Quesnill and Cook." Cook's body was not recovered. His father, John Cook, lived in New York and, presumably, Cook had enlisted there. May 24, 30, 1868 entry, Diary, Lt. Andrew Canfield, MHS, MF 73.

Courtney, Bill

Born in London in 1834, Courtney received a fair education before emigrating to the United States in 1859. After seven years of "operating a business" in New York City, he purchased a stock of goods and moved, first to the Yellowstone valley, and then to the Judith Basin where he exchanged his goods for furs and robes obtained by the Indians of the area. In 1870 the census taker found him located in Fort Benton, operating as a wood dealer. Later that year Courtney acted as bookkeeper for a group of men sent down river to erect trading posts at Fort Belknap, Wolf Point, and the Pouchette. (Others in the party were Jerome Higbee, William Skelton, George Powell, William Ivey, and Bill Benoir.) That winter (1870-71) Courtney was wounded by an Indian who "shot him through the thigh with an old trade gun ... loaded with a ball wrapped in an old rag." The wound finally healed, treated according to instructions sent from Clendenin at Musselshell. In the late 1870s, Courtney moved to the new town of Miles City on the Yellowstone and opened a pioneer real estate office. Leeson, 1036; U.S. Census, 1870, Chouteau County, Benton City; Skelton, Reminiscenses, 3,

4; "Life at Pouchette," University of Montana Clipping File No. 7.

Crittenden, Henry

Crittenden is mentioned as being a member of a buffalo hunting expedition to the Musselshell in 1867 (from Helena) and listed in the 1870 U.S. Census (Thomson Gulch/North Deep Creek) as a 28-year-old miner from Virginia. Leeson, p. 816.

Cutter, William B.

Cutter was one of the partners in the firm of Cutter and Taylor, post traders at Fort Shaw. In 1870 he was 42 years old and had amassed a personal estate valued at $15,000 since leaving his native Ireland. U.S. Census, 1870, Sun River Valley, Lewis and Clark County.

Dennis, Fountain M. ("Pomp")

A former Confederate soldier who, with three other Southerners, discovered the fabulously rich Confederate Gulch strike in late 1864. Estimates of the value of gold taken from the area vary from 10 to 30 million dollars. Dennis apparently did not prosper from the strike for three years later he was seeking employment as a rider for the Pony Express. Lt. James H. Bradley, a contemporary, states that Dennis was born March 10, 1836, in Boone County, Missouri. The 1870 Census indicates a birth date eight years later, a birthplace in Kentucky, and identifies him a woodcutter. Described as a "slow-moving and slow talking ex-Southern soldier," Dennis moved fast enough to later earn the distinction of being one of the principal stockmen on the Musselshell range in 1882-83. Malone and Roeder, 52; Banks, Wandersong, 76; Bradley, "Attempts to Build a Town ...," Montana Historical Society *Contributions,* 2, 307, note; U.S. Census, 1870, Dawson County, Missouri River; Leeson 595. Grey, John Northern Overland Express *Montana, The Magazine of Western History,* 16(4) (1966) 71.

Denton, Drew

Identified only as "an Oregonian," Denton narrowly escaped death when, with Joseph Lee and Charles Williams, he was attacked by Teton Sioux some 25 miles up the river from the mouth of the Musselshell. As reported in the Helena newspaper, "Denton was nearly knocked down by a bullet in the breast, his life being saved by the mail package and a plug of tobacco, both of which were perforated by the missile." Joseph Lee was killed in this attack and Denton reportedly told a friend, "I am sure I have got enough. I am going back to Oregon, it is too bloody for me." *Helena Daily Herald,* May 18, 1871; J. J. Healy, Interview, MHS.

Dexter, Wheeler 0.

Born in Steuben County, New York in 1843, Dexter fought the last year and a half of the Civil War. A year later, 1866, he came West with the Fisk Wagon Train and held a variety of jobs in Helena and Fort Benton before establishing several woodyards along the upper Missouri River. In 1870 the census taker found him twice; once he listed him as 28 years old, following the trade of woodchopper, and later reduced his age to 24 and promoted him to operator of a woodyard. When the river trade diminished, Dexter turned to freighting, threshing, and lumbering. In the 1880s he was operating ferries on the Missouri and Sun rivers, and by the early 1890s he had established himself as a farmer and horsebreeder in the Gallatin Valley. Sometime in the 1920s he returned to Fort Benton and died there. U.S. Census, 1870, Benton City and Dawson County, Missouri River; Sanders, Helen. *A History of Montana* 992; Stout, Tom, *Montana, Its Story and Biography* 673-74; *Mineral Independent,* April 27, 1936.

Durfee, E. H. ("Hicks")

Durfee, with his brother-in-law Campbell Kennedy Peck, organized and operated the Northwestern Fur Company which replaced the Pierre Choteau & Company on the upper Missouri. The company secured government contracts to supply military posts and Indian agencies and at one time held monopolies on military suttlers at Forts Sully, Rice, Stevenson, and Buford; the firm also operated trading posts at the Standing Rock and Cheyenne agencies as well as several smaller posts along the Missouri and Milk rivers. The company, headquartered in Leavenworth, was dissolved in 1876 when the partners refused to cooperate with the illegal schemes of Secretary of the Interior Columbus Delano and President Ulysses Grant's brother, Orvil. Leeson, 194, 99, 200; Robert Ege, "Braves of All Colors ..." *Montana, The Magazine of Western History*, 16 (1) (1966) 35-40; William Lass, Elias H. Durfee and Campbell K. Peck: Indian Traders On the Upper Missouri Frontier, *Journal of the West* 43 (2) (2004) 53-67.

Enos, M.

M. Enos was noted in the 1870 Census, Thompson Gulch/ North Deep Creek, Meagher County. The census taker listed his age as 50 and indicated that he, with his two sons, George, 25, and John, 30, supported themselves by hunting. A year earlier an item in the Helena newspaper referred to him as "the old Red River breed." *Helena Weekly Herald*, March 25, 1869.

Etlinger

Mr. Etlinger just barely makes the historical record. Five days after leaving the Musselshell (February 2, 1872) James Stuart recorded in his diary at Fort Browning that Etlinger had arrived from the Musselshell and an item in the Helena newspaper noted the amputation of the tips of three fingers from "Mr. Etlinger, an Indian trader," fingers "which were frozen last winter during the severe weather." Stuart diary, MHS; *Helena Daily Herald*, March 28, 1872.

Farwell, Abel

Born in 1842 in Massachusetts, Farwell was a well-known trader in central Montana and southwestern Canada. He helped construct Fort Peck for the Durfee and Peck firm and ran the post for several years. In 1872 he and his Indian wife moved north into Canada, constructed a post he called Fort Farwell on the banks of Battle Creek, and traded as a representative of the T. C. Power Company. In the formal investigation that followed the Cypress Hills Massacre of May 1873, Farwell was a controversial witness against two of his former friends, Tom Hardwick and George Hammond. So unpopular was his testimony that threats were made on his life in Fort Benton. He died in May 1886. U .S. Census, 1870, Missouri River, Dawson County; John S. Grey, "George Boyd, Montana Frontiersman, Chicago Westerners *Brand Book*, 22, (5) (1965) 38; Paul Sharp, *Whoop-Up Country*, 60,61; *Helena Daily Independent*, July 15, 1875

Fattig, John

Born in Indiana around 1838, Fattig was a prospector, trapper, and trader and described as "a burly middle-aged giant, whose rugged features glowered from a brush of black beard and whose thunderous voice roared in mighty oaths.... He had the reputation of being a skillful huntsman and, to his own deep shame, of having a heart as tender as a child's." Sometime after 1880, Fattig joined forces with J. H. Healy, and they, with their Indian mates, operated a roadhouse in the vicinity of present-day

Melstone, Montana. There they "served meals and allowed travelers to spread their beds on the dirt floor in stormy weather. However, if the weather was pleasant you were far better off under the stars," according to one observer. U.S. Census, 1870, Thompson Gulch and North Deep Creek; Banks, *Wandersong* 54; Charles M. Jacobs, *Horizons O'er theMusselshell,* 109.

Fisher, John

Listed as being 32 years of age, occupation a wood-chopper, and having been born in New Hampshire by the census taker in 1870, Fisher came to Montana following his military service in the Civil War. One cryptic source suggests that he was in the "government service many years" and that following the Custer fiasco, he "helped rid the country of its hostile Indians." In 1921, Fisher was still alive and residing in the Old Soldiers' Home at Columbia Falls, Montana. U.S. Census, 1870, Missouri River, Dawson County; Tom Stout, *Montana, Its Story and Biography,* 3, 856.

Fitzpatrick, "Big Dan"

Identified as a laborer, born in New York and 28 years of age in 1870, and occasionally referred to as Fitzgerald, Big Dan was described by Henry McDonald as a "stalwart, rollicking, jolly Irishman ... so awkward that he could scarcely run a hundred yards without falling, or cock a revolver without using both his huge hands." The wound he received never completely healed and bothered him the rest of his life. U.S. Census, 1870, Fort Benton;, *Forest and Stream*, August 2, 1888; James Willard Schultz, *Friends of My Life as an Indian,* p. 114.

Foster

One of the three men hired to work for Henry McDonald and his partner, Joe Bushaway. McDonald remembered that Foster possessed several letters of introduction to "prominent gentlemen of Denver," and that he was a "born mathematician" whose sole recreation was the working of problems in algebra. For some unexplained reason, McDonald preserved the problem that Foster was working on the evening before he was killed: given $\frac{x^2}{6} - 12 = X$, to find X. Presumably Foster arrived at the number 12 prior to his death. *Forest and Stream*, August 2, 1888.

Freebairn, Jack

Identified only as a miner, Freebairn was born in 1835 in Scotland. U.S. Census, 1870, Thompson Gulch and North Deep Creek, Meagher County.

Friday (Arapaho)

At age seven, Friday was accidentally separated from his family near the Arkansas River in Colorado Territory. Found by Thomas Fitzpatrick, a noted trader, and named for the day of the week he was found, the boy was taken to St. Louis and there turned over to the Jesuits, who educated him with the intention of making him a missionary. Friday "became a respectable scholar in Hebrew, Greek, and Latin." Returned to his tribe at the age of 16 at the request of his parents, he cast off his educated ways and reverted to the nomadic life of his people. George Woodward, "The Northern Cheyenne at Fort Fetterman," *Montana, The Magazine of Western History,* 9, (1959) 16-27.

Frost, Jack

One source indicates that Frost was a pony express rider operating out of Fort Hawley in 1867-68 and mentions that he often went wolfing with Henry McDonald.

Another relates the death of a man named Frost, who, with his Crow Indian wife and child, were killed by a marauding band of Sioux in September of 1871. Banks, *Wandersong,* 78; Leeson, 177.

Garrigan, Owen

A native of Ireland, Garrigan was active in the Sarsfield Center of the Fenian Brotherhood, organized in Diamond City in 1865. In 1870, the census listed him as a probate judge, age 43, in Diamond City. Two years later he was a member of the Territorial Council and in 1874, he was admitted to the Territorial bar. Census, 1870, Diamond City, Meagher County; Leeson, 321, 813, 616; Letter to editor from More Mort of the Montana *Radiator,* Diamond City, January 27, 1886, in *Montana, The Magazine of Western History* 7 (2) (1957) 53.

Gates, R. R.

An employee of the Montana Hide and Fur Company, Gates received an appointment as Deputy United States Marshal the same day that he departed the Musselshell settlement. In Lt. Bradley's account of life at the mouth of the Musselshell, he describes the death of a Christopher Gates at the hands of raiding Indians. *Helena Weekly Herald,* November 5, 1868; February 25, 1869; Bradley,*"Account of the Attempts to Build a Town,"* Historical Society of Montana, *Contributions,* 2, 313.

Gerard, Joe

One reminiscence refers to him as "Joe Girard, a little Frenchman," but the 1870 Census for the Missouri River District, Dawson County, spells his name Gerah and notes that he was 24 years old, Canadian-born, and worked in a woodyard. Joe Mosser in Noyes, *In the Land of Chinook,* 100.

Gordon, Bob

The census taker either counted one Robert Gordon twice, or there were two remarkably similar young men with the same name living on the river. One is identified as living in Fort Benton, age 21, born in New York and working as a laborer; the other is listed in the Missouri River District, age 22, born in New York, employed in a woodyard. U.S. Census, 1870 Missouri River, Dawson County; U.S. Census, 1870 Benton City, Choteau County.

Greenwood

There were several Greenwoods in the vicinity according to contemporary sources: Isaac, Tom, John, and perhaps the most likely one mentioned in the Lee Diary, D. H. Greenwood. D. H. was 29 in 1870, working in woodyards "below Fort Benton." U.S. Census, 1870, Choteau County. For other Greenwoods, see: Leeson, 816, 1215; Banks, *Wandersong* 102; U. S. Census, 1870, Prickley Pear Precinct, Jefferson County

Grinnell, George

Described as having been "not a very desirable citizen" by one who knew him, George Grinnell was 35 years old in 1870. Born in Wisconsin, Grinnell teamed with Jim Wells in operating a woodyard and later established a small ranch. George Bird Grinnell, the author and conservationist (and no relation) later related that he had met the other Grinnell in 1875 and "looked on him rather as an old man. He may have then been forty ..." One account has Grinnell killed by Indians, another simply places his death "not very long after 1890."

George Bird Grinnell to Dan Bowman, March 11, 1921, Montana Historical

Society; U.S. Census, 1870, Missouri River District, Dawson County; Noyes, *In the Land of Chinook* 91; Joseph Taylor, *Sketches of Frontier and Indian Life* ... (Washburn, North Dakota; author, 1895) 116.

Grubb, Jim

Grubb, age 32 in 1870, had come to Montana, via the Colorado mines, from his native state of Virginia. He was occasionally a bullwhacker, but most often a miner. U.S. Census, 1870, Diamond City, Meagher County; Coates, Grace Stone, "Biography of Charles W. Cook," *Mineral Independent*, n.d., Clipping File, University of Montana Library.

Halpin, Dennis

When Lee met him, Halpin was a 32-year-old journeyman blacksmith from Ireland. Twenty years later Halpin was still in Montana and working as janitor in the courthouse at Fort Benton. One of his wolfing partners escaped an Indian attack by digging his way down a badger hole and remaining underground until his aggressors had departed. U.S. Census, 1870, Sun River Valley, Choteau County; Ft. Benton *River Press,* December 11, 1889.

Hammond, George L.

George was a brother of the timber baron A. B. Hammond and had been born in New Brunswick around 1844. He came west to Fort Benton in 1867 and there contracted to supply wood to the United States Government. A year later he journeyed west to California and visited Salt Lake City before returning to Montana. In 1869-1870 he turned north, traveled into the Northwest Territories and helped build the soon-to-be-notorious Fort Whoop-Up. While in Canada he became involved in the whiskey trade and, along with companion Tom Hardwick, played a central role in the Cypress Hills Massacre of 1873. He continued in the Canadian trade until 1878, when he returned to Fort Benton. In 1882 he moved to western Montana and worked for his brother several years before establishing a ranch in the Ovando valley. *Progressive Men of the State of Montana*, 1678; Sharp, *Whoop-Up Country*, 63-69.

Hard, Charles D.

Born in New York in 1841, Hard traveled to California via the Isthmus of Panama in 1864. After clerking in San Francisco for three years, he headed east and ended up in Montana. There, after working for the election of William Clagett as Territorial Delegate to Congress, and with the assistance of political connections, he was appointed Deputy Collector of Internal Revenues for the 5th District. He held that office for a year, then accepted appointment as Deputy U.S. Marshal and later, U.S. Marshal. One historian described Hard as an able and conscientious peace officer and states that he was the first to challenge successfully the power of the Whoop-Up whiskey traders. Joaquin Miller, *An Illustrated History of the State of Montana* 1, 134; Sharp, *Whoop-Up Country*, pp. 46, 122; Stan Davidson, "1871; Montana Year of Political Fusion," *Montana, The Magazine of Western History* 21 (2) (1971) 51.

Harding, J. A.

Fourteen years older than his 19-year-old bride, Harding is simply identified as an Ohio-born "retired merchant" by the 1870 census taker. A Helena newspaper contains numerous references to Harding's visits to that town throughout the 1870s. U.S. Census, Diamond City, Meagher County; *Helena Weekly Herald*.

Hardwick, Tom

This man comes as close as any of Lee's acquaintances to the stereotypical frontier hard case. Occasionally referred to as "Green River Renegade," he was born in Missouri in 1844 and eight years later traveled to California and back with his parents. At the age of 14, he worked with his father trailing cattle from Texas to Missouri. When 16, he joined the Confederate Army, served until 1864, and then, in November of that year, he appeared in Virginia City, Montana. After prospecting and mining for several years, he began trading with the Crow Indians in the Yellowstone Basin. Captured and held captive by the Arapaho on two different occasions, he appeared on the Musselshell in August 1870. His next two years were spent in north-central Montana, trapping, wolfing, and fighting Indians. He experienced several bloody encounters with the Sioux, the Assiniboine, and the Crow. On one occasion he followed (on foot) a group of Sioux who had stolen his horses; 150 miles later he recovered his stock. Another time the distance was 200 miles on foot and, again, he reclaimed his animals. In 1872, Hardwick traveled north into Canada on a hunting and wolfing expedition and while there played a central role in the Cypress Mountain Massacre, and numerous other White/Indian conflicts. By 1876 he had returned to Fort Benton and was operating a livery stable there. Soon he was on the road again, this time leading a party of prospective miners to the Black Hills. Employed by General George Crook for a time, he soon opened a saloon in Deadwood, operated as a private detective, served as a deputy sheriff and arrested several murderers. In 1882 he moved back to Montana, this time to Butte, where three years later he was reported to be dealing "in fine stock." He died at Excelsior Springs, Missouri, in July, 1901, but was reincarnated by Guy Vanderhaeghe in his excellent novel, *The Englishman's Boy* (1996).

Fort Benton Record, June 12, 1876; Leeson, 1336-1337; Sharp, *Whoop-Up Country* 57, 64, 69; Hugh Dempsey, Cypress Hills Massacre, *Montana, The Magazine of Western History* 3 (4) (1953) 1-9; Dempsey, Sweetgrass Hills Massacre, *Montana, The Magazine of Western History* 7 (2) (1957) 13-18.

Harris, Dick

A couple of men named Dick Harris were in the vicinity of the Musselshell, but the one most likely mentioned by Lee was a 28-year-old, born in Missouri, and one who had some experience as an engineer working the steamboat trade. U.S. Census, 1870, Missouri River, Dawson County.

Hayes, Joe

Joe was one of the young Pony Express riders who had spent the previous winter (1868) at Fort Hawley. The supervisor there, writing to his employer, described the Fort Hawley scene: "... The Indians have been raising hell here and frightening all the mail riders so they dare not go outside the door ... The boys have done everything contrary to my instructions ... a number of them have traded off your horses. Joe Hays has sold your Henry rifle others have attempted to leave your employ and run off with your stock." A. E. Bradbury to S. S. Huntley, February 29, 1868, reproduced in Banks, *Wandersong,* pp. 77-78.

Higbee, Jerome

Higbee was in charge of the party that constructed the new post at the mouth of Pouchette Creek (also called Fouchette) in 1870-1871. He was later replaced by A. Juneau. Clipping, n.d., "Ft. Pouchette," Reel 7 microfilm, University of Montana

Clipping File.

Higgen, Samuel S.

A lifetime friend of Oliver Robie, Higgen died in 1914 and was buried next to Robie in the Chesnut Valley cemetery where his tombstone carries the epitaph: "Nature's Scholar and Man's Friend." C. J. Rowe, *Mountains and Meadows Pioneer History* 46.

Higgins, Jonas P.

"Old Man" Higgins was born in England in 1815, emigrated to Ohio in 1842, and spent the next five years mining lead in Illinois before moving to Wisconsin and farming there for the subsequent fifteen years. In 1864 he drove a herd of cattle to Colorado, lived there for two years, returned to Indiana, purchased a number of mules and started them for Montana. Some died, some were stolen by Indians, and some made it all the way to Diamond City, Montana Territory. Higgins sold the mules and began a merchandising business in Diamond City that he operated until 1878 when he moved his business to White Sulphur Springs. He retired in 1882, but two years later he built the Higgins House, described as having been "a fine brick structure, three stories high, 80 x 50 feet, at a cost of $30,000 containing thirty-seven sleeping rooms." U.S. Census, 1870, Diamond City, Meagher County; Leeson, 295, 806, 1287

Hitz, Rudolph B.

The contract post surgeon at Fort Shaw, Hitz was described as "a surgeon of great skill," "a man of kind disposition," and the owner of one of the fleetest blooded horses in the Territory. Born in Switzerland, the young doctor died – at the age of 28 – on New Year's Eve, 1869, as a result of "softning of the brain." *Helena Weekly Herald*, January 16, 1868; *Montana Post* (Helena), April 23, 1869; Paul Phillips, *Medicine in the Making of Montana*, 339; Census, 1870, Microform #108, Montana Historical Society.

Hoover, Harry

The census taker discovered only one Harry Hoover on the river. That one was 40 years old following the grueling occupation of woodchopper and had been born in Missouri. U.S. Census, 1870, Missouri River, Dawson County.

Horn, George

In 1870 a George Horn, age 40, born in Pennsylvania, was operating a woodyard on the Missouri and may be the same George Horn who was killed by the Santee Sioux or the Assiniboine five years later on Cow Creek. U.S. Census, 1870, Missouri River, Dawson County; Leeson, 180, 496; Luther S. Kelly, *Yellowstone Kelly,* 108-109; *Helena Daily Independent*, Mar 5, 1875.

Horse Guard

A distinguished River Crow, described by T. A. Culbertson who met him in 1850 at Fort Union, as "a great warrior and although not 30 years old he has been engaged in about 30 expeditions, always returning with scalps or horses and getting his party back in safety. He is a half-breed, and has the features of a white man ... he is very brave." Seven years later an agent for the Upper Missouri Indians reported that Horse Guard was then a chief of some 70 lodges. In 1868 Horse Guard signed the River Crow treaty at Fort Hawley and was reported in the Judith Basin during the winter of 1873-74. Historical Society of Montana, *Contributions*, 10, 287

Howard, Jas

Lee may have been referring to a 33-year-old man, identified by the census taker as "Jas Howard laborer, personal estate $500.00, U.S. citizen." Howard was further described as a half-blood. U.S. Census, 1870, Fort Benton, Choteau County.

Hunter, Frank

Several contemporary accounts refer to a man named Hunter on the river. The 1870 Census, Fort Benton District, Choteau County, lists a 28-year-old, born in New York and working as a laborer. Another source refers to "a white man named Hunter"; another to Frank Hunter arriving or departing for Musselshell, and yet another mentions Frank Hunter, who was wounded in a Sioux attack near Carroll, and who later drowned in a rafting accident on the Missouri River. Bradley, "Attempts to Build a Town ...," 313; James Stuart, Diary at Fort Browning,MHS; Skelton, Reminiscences, MHS, Vertical File

Ivey, Bill

Ivey was one of the men sent down river to construct Fort Pouchette in 1870-71 and appears briefly in the historical record when he visited Fort Browning in November 1872. "Ft. Pouchette," n.d., Clipping File, University of Montana, Reel #7; James Stuart Diary, MHS.

Jackson, Andrew

Usually referred to only as "Andrew" or "Andy the Negro," he later cooked for Pike Landusky and Jo Hamilton on Flatwillow Creek in the 1880s. While at Carroll, prior to this, he had badly frozen his hands and feet. G. Stuart, *Forty Years on the Frontier*, 2, 127

Jenkerson, William

Credited, along with J. S. Brewer and R. W. Andrews, as being the first to "open up" the Musselshell country. Four months before being noted by Lee, Jenkerson had received two arrow wounds in his left hip during an Indian raid. In 1870 he was listed in the census as being 40 years of age, residing in Fort Benton and working as a woodchopper. *Helena Weekly Herald,* February 3 and June 4, 1868; U. S. Census 1870, Fort Benton, and Missouri River, Dawson County.

Jim, Slim

On the 9th of November 1871, Lee notes that Slim Jim "took several articles off with him that belonged to different ones." Continuing his thieving propensities, Slim Jim made the newspapers on at least two occasions: the Fort Benton *Record* advised readers to be on the alert for "the notorious Slim Jim" who was wanted by the authorities for the theft of a horse at Blackfeet Agency and a rifle from Benton on the 4th of September 1875; a month later, on the 9th of October, the same paper reported that "Slim Jim, the notorious horse thief, escaped jail at Diamond City.

Joe, Santee

Also referred to as "Indian Joe" and "Half-Breed Joe" by Lee, Santee Joe was not particularly liked by some. On October 14, 1871, James Stuart, then living at Fort Browning, entered in his diary: "Santee Joe departed this morning for his dearly beloved tribe – and it is to be hoped that many snows will come and go before we will again see his pleasant open countenance. It would afford me a great deal of pleasure to mark his last resting place with a tombstone and to write his epitaph thereupon." James Stuart Diary, MHS; also quoted by Edward Barry, *The Ft. Belknap Indian Reservation*

... 21.

Houk, George

Houk was born in 1843 or 1846 or 1848 in either Iowa, Missouri, or some unidentified place. According to one sketch, he attended school in St. Louis, worked on steamboats on the Mississippi, moved to California and from there prospected in Nevada and Utah. He also rode for the Pony Express and drove stage for Wells Fargo; all of this accomplished before he was 16 or 18 or 21 years of age. In 1866 he arrived in Fort Benton in the employ of the Northwestern Fur Company. Later he ran a livery business, worked as a teamster, and in 1872 he became sheriff of Choteau County. Retiring from the law business three years later, he successively ran a saloon in Benton, participated in the illegal Whoop-Up whiskey trade, drove teams for T. C. Power and for the Helena and Fort Benton Stage Company. Still later, he became a rancher and reentered the law business as deputy sheriff. He was described – by a contemporary – as a "typical frontiersman." U.S. Census, 1870, Fort Benton and Missouri River, Dawson County; Leeson, p. 1014; Joliet *Independent*, n.d., Clipping File "Ft. Browning," Reel 7, University of Montana.

Johnson, John ("Liver Eating")

Johnson was a well-known hunter, trapper, and wolfer in central Montana Territory during the late 1860s and 1870s. According to J. J. Healy, Johnson had been a sailor and whaler until he was nearly 40 years old. One source says that he was a former Pony Express rider, but if one accepts Healy's physical description of him, this seems unlikely: "He was a giant and a wonder in his way ... a man about six feet two inches and weighed about 250 pounds and did not have a bit of spare flesh on him ... he was a fine offhand shot ... and had a voice on him like a buffalo bull." Johnson earned his nickname during a Sioux attack on the small group living at the mouth of the Musselshell (May 8, 1869) and while several varying accounts of the incident appear in the record, all agree that the name stemmed from Johnson's mutilation of an Indian body after the fight.

In 1877 he served as an Army scout for Generals O.O. Howard and Colonel S. D. Sturgis during the Nez Perce War. In the early 1880s he served as a deputy sheriff at Red Lodge, Montana, and while there he farmed a bit, but claimed not to have liked the occupation. J. J. Healy, "Interview," MHS Banks, *Wandersong* 97-98; Noyes, *In the Land of Chinook,* 100; *Mineral Independent*, August 1, 1929, June 2, 1932; Raymond Thorp and Robert Bunker, *Crow Killer*, passim.

Jordan, Bill

Jordan and two other men – Long and Foster – were employed by Henry McDonald and Joe Bushaway to work in their woodyard. An account of the three employees' deaths is related by McDonald who found and buried their bodies. Jordan arrived on the river in the fall of 1868 and, coming down from Fort.Benton, had escaped a previous Indian attack by his swimming and diving ability. *Forest and Stream*, August 2, 1888.

Judd, William B.

Born in Canada, Judd was for a time Deputy Collector of Internal Revenue before turning to his occupation of Indian trader at the Montana Hide and Fur post at the Musselshell. He spent much of 1871and 1872 at Fort Browning, working with James Stuart and Jim Mabbett. Edward Berry identifies Judd as an Indian half-blood but that is unlikely. One Helena newspaper mentioned that Judd was in that town and "In consideration of his long residence among the aborigines, Mr. Judd believes he is entitled to annuities." A Deerlodge newspaper later mentioned that Judd's elderly father lived in Vermont and "eagerly awaits the return of his long absent son." In 1877 Judd was one of the volunteers fighting the Nez Perce at the Battle of the Big Hole. Leeson 260; U.S. Census, 1870, Missouri River, Dawson County; Berry, "From Buffalo to Beef," *Montana, The Magazine of Western History* 26 (1) (1976) 21; *Helena Daily Herald*, February 29, 1872; *New Northwest*, August 9, 1873; Leeson, 143, 149; Edward Barry, *The Fort Belknap Indian Reservation; The First Hundred Years.* (Bozeman: Big Sky Books, 1974) 78.

Keiser, Henry

Keiser is a fine example of those mobile teenagers who peopled the Trans-Mississippi West. Born in West Virginia in 1849, he waited until he was 15 before heading West in 1864. Traveling through Omaha to Denver, he turned north and after spending several months at the Gros Ventre Agency and Fort Union he devoted the next three years to hunting and trapping throughout central Montana. He lived a year with the Crow, then in 1869 signed on at Fort Hawley as an interpreter for Durfee and Peck's Northwestern Fur Company. A year later he was seeking gold in western Montana (Cedar Creek mines) before trading with Indians in southern Canada. He worked for T. C. Power and Company as a trader at Fort Clagett until 1874 and for the next two years he was sub-agent at the old Crow Agency on the Yellowstone. In 1876 he established his own trading post on Keiser Creek (named for him) at a point where Columbus, Montana, now stands. While trading, he also worked as a guide and interpreter at Fort Custer between 1877 and 1879. In 1880 he accompanied a group of his Indian friends East in an attempt to show tenderfeet what the West was all about. The following four years he was employed as chief guide and scout for Colonel Nelson Miles. He began raising cattle and contracting with the Northern Pacific Railroad, a process that he continued until 1900. He also constructed irrigation ditches on the Crow Reservation, continued to trade with Indians and maintained a financial interest in three mercantile establishments. At the turn of the century, he sold all of his holdings but continued working with the Northern Pacific. Eighty years old in 1929, he was living in Bowman, North Dakota. *Progressive Men of Montana*, 1597; *Mineral Independent*, August 1, 1929.

Kelly, John

Lt. Canfield's diary carries the terse entry for June 14, 1868: "Crossed the river and broke up a wood-chopper's ranch. Ordered Mr. Keller to leave the place and not come back." Presumably Keller and Lee's Kelly are one and the same. Canfield Diary, MHS. MF 73.

Kendrick, Frederick Monroe Hill

Born in New York in 1839, he entered the U.S. Army in 1862 and after service in the Civil War was stationed with the 7th Infantry at Fort Shaw during the late 1860s and 1870s. He retired from active duty with the rank of major in 1900. In 1873, he was the Post Quartermaster and Commissary at Camp Baker. U.S. Census, 1870, Fort Shaw, Lewis and Clark County; Joseph Hanson, *The Conquest of the Missouri*, 402; Heitman, 1, 591; *Helena Daily Herald*, December 13, 1873.

Kennedy, John

Described as a "holy terror" by one of his early day comrades, Kennedy came West at the tender age of 17 in 1857. Born in Richland, Ohio in 1840, he worked as a freighter between Nebraska and Utah before turning his attention to the mineral wealth of the Rocky Mountains. Between 1861 and 1865 he tried his luck in the mines of Montana, British Columbia, and Idaho before becoming a ferry operator, freighter, and finally rancher in the 1880s. J. J. Healy Interview, MHS, MF 64; Leeson, 1015.

Koch, Peter

Born Hans Peter Gyllembourg Koch in 1844 in Denmark, young Koch came to America in 1865 seeking, as were so many, his fortune. After a few disappointing months in New York City, the 21-year-old Dane traveled to an uncle's farm near Bogue Homa, Mississippi, where he fell in love with a cousin. Two years later he headed West with the hope of making enough money to support a wife; 1869 found him on the boat *Tacony,* steaming slowly up the Missouri River. He arrived at the Musselshell in August and spent the following fall and winter chopping wood, hunting, and trapping. When the Indians burned all of his corded wood that spring, he found himself in debt to Clendenin and agreed to work off that debt in the trading post that summer. Late in 1870 he transferred to Clendenin's sutler store at Fort Ellis. For the next four years he combined clerking and surveying and in 1874 had accumulated sufficient funds to return to Mississippi and marry his cousin Laurentze. The couple returned to Montana, settling in Bozeman where Koch eventually became a successful banker. He played a prominent role in civic and state affairs before retiring to California in 1908. He left behind a son, Elers Koch, who was to contribute a great deal to Montana and the United States Forest Service. Carl Cone, ed. "Letters from the Musselshell, 1869-1870 *Pacific Northwest Quarterly* 37 (4) (1936) 313-335. Peter Koch, 'Life at Muscleshell in 1869 and 1870 'Appended; Leeson, 1137.

Larson, Louis

Born in Denmark, Larson, at 25 years of age, was a year younger than Peter Koch with whom he worked during the summer of 1870. U.S. Census, 1870, Missouri River, Dawson County; Cone, ed., "Letters from the Musselshell, *Pacific Northwest Quarterly*, 37, 328-329.

Leader, Jake

Born in Germany, Leader was one of the few white men who were in the vicinity of the Little Rockies as early as 1865. Married to a Crow woman, he was employed by Clendenin as an interpreter. Bradley, "Attempts to Build a Town," MHS, *Contributions,* 2,. 309; Noyes, *In the Land of Chinook* 24; Banks, *Wandersong,* 100.

Lee, Joseph

Missed completely by the census taker, "Old Man Lee" enters the historical record only through the details of his death. Citing a letter from the Musselshell settlement dated May 10, 1871, the Helena newspaper provided details of the Indian attack upon Lee, Drew Denton, and Charley Williams. The three were carrying mail for the Benton post office when they were attacked ten miles above Ft. Hawley by 45 Teton Sioux. *Helena Daily Herald*, May 18, 1871.

Long

Killed with Jordan and Foster, Long was later described by Henry McDonald as having been "a magnificent specimen of manhood, over six feet four inches; he had a daughter in the States who was notified of his tragic fate." *Forest and Stream*, August 8, 1888, 22.

Mabbet, James P.

Born in New York the 28-year-old bookkeeper served as a member of a Grand Jury for the 3rd Judicial District of Montana in October of 1869. The following spring he and William Judd were in charge of the Montana Hide and Fur trading post at Musselshell. The fall and winter of 1871-72 Mabbet, his Indian wife, and child were at Fort Browning, returning to the Musselshell in January. In April 1873 he is located at Fort Peck; three years later, news reached Montana from New York that Mabbet was working as either the proprietor or clerk of the Palisade Mountain House on the Hudson. Leeson, 24; *Helena Daily Herald*, March 5, 1870; James Stuart Diary, Fort Browning, MHS; the *New Northwest* (Deer Lodge), May 12, 1876.

McDonald, Henry

"Little Mac" as he was known during his frontier days, was born in 1848 in Kingston, Ontario. Later orphaned, he ran away from an uncle and enlisted in the Union Army in 1863. He participated in four major battles before a severe wound ended his active service a year later. He was 16 years old. Two years later he appeared in Montana and with William Bent headed for the Musselshell country where the two hunted, trapped, wolfed, and traded. Both wintered at Fort Hawley in 1866-67, where they rode for the Pony Express. Described as being daring, successful, and somewhat irresponsible, McDonald tried his hand at mining (unsuccessfully) before returning to hunting and scouting. In 1875, now 27 years of age, McDonald determined to make something of himself and he devoted the next 12 years to building a successful sheep ranch on Arrow Creek in Choteau County. In 1887, married, with a child, he sold his ranch and took his family back East where he embarked upon a career as a journalist and author. In New York City he was described as a man "much given to haunting galleries and museums of science, he is a slender gentleman, under medium height, with dark piercing eyes and iron-gray hair ... now the owner of one of the largest sheep ranches in Montana ... having at his ranch one of the best selected libraries in the west, he is a very quiet, reserved man, but has that in his bearing and eye that creates observation and commands respect. He moved back West in 1917 – to Portland, Oregon – where he died in 1920. His daughter, Eleanor Banks, wrote his biography, *Wandersong*. Noyes, *In the Land of Chinook*, 90; Bradley, "Attempts to Build a Town ," MHS, *Contributions*, 2, 306; U.S. Census, 1870, Missouri River, Dawson County; New York World, December 30, 1888, quoted in *The River Press* (Fort Benton), January 9, 1889.

McDonald, John

Called "Big McDonald" to differentiate him from "Little Mac" or Henry McDonald, John was a 29-year-old (in 1870) woodcutter who placed Scotland as his birthplace. He is probably Lee's George. U.S. Census, 1870, Missouri River, Dawson County.

McGinnis, James

Actually there were two McGinnis brothers at the Musselshell, Jim and Tim. They were described as being red-headed, rollicking and constantly scrapping with one another. Noyes, *In the Land of Chinook*, 83; Banks, *Wandersong*, 50.

McKnight, Charles

Described only as "a young man lately from the states" and as "an employee of the fort" McKnight escaped further notice. Koch, "Life at the Musselshell," 299; Bradley, "Attempts to Build a Town" 313.

McKnight, Joseph H.

Born in Dubuque, Iowa, McKnight came upriver to Montana in 1864 in the company of T. C. Power, a friend and business associate. Twenty years old at the time of his arrival in the West, he was to amass a sizeable fortune before his death 39 years later. Between 1866 and 1871, he worked as a clerk in sutler's stores at Fort Buford, Camp Cook, and Fort Benton. In 1871, backed financially by T. C. Power, he took charge of the trading post at Fort Shaw, where he remained until 1887. Paul Sharp, (*Whoop-Up Country*), considered McKnight's operations a "case study of a typical sutler during these years. He carried varied stocks of goods for both soldiers and civilians, served as banker for a community lacking formal banking institutions, and worked closely with the merchant princes of Fort Benton." McKnight also carried on a profitable whiskey trade with customers across the Canadian border. In 1887 he sold his Fort Shaw post, moved to Great Falls, Montana, constructed the McKnight block and maintained investments in steamboats, the Bogy Mercantile, and the Judith Cattle Company. He never married and died at Havre, Montana, January 20, 1903. J. H. McKnight Papers MHS Archives, Manuscript Collection #56.

McNeal, Eli

Lee's "Mr. McNeal" may have been Eli W. who came to Fort Benton in 1862, Born in Niagara Falls, New York, in 1835, McNeal worked as a carpenter, store operator, and miner before turning to ranching. A typescript of his reminiscences are in the Montana Historical Society, SC258.

Mail, Jack

One is inclined to believe Luther Kelly, who remembered Jack Mail as "an all around good fellow and clever hunter," for no one else seems to have mentioned him. Kelly made a trip up the Yellowstone "around 1870" with Mail. Kelly, *Yellowstone Kelly*, 84-85.

Marsh, Grant P.

Considered by many to be the dean of the Missouri River steamboat pilots, Marsh was born in Pennsylvania in 1834 and began his career on steamboats 12 years later in 1846. By the 1850s he was piloting boats on the Mississippi and in 1858 he worked the river with Samuel Clemens. Marsh piloted boats for the Union Army on the Ohio River during the Civil War and in 1866 he made his first trip into Montana as Captain of the *Luella*. This marked the beginning of a long career on the Missouri. So proficient was Marsh that it was said he was "capable of navigating on a heavy dew." In 1876 he set a speed record transporting the wounded from the Battle of the Little Big Horn to Bismarck. He prided himself on the fact that he never lost a boat – a considerable feat given that he remained active in steam-boating well into his 70s. He died in 1916, His biography, *Conquest of the Missouri*, (Chicago: A. C. McClurg and Company, 1909) was written by Joseph M. Hanson in 1909. Mark Brown, *Plainsmen of the Yellowstone*, 203; Clifton B. Worthen, "Judith Basin in Central Montana," MS #760, Special Collections, Montana State University.

Martin, Bill

Born around 1835, Martin was in his early 30s when he worked for A. E. Bradley as an express rider in the winter of 1868. While at the Musselshell, he worked as a hunter and cut wood with Dennis Halpin, Later, with Henry Keiser, he was forced to work as a wolfskinner at the rate of $5.00 per day at Fort Peck. In 1887, now 52 years old and known as "Old Bill Martin," he barely survived a flood on Arrow Creek where he was then living. A newspaper account stated that during the flood, "Everything was swept away, even his wearing apparel. The old man barely escaped with his life, being compelled to crawl up the chimney his condition now is really pitiable." Banks, *Wandersong*; 80 Noyes, *In the Land of Chinook*, 84, 87; The *River Press* (Fort Benton), June 6, 1887.

Matt, Cyprian

Identified by A. J. Noyes, *In the Land of the Chinook*, 24, 35 as one of the few white men living in the Little Rockies area in 1865, Matt was probably a member of the Flathead/French family that included a number of well-known scouts and hunters. Leeson, 149.

Mefford, George

An iniquitous young man, age 22 when Lee met him and working for awhile as a woodchopper, Mefford met a violent death shortly after attaining the age of 25. While in the process of smuggling whiskey to the River Crow, he and his partner George Owens drank a considerable amount of it themselves. Thoroughly drunk, the two argued and Owens shot the unarmed Mefford. U.S. Census, 1870, Fort Benton; *Helena Daily Herald*, January 2, 1874.

Mills, William

Mills was 32 years of age in 1870, had been born in Scotland, and was employed in a woodyard on the Missouri. U.S. Census, 1870, Missouri River, Dawson County.

Missouri

While there were undoubtedly a number of men carrying the sobriquet "Missouri," Luther Kelly knew one who could have been the same one mentioned by Lee. Kelly described his Missouri as an "esteemed trapper friend" but one who "awakened mild scorn [by] the fact that he drank gruel in place of coffee. Otherwise he was a good fellow, full of that quaint personality one attaches to Pike County." Kelly, *Yellowstone Kelly*, 80-83.

Morrison, Charley

An Iowa born 21-year-old, Morrison is listed as an Indian trader in 1870. U.S. Census, 1870, Missouri River, Dawson County.

Mosser, Joe

Mosser was born in Alsace, France, in 1840 and emigrated to the United States six years later, settling in Kenton County, Kentucky. Refused entrance into the Army with the outbreak of the Civil War, Mosser headed West. He reached Fort Benton before returning to St. Louis and finally spent several years "in business" in Cincinnati. In 1868 he worked his way back up the Missouri and spent the next several years working the woodyards at the Musselshell and at Rocky Point. As the steamer traffic dwindled, and the Indians burned his wood and killed his cattle, Mosser convinced himself that there were better ways to make a living. He prospected, clerked, traded, cut hay, freighted, and worked as a watchman before locating a ranch on Clear Creek, some 30 miles from the town of Chinook. In 1916, he retired from the cattle and horse business and moved to town. Noyes, *In the Land of Chinook,* 99-105.

Norris, G. R.

"Bill" Norris, as Gilman R.was called, had enlisted in the Army during the Civil War when only 14 years of age. At the end of that conflict he turned toward the West and by 1869 was working at Fort Browning. In 1874 he was operating a wood yard above Carroll. (*Helena Daily Independent,* June 23, 1874) After wolfing, trapping, and trading he made himself useful to the Army by carrying messages and scouting for Custer's command; he performed the same duties for Nelson Miles and claimed later that his greatest achievement was the location of the Nez Perce camp for Miles. Norris was, for a time, deputy customs collector stationed at Wolf Point and claimed to have carried General Terry's order to surrender into Sitting Bull's camp. Later, he accepted a $30.00 per month pension, and with it lived out his life in retirement in Lewistown, Montana. *Joliet Independent,* n.d., clipping; *Silver State Post,* December 12, 1933, Clipping File, Mansfield Library, University of Montana; *Helena Daily Independent,* June 23, 1874.

Nugent, Robert

Born in Ireland, Nugent served in the Civil War as an officer in the 13th Infantry, entering service from New York. He retired from active service in 1879 and died in 1901. On the return journey back to Camp Cooke from the post at the mouth of the Musselshell, one of his junior officers noted in his diary: "Col. Nugent walked all day!!!! Heitman, 1, 754; Canfield Diary, July 5, 1868, MHS, MF 73.

Oleson

When Clendenin related the story of the 1869 Indian raid at the Musselshell, he mentioned Halvor Olson who may be Lee's Oleson. Bradley, "Attempts to Build a Town MHS, *Contributions,* 2. 311.

Orcutt, W. H.

Orcutt was one of the earlier settlers in the boomtown of Bannack, Montana Territory, in 1862, and was a member of the 1863 prospecting expedition led by W. W. DeLacy into the area that would become Yellowstone National Park. He was later an unsuccessful candidate for territorial representative from Montana. Walter W. DeLacy, "A Trip Up the South Snake River,"MHS, *Contributions,* 1, 124; Leeson, 467-68, 553.

Patterson

Little is known of Patterson, other than the minor fact that he was working at Fort Browning during the spring of 1872. James Stuart, Diary, MHS, entry May 6, 1872.

Peck, Campbell Kennedy

Colonel Peck, brother-in-law and partner of E. H. Durfee. In 1864 Pierre Choteau and Company sold its interests in what had previously been the American Fur Company to a group who called themselves the Northwest Fur Company. A year later, Durfee and Peck bought the company, renamed it the Northwestern Fur Company, and embarked upon an active trading business that continued until 1876. Peck traveled to Washington, D.C., in 1875 to testify before the Indian Affairs Committee concerning the Secretary of the Interior, Columbus Delano, and the President's son, Orville Grant, and their nefarious scheme involving kickbacks on government contracts. Leeson, 112, 194, 199-200; Robert Ege, "Braves of All Colors: The Story of Isaiah Dorman," *Montana,*

The Magazine of Western History, 16 (1) (1966) 35-40; William E. Lass, Elias H. Durfee and Campbell K. Peck: "Indian Traders on the Upper Missouri Frontier." *Journal of the West,* 43 (2) (2004) 9-19.

Porcupine

Identified as a Crow by Lee, another account refers to him as "a reliable Sioux." L. F. Crawford, *Rekindling Camp Fires* (Bismarck: Capital Book Company, 1926) 141-142.

Power, Thomas C.

T. C. Power was born in Dubuque, Iowa, to immigrant Irish parents in 1839. He attended college in Wisconsin and worked as a schoolteacher for three years before heading West as a member of a survey party in 1862. In 1864 he made his first trip to Montana. Three years later he opened a general merchandise store in Fort Benton, supplying settlers and military posts. He also carried on an active trade in furs and hides, and in 1868 he began a freighting business to serve the mining areas to the south. By 1874, Power had expanded into stage lines, more stores, and – with I. G. Baker and Brother – steamboats. He later joined with his close friend and business associate, J. H. McKnight, to form the Judith Cattle Company, a development that marked the beginning of extensive grazing in the Judith Basin. He also invested in sheep. In 1878 he served as a Republican delegate to the first territorial convention and in 1884 was involved in the first constitutional convention. He lost his bid for governor to J. K. Toole in 1889, but was elected the following year as one of the state's first United States Senators. He remained active in Republican politics until his death in 1923. James Hamilton, *From Wilderness to Statehood*, 389, 406, 528, 587; Helen Sanders, *A History of Montana* 998.

Puett, Bill

A. W. Puett had been born in Kentucky and called himself a sawyer instead of a woodcutter. Perhaps this was due to his age (42 in 1870) or to the fact that he had saved his money and could claim an estate valued at more than $8,000. U.S. Census, 1870, Missouri River, Dawson County.

Quesnell, Constant

Only 25 years old when he met his death, Quesnell's army records describe him as a tinsmith from Montreal, five feet six inches tall, blue eyes, brown hair, enlisting from Boston on April 14, 1866. Cited by Tom Bryant, *The Montana Journal*, November 1987.

Reed, Alonzo S.

Described as a "large stocky man of from 170 to 190 pounds in weight and 5 feet seven inches tall, usually clad in a buckskin shirt and moccasins wearing a mustache and goatee ... a daredevil in all walks of life ... a man of education and a gentleman when sober but a fiend when drinking or drunk," Reed was a notorious trader and Indian agent in the late 1860s and 1870s. In late 1868, 31-year-old Reed recruited a number of men to help in salvaging goods from the wrecked steamboat, *Amelia Poe*. This group was attacked by nearly 300 Sioux, who killed W. H. Taber and others. Lee reports the attack in his January 24, 1869, entry. Appointed acting agent for the Fort Peck Agency in 1869, Reed began his duties with a sincere attempt to help the Indians. He soon regressed to the state of many agents and began cheating them by taking their flour for his own profit in sale or trade. In 1874 Reed established a trading post with a man named Bowles near the present site of Lewistown, Montana. Some considered Reed to have been entirely unscrupulous and rumors abounded about his killing peaceful Indians and stealing their horses. The Reed and Bowles partnership ended in a fist and knife fight in 1880. Oscar Mueller, quoted in the *Meagher County News,* January 25, 1950; Edward Barry, *Fort Belknap* 17; U.S. Census, 1870, Missouri River, Dawson County.

Remming, Antoine

The only Antoine in the record is Remming, listed as 30 years of age, a laborer from New Mexico. U.S. Census, 1870, Missouri River, Dawson County.

Robie, Oliver G.

Known as "Yank," due to his sympathies for the North, Robie was born in Michigan and in 1870 was working as a teamster. Robie was murdered, shot in the back, in 1897. His only known enemy was Robert Chesnut, former Confederate soldier, who quarreled repeatedly with Robie about the Civil War. The census taker listed his age at 33 in 1870, but his tombstone carries the birth year 1828. C. J. Rowe, *Mountains and Meadows,* 246; U.S. Census, 1870, Benton City, Choteau County.

Ross, John K.

Employed by Clendenin, Ross was simply described as "an old mountaineer" by two different sources. He may have been the same Ross who lived in the Big Hole/Beaverhead area of southwestern Montana in the late 1850s. Clendenin provided the Helena newspaper with an account of his death. Bradley, "Attempts to Build a Town ...," Koch, "Life at the Musselshell," MHS, *Contributions,* 2; Leeson, 587; *Helena Daily Herald*, February 1, 1871.

Schaff, Ed

Lee had a particularly difficult time in getting the spelling of Schaff correct (Schauf/Schauffer/Scharf/Sharp, etc.). Born in Prussia, Schaff was living with Frank and Jennie Smith in 1870 and following the life of a woodchopper. He was 30 years old. Previously he had lived on the north side of the river, working a woodyard with Pomp Dennis and Bill Martin. U.S. Census, 1870, Missouri River, Dawson County; *Helena Weekly Herald,* February 25, 1869.

Scott (James; G. W.; William)

One can choose between James R. Scott, 29, a clerk born in Virginia, or G. W. Scott, age 39, blacksmith, born in Maryland, or William Scott, a 27-year-old laborer born in Louisiana. U.S. Census, 1870, Missouri River, Dawson County

Secord, George

Lee's Secord may have been George Secord whose death was reported in the *Montana Gazette* (Helena) August 13, 1873. He is there described as "an old pioneer of our Territory ... a kind natured man ... no warmer hearted man lived."

Seymour, French Jo

In 1870 French Jo was 25 years old, a noncitizen, and listed his birthplace as Eastern Canada. Later he established a ranch and trading station in the Fox Creek valley near the present site of Newlon, Montana, along the Yellowstone. Still later, (1881) he sold the entire outfit to John W. O'Brien. U.S. Census, 1870, Jefferson Valley, Jefferson County; Tom Stout, *Montana, Its Story and Biography* 3, 723-724, 1365.

Sillcott, Louis
A 35-year-old woodcutter from France. U.S. Census 1870, Missouri River, Dawson County.

Simmons, Andrew Jackson
A partner in the Montana Post Publishing Company, Simmons was appointed special Indian agent by President Grant and given the job of securing right-of-way for the Northern Pacific Railroad through Indian land. According to one source, Simmons teamed with banker Samuel T. Hauser and "A mutually profitable exchange of favors began in 1870 and continued until 1873." In 1871 Simmons became the agent at Fort Browning and used his influence to obtain the post tradership for James Stuart, who was, at that time, in debt to Hauser's Helena bank. *Helena Herald*, July 23, 1869; Edward Barry, *Fort Belknap*. 19.

Skelton, William
"Skelly," as Lee calls him, was a wolfer and trapper who roamed throughout central and northern Montana in the 1860s and 1870s. Born in Cumberland, England, in 1850, he emigrated to the United States 15 years later. He immediately came West, was working steamboats on the Missouri River in 1866, and soon obtained a job as guard at Fort Peck. In 1870 he joined the expedition to build a post at the Pouchette, before turning to wolfing and hunting with his partner, Joe Valentine. He operated a woodyard at Cow Island, prospected unsuccessfully in the Black Hills, and ultimately ended up ranching successfully in Fergus County. He died in December 1943. Tom Stout, *Montana, Its Story and Biography* 3, 1295-1296; Skelton, Reminiscences, MHS, Archives, Vertical File.

Smith, Frank
The 1870 Census, Missouri River, Dawson County, records a Frank Smith, age 32, owner of a woodyard, born in Wisconsin and living with Jennie Hawley (Smith) and Ed Schaff.

Smith, Jennie
Sometimes known as Jennie Hawley, the census taker gave her brief notice, listing her birthplace as Wisconsin, her age as 28, and added: "... scalped by Indians last year, left for dead. Well and hearty now ... hates Indians." One who knew her better wrote that "Many women may have excelled her in rigid virtue, but few in generosity, hospitality and womanly sympathy ... may she flourish forever." Peter Koch was less generous and remembered her as the single white woman living below Fort Benton, "called Mrs. Smith, but better known throughout Montana under a sobriquet not fit for polite ears." Henry McDonald's daughter, Eleanor Banks, was even less kind: "her reputation was as ill-favored as her face and figure [her] nickname was too vile for print. McDonald, who knew her as his daughter did not, portrayed her as generous, loyal, and tough but not so tough that she could bear having known that she had been scalped. Long after the incident, she begged McDonald not to betray her secret, hiding, as it were, under a horrid, red, ropy wig. Peter Koch thought that she had gone to Michigan with Frank Smith and was married there; McDonald, writing in 1888, said she had been married twice since her scalping and "may be now alive." Another source says that Jenny lived in western Montana until the early 1900s. U.S. Census, 1870, Missouri River, Dawson County; McDonald, *Forest and Stream*, August 2, 1888; Koch, "Life at the Musselshell," MHS, *Contributions* 2, 303; Banks, *Wandersong*, 98-

99; Geneva Highland, *Big Dry Country,* Billings Print Company, Billings 39.

Standing Buffalo

In the early 1860s Standing Buffalo held the rank of head chief of the Sisseton Sioux, but he refused to take part in the Sioux uprising in 1862 and, according to an agent, "went far to the West ... eventually close to the hunting-grounds of the Crows ... the hereditary enemies of all Sioux ... He probably affiliated with the Assiniboines." Another agent identified him as Tah-tunga-ne-sha (Standing Buffalo Bull), head chief of the band of Santee Sioux and describes his heroic warrior death at the hands of the Gros Ventre and Upper Assininiboines in June, 1871. James McLaughlin, *My Friend the Indian,* (Boston: Houghton Mifflin 1910) 24; A. J. Simmons, Agent, Milk River Agency to J. A. Viall, Superintendent, Montana, June 20, 1871, in *House Executive Document* 23, 42d Congress, 2d Session, 6 Serial 1510. See Dennis Smith, "Convergence: Fort Peck Assiniboine and Sioux Arrive in the Fort Peck Region, 1800-1871," 58-60, in Miller, Smith, *et. al., The History of the Assiniboine and Sioux Tribes,* for more.

Stewart, Tom

Tom's Crow wife was the woman shot through the neck during the Indian attack of March 22, 1869, in which Jenny Smith lost her scalp. Stewart later served as interpreter for the Crow agency and in 1879 traveled to Washington, D.C., with a Crow delegation. He may have been the Brackett E. Stewart, known as Tom Stewart, who was hanged by a lynch mob near Choteau, Montana, in 1881 after having murdered two people. Then again, he may not have been. Granville Stuart, *Forty Years* ... 2, 139; Frederick C. Krieg, "Chief Plenty Coups; The Final Dignity, *Montana The Magazine of Western History,* 16, (4) (1966) 31; Helen West, "Tragedy on the Teton; 1881," *ibid.,* 12 (3) (1962) 21.

Red Stone

Chief of the Canoe band of Lower Assiniboine, who often camped at the mouth of the Milk River, Red Stone is a good example of two conflicting contemporary views of the Indian. James Stuart, post trader at Fort Browning, referred to Red Stone and four other Assiniboine leaders as "dead beats," yet another one who knew him described him as an admirable leader who was attempting to convince his people to accept the agricultural life of the white man as the way of the future. James Stuart, Diary, MHS; Edward Barry, *The Ft. Belknap Indian Reservation* ... , 18, 23; Leeson, 112; Dennis Smith, in "The Sioux Transform the Milk River Agency, 1871-1877," in *The History of the Assiniboine and Sioux Tribes* ... 80-89, supports the latter assessment. See also, C. M. Oehler, *The Great Sioux Uprising,* (New York: Oxford University Press 1959) 4.

Stubbs, Chauncey C.

Born in New York in 1840, Stubbs came to Montana in 1865. After teaching school and working as a civil engineer for two years, he established a ferry on the Missouri where Trout Creek empties north of Helena. In 1871 he was operating the Stubbs or "Spokane" ferry connecting the road from Diamond City to Helena. *Progressive Men of Montana,* p. 1262; Helena *Daily Herald,* September 10, 1873.

Swan, Edward

Ohio born Swan waited until he was 30 years old before moving to Montana in 1862. After seeking the elusive gold in Bannack and vicinity, he turned to freighting. In

1870 he established a ranch in the Gallatin Valley and raised cattle for six years before moving to Idaho. He died in 1915. *Pony Express Courier*, July-August 1943, copy in Vertical File, MHS.

Sweeney, Ed

Twenty-four years old in 1870 and working as a laborer, Sweeney had been born in New York. U.S. Census, 1870, Missouri River, Dawson County.

Synix, Joe

Lee used various spellings (Sennix/Sannox) for this woodcutter. Synix had been born in Michigan. U.S. Census, Missouri River, Dawson County.

Taber, W. H. ("Steve")

Taber may have been the liar that Lee thought he was. A Helena newspaper carried the report that Taber and George Horn had been attacked by Indians at their woodyard on the Missouri, their horses stolen, and they had been forced to walk 250 miles in five days "during which time they had but three meals, and a fight with the Indians for every meal." A later encounter with the Indians did not prove so fortuitous; Taber was with A. S. Reed and six others attempting to salvage the wreck of the steamboat *Amelia Poe* when they were attacked by a large number of Sioux. Taber, "McGregor," "Thomas," and "Steve the stutterer" were killed; Moses Solomon was wounded. *Helena Weekly Herald*, October 29, 1868; January 7, 1869.

Theodore, George

Identified only as an employee of T. C. Power and Bros. Company by the Fort Benton *Record*, May 15, 1875.

Thompson, W. A.

"Billy" Thompson shared a dwelling with R. C. Warring in 1870. He was 28 years old, born in Ohio, and listed as a saloonkeeper (as was Warring) by the census taker. U.S. Census, 1870, Missouri River, Dawson County.

Thum, Col. M. C.

Described as that "rotund bundle of jolly good fellowship" and the "right hand man of Durfee and Peck and chief in charge of their northwestern trading posts," Thum managed the affairs at Fort Peck for a number of years. James Stuart thought him a "good fellow to travel with, but very hard to get out of camp in the morning." *Helena Daily Herald*, October 1, 1873, January 9, 1873; Fort Benton *Record,* March 1, 1875; James Stuart diary, MHS.

Town, George H.

Born in 1847 in Illinois, Town headed west at the age of 19 and reached Fort Buford one year later. There he found employment as a freighter for Abe Farwell and followed him to Fort Peck where he worked as a government scout and guard. It was at Peck that he met "Yellowstone" Kelly, whose Indian-maimed finger he amputated using "a little booze and a chew of tobacco" as anesthetic. After his stay at the Musselshell, Town built a small trading post near the present site of Lewistown, Montana. He followed a variety of enterprises in the Billings-Red Lodge-Bozeman areas for the next 30 years. He died in the Old Soldiers' Home in Columbia Falls in 1914. There is no record of his ever having served in the military. Autobiography, MHS, MC64; *Encyclopedia of Northwest Biography*, 461.

Two Belly

A River Crow medicine man, Two Belly played a prominent role in the life of the fabled warrior, Two Leggings. A photograph of Two Belly, taken in 1879, appears in Peter Nabokov, *Two Leggings: Making of a Crow Warrior* (New York: Crowell, 1967).

Tyler, August

Twenty-one years old when Lee first met him, Tyler hunted, wolfed, and chopped wood for seven or eight years before starting a small trading outfit at Carroll. Once, when traveling from Fort Belknap to Fort Benton, Tyler and M.W. Alderson became lost and wandered northward for five days before being found. U.S. Census, 1870, Missouri River, Dawson County; *Helena Herald*, April 8, 1868; *Great Falls Daily Tribune*, July 5, 1914; *Fort Benton Record,* April 15, 1875.

Valentine, Joe

Lee's "Valentine the Spaniard" was Joe – hunter, wolfer, trapper, and frequent partner of William Skelton during the decade of the 1870s. He and Skelton visited the Bear Paw Battlefield in 1877 and, contrary to Roberta Cheney's explanation, the name of Rock Springs was changed to Valentine Springs in honor of Joe. The present town of Valentine, Montana, can trace its name back to Valentine the Spaniard. James Stuart Diary and Skelton Reminiscence, MHS, Vertical File; Tom Stout, 31295-1296; Roberta Cheney, *Names on the Face of Montana*, 231.

Veits, C. M. ("Cash")

This surname presented considerable difficulty to Lee and others. He appears as "Vaity," "Veity," and even "Cash Netes." The Helena newspaper refers to him as C. M. Veits, and Henry McDonald described him as Cash Veits, "a young man of as consummate coolness in the face of danger as I have ever seen, a dead shot and a magnificent oarsman." Eleanore Banks, *Wandersong,* 97; *Helena Weekly Herald*, April 27, 869; McDonald, *Forest and Stream*, August 2, 1888.

Viall, Jasper A.

Superintendent of Indian Affairs for Montana (1870-1872). Viall was described as an "energetic and honest officer." He may well have been, but a close reading of official documents pertaining to his tenure as superintendent suggests the possibility that Viall may have succumbed to the corruption endemic among Indian Bureau officials of this time. Oliver W. Holmes, ed., "Diary of James A. Garfield's Trip to Montana, 1872," *Montana The Magazine of Western History* 6, (4) (1956) 40, fn. 16. For charges of corruption, see: M. M. McCauley, Agent for the Blackfeet, to E. S. Parker, Commissioner of Indian Affairs, February 13, 1871 in *House Executive Document,* 15, 42d Congress, 1st Session, 2, Serial 1471.

Warring, R. C.

Occasionally in trouble with what few authorities there were – for selling whiskey to soldiers and Indians – Warring was a saloonkeeper who had been born in 1828 in Kentucky. Canfield Diary, entry July 4, 1868, MHS, MF 73; U.S. Census, 1870, Missouri River, Dawson County.

Wells, Jim

Wells spent 20 years in north central Montana, coming to the Territory in 1865 at the age of 31, after having toured California and Oregon. While he would occasionally hunt and poison wolves, he was essentially a trader. In 1868 he was operating out of his post on the Milk River about 20 miles above old Fort Browning; the following year he went to work for T. C. Power and served at various places along the river. After wintering at Fort Hawley in 1867-68, he went down river and constructed a stockade and established a wood yard on the north side of the river across from the mouth of the Musselshell. In 1874 he was running a Power trading post near Black Butte, and the following year he replaced Tom Bogy at Fort Claggett. He purchased an interest in this establishment, operated a small cattle ranch, and died following "a long and painful illness" in 1885. Described as "gaunt and swarthy," with "piercing eyes ... as black as his straight shoulder-length hair and a heavy moustache that drooped over his chin whiskers," (Fort Benton River Press) he dressed in buckskin and was considered to be a man of first class business ability whose generosity prevented him from becoming wealthy. One who knew him well wrote that "His moral character might not have passed muster before a theological board, but no saint possesses a tithe of his magnanimous spirit." (McDonald, in *Wandersong*) He was born in Pennsylvania around 1835. Noyes, *In the Land of the Chinook* 24; Banks, *Wandersong,* 75; Fort Benton *River Press,* February 11, 1885 and January 24, 1887; U.S. Census, 1870, Missouri River, Dawson County; *Helena Daily Independent*, May 7, 1875. W. F. Wheeler (next entry) provided the Montana Historical Society with a lengthy, informative narrative, derived from an interview with Wells completed shortly before his (Wells) death. W. F. Wheeler papers, MHS, MC 65.

Wheeler, William F.

Born in Warwick, New York, on July 6, 1824, Wheeler began his westward migration 18 years later when he moved to Columbus, Ohio, where he worked as a printer and newspaper reporter while studying law. Admitted to he bar in 1848, he moved to Minnesota where he served as secretary to the territorial governor. After serving in the Union Army he traveled further west and in June 1869 he arrived in Montana as the newly-appointed United States Marshal. He held that post until 1878, when he returned to journalism. Later, he provided biographical information on early fur traders to the Montana Historical Society and from 1889 until his death in 1894, he served as librarian of that Society. William F. Wheeler. William F. Wheeler Papers, MHS, MC 65.

White Eagle

Son of Eagle Chief, White Eagle was second in authority only to Sitting Woman, head chief of the Gros Ventre in 1866. Described as "dignified and cordial in manner" he and his father were both spokesmen at treaty talks held by I. I. Stevens in 1853. White Eagle was a signatory to the treaties of 1855, 1865, and 1868. He died at Clagett, Montana, in 1881, at an estimated age of 60. MHS, *Contributions*, 10, 276; James Hamilton, *From Wilderness to Statehood* (Portland: Binfords and Mort, 1957) 101.

Whitson, James B.

"Bert" was listed as a 28-year-old miner, born in Illinois, by the 1870 census taker. U.S. Census, 1870, Thompson Gulch/North Deep Creek.

Williams, Charley

Wounded in the fight with Indians in May of 1871 (the one in which Joseph Lee was killed), Williams suffered further indignity when some cartridges he was carrying were struck by an Indian bullet and exploded. According to the other survivor of the fight, Williams cried out: "God, Drew, I'm blown up!!" Drew /Denton/ replied: "Never mind that, keep shooting!" Older than most of the boys on the river, Williams had been born in Michigan around 1823. Noyes, *In the Land of the Chinook*, 101; U.S.

Census, Missouri River, Dawson County.

Woodward, Harry

Employed as a bookkeeper by Abe Farwell, young Harry had been born in Missouri 23 years before the census taker found him on the Missouri River. U.S. Census, 1870, Missouri River, Dawson County.

NOTES

1. Montana's counterpart to Nevada's more famous one. Gold discovered in Alder Gulch in 1863 gave birth and reason to the resulting town.

2. The settlement resulting from gold discoveries in 1864 in Confederate Gulch and described as one of the "wealthiest, gayest, and toughest places in Montana". Roberta Cheney, *Place Names in Montana*, (Missoula, University of Montana, 1971), 61. A contemporary reported that "Diamond City cannot boast of beauty in architecture, or convenience of access, being surrounded on all sides with immense piles of tailings" *Montana Post*, Helena, June 8, 1867). The camp flourished through the 1870's as gold production continued, but by 1880 a visitor reported: "Diamond City is desolate, deserted and dreary ... there are only four families left…" Michael Leeson, ed., *History of Montana*, (Chicago, Warner, Beers and o. 1885), 808.

3. Site of the first copper ore discovery in Montana in 1866. The town that resulted from this discovery lasted until the turn of the century when low copper prices determined its demise. Muriele Wolle *Montana Paydirt (Denver: Sage Books, 1963)* 338-39. George Davis, Autobiographical Sketch, MC 64. Montana Historical Society. (Hereafter, MHS)

4. One of the fourteen gold-producing gulches that surrounded Diamond City.

4. Present day Smith River.

6. A side-wheel steamship that plied the Missouri until her demise at Bellefontaine bend, near the mouth of the Musselshell August 16, 1869. Philip Chappell, "A History of the Missouri River." *Transactions, et al*, Kansas State Historical Society, 9 1905.

7. Camp Cooke was the first permanent military camp in the Territory. Established in 1866 on the south bank of the Missouri, 160 miles below Fort Benton, it was permanent for only four years. One army officer complained that: "The post at the mouth of the Judith River is at a point where neither white nor red men ever go, and the location is subject to ridicule wherever I go". (Major General Frank Hazen) Another wrote: "This unfortunate post is situated…upon sage bottoms, saturated with alkali. It is entirely overrun with rats…[and] the Indians have moved away and left it alone" (Lieutenant Colonel S. B. Holabird). Both quoted in McElroy, Harold. "Mercurial Military: A Study of the Central Montana Frontier Army Policy" *The Montana Magazine of Western History* 4 (4) (1954) 14.The temporary stockade constructed at the Musselshell was called Camp Reeve.

8. The two soldiers killed were James Cook and Constant Quesnelle, privates in Company E, 13th Infantry. Cook's body was not recovered. (Canfield Diaries, May 30, 1868 MHS, , MF 73 & 73a) and Tom Bryant, *The Montana Journal*, November 1987 (Missoula, Montana).

9. A French-Canadian fur trader, Louis Rivet, constructed Fort Hawley for Hubbell and Hawley of the Northwest Fur Company approximately fifteen miles above the mouth of the Musselshell. Abandoned as a fur trade post in 1868, the site was later used as a station on the Northern Overland Trail Pony Express that connected Fort Abercrombie to Helena. In 1882, it had become a telegraph station on the military line between Fort Buford and Fort Maginnis. It is sometimes referred to as Ft. Holly in memoirs and reminiscences. A. J. Noyes, *In the Land of the Chinook: The story of Blaine County*, (Helena, State Publishing Company, 1917) 82.

10. West of the Musselshell, near the headwaters of Crooked Creek.

11. Relegated to the lower river after 1869, this boat sank below Leavenworth, Kansas in 1873. (Chappell, 302).

12. Fort Peck, a trading post some 70 miles downriver from the mouth of the Musselshell, established in 1867 by Campbell K. Peck and E. H. Durfee and named for the former. Abel Farwell constructed the fort and carried on trade there until 1872. The firm, Durfee and Peck was one of the major trading and shipping organizations along the river in the 1860's and 70's. (Leeson,) 191, 199-200; William Lass, "Elias H. Durfee and Campbell K. Peck: Indian Traders on the Upper Missouri Frontier," *Journal of the West* 43 (2) (2004) 9-19.

13. Round Butte, midway between Fort Peck and the Musselshell.

14. The Little Rockies are a small range of mountains 50 miles northwest of the mouth of the Musselshell.

15. Between Diamond City and Copperopolis.

16. A small settlement of wolfers and woodcutters located 25 miles up the river above the Musselshell.

17. The Beaverhead is a tributary of the Jefferson River, which, in turn, joins the Madison and the Gallatin to form the Missouri River. The "falls" refer to the Great Falls of the Missouri, now inundated.

18. Located just below the confluence of the Yellowstone River and the Missouri and downstream from the old fur trade post Fort Union. Constructed in 1866, this military fort was named after Major John Buford, who had died three years earlier. Robert Athearn, *Forts of the Upper Missouri* (London, Prentice Hall, 1967) 227.

19. Located north and slightly west of the Musselshell on the Milk River. The government established the agency to serve the Gros Ventres and Assiniboine; River Crow, Sioux, and other Indians also lived in its area. In 1873 the government moved the agency to Fort Peck and renamed it the Fort Peck Agency. See David Miller, Dennis Smith, et. al., *The History of the Assiniboine and Sioux Tribes of the Fort Peck Indian Reservation*, Montana, 1800-2000, (Popular, Montana, Fort Peck Community College, 2008), 41-109.

20. Central Montana, the area drained by the Judith River.

21. Fort Abercrombie was a military post located on the west bank of the northward flowing Red River of the North, thirty-four miles south of present-day Fargo, North Dakota. Established in 1858, the Army abandoned it in 1877. Linda Slaughter, "Fort Abercrombie", *Collections*, State Historical Society of North Dakota, v. l, (1906) 412-429.

22, Some twenty miles below the mouth of the Musselshell the Pouchette (occasionaly spelled Fouchette) enters the Missouri from the north. The trading company of Durfee and Peck constructed a post here in 1870. Thomas Curry, one of the party who helped erect the fort, later recalled that "The location of the post was chosen because of the heavy and plentiful timber in that locality". Also in the vicinity was a stranded steamboat, the *Trosper*. "One night a few years previously," Curry continued, "the Trosper tied up here for the night…during the dark hours the treacherous current of the Missouri shifted, and when morning broke, the Trosper was high and dry and the cook had to walk quite a distance to get water enough for breakfast". Unable to refloat the boat, the owners abandoned it and Curry related that the wood from the stranded boat was of "great assistance to us in building our post and we utilized much of the old steamer". *Jefferson Valley News*, "Life at Old Fort Pouchette" Clipping file, K. Ross Toole Archives, University of Montana.

23. The abandoned Camp Reeve.

24. The United States government officially split the Crow Nation into two groups, the Mountain Crow and the River Crow and did so due to customary hunting areas. There were neither ethnic nor linguistic differences between the two groups. Robert Lowie, *The Crow Indians* (New York, Rinehart and Co., 1935) 4.

25. The Flathead's traditional land lay west of the mountains in the Bitterroot Valley. They traveled to the plains in search of bison. John Fahey, *The Flathead Indians* (Norman: University of Oklahoma Press, 1974).

26. This was the *Amelia Poe*.

27. Most of the contemporary Montana literature contains a description of this battle and the episode of Jennie's lost scalp. Teddy Blue Abbott, cowboy, who spent the winter of 1884 at the mouth of the Musselshell, repeats the story and relates that he had seen Jenny in Forsyth, Montana, the year before. E. C. Abbott and Helena Huntington Smith, *We Pointed the North* (Chicago: R. R. Donnelley and Sons Co, 1991) 179-182.

28. Again, most contemporary literature report this battle. It was a result of this episode that John Johnson received the name "Liver Eating Johnson". See Raymond Thorpe and Robert Bunker, *Crow Killer: The Saga of Liver-Eating Johnson* (Bloomington: University of Indiana Press) 1969.

29. The *Deer Lodge* was an upper river or "mountain" steamship and worked the Missouri between 1865 and 1870. *Contributions*, MHS 1& 2 ,285-286.

30. The *Importer* was on the upper river in the 1868 and 1869 seasons; the *Nile* reached Fort Benton in 1867, 1868, and 1869; the *Ida Reese* operated between 1868 and her sinking by ice at Yankton in 1871; the *Fanny Barker* made trips to Fort Benton in 1868 and 1869 before retiring to the lower river where she sank in 1873. Chappell, 302.

31. One of the most informative pieces of literature pertaining to steamboat travel on the Missouri River is the "The Log of the Henry Shreve", *Mississippi Valley Historical Review*. 31, March, l945). The entry in the log for this date indicates that the boat loaded 16½ cords of pine at $8.00 per cord, "less $61.90 Mr Lee's freight bill".

32. The *Huntsville* worked the upper river between 1866 and 1869. The *Sallie* (next entry) was in commission 1868-1870. *Contributions* MHS, v 1 and 3.)

33. A substantial military post established in 1867 near the new town of Bozeman. The garrison varied between three and five companies and was finally abandoned in 1886. (Francis P. Prucha, *Guide to the Military Posts of the United States,* (Milwaukee: State Historical Society of Wisconsin, 1964), 73.

34. Clendenin's trading post was called the Hide and Tallow post to differentiate it from the rival Montana Hide and Fur Company's establishment. Lee occasionally refers to it as the "Skin and Grease."

35. This was the last trip for the *Columbia.* She sank near Napoleon, Missouri, a few month later. (Chappell,) 300.

36. The only *Tempest* located in the literature is *Tempest #2* and listed as sunk at Bonhomme Island, South Dakota, in 1865 (Chappell, p.311).

37. He may have, for it was.

38. This was the *Tacony* that had traveled the upper river since 1866 and sunk at Ft. Peck. Chappell (p. 316) lists her as *Tacorny.*

39. Crooked Creek flows into the Musselshell from the west a few miles above Lee's small settlement.

40. Located on the Milk River a short distance downstream from the mouth of People's Creek and west of present-day Dodson. Constructed by Hubell and Hawley of the Northwest Fur Company (the builders of Fort Hawley) in 1868, this trading post – constructed of cottonwood logs, complete with stockade, bastions, and two small brass cannons – operated until 1872 when the firm moved its operations to Old Fort Belknap, 50 miles up the Milk on the opposite side of the river from present-day Chinook. Designed for trade with the Gros Ventres and the Assiniboine, the trading post was moved due to increasing pressure from the Sioux (Noyes,7-8).

41. Horace E. Dimick was the proprietor of a St. Louis company that manufactured firearms and munitions (*American Rifleman*, 1958) 29.

42. The Crow Agency was established in 1869 for the Mountain Crows but eventually became responsible for the River Crows as well.

43. This was F.W. Wheeler who, while U.S. Marshal, was also busy taking the 1870 census. He incorrectly listed Lee as being 40 years old and noted that "Jane Smith ... Scalped by Indians last year. Hale and Hearty now ... hates Indians" (U.S. Census, 1870).

44. Cut Heads were the Yanktonai, one of seven divisions of the Dakota Sioux (Frederick Hodge, *Handbook of the American Indians*, 2 vols., 1965 reprint (Washington: Government Printing Office (1907-1910) 990.

45. Mountain fever was originally a general term to describe a variety of diseases. By the latter part of the 19th century, the term was used to describe a specific illness: a "disease [that] occurred primarily in the spring ... with one to three episodes of fever lasting roughly forty-eight hours separated by two to eight days of seeming good health ... Constipation, severe muscle and chest pains particularly in the back and loins and joint pains, headache, and retro-orbital pain were also common symptoms." A Medical Corps officer demonstrated in 1906 that the disease was transmitted by wood ticks. Since 1926, the infection has been termed Colorado Tick Fever. Peter Olch, "Treading the Elephant's Trail; Medical Problems on the Overland Trail," *Bulletin* of the History of Medicine, 59, (1985) 202-03.

46. A similar account of this episode, recounted by George Clendenin, appears in James H. Bradley, "Account of the Attempts to Build a Town at the Mouth of the Musselshell River," *Contributions*, MHS, 2, 312-313. See Appendix.

47. The record indicates some confusion concerning the *Nick Wall*. Lee notes her arrival here and departure on the 31st. A list of steamboat arrivals at Fort Benton marks her arrival there on the 26th of May, 1870. So far so good. But Chappell (p.315) claims that the *Nick Wall* "sank on the upper river April 25, 1869."

48. The *Ida Reese* carried freight up the river for four years, 1868-1871. She was sunk by ice at Yankton in 1871 (Chappell, p.303).

49. A landmark on the south side of the river, some 40 river miles downstream from the mouth of the Musselshell.

50. This is in reference to General Phil Sheridan, then commander of the Army's

Division of the Missouri. This is one of the few acknowledgments of the military presence in the Territory. Lee makes no mention of the much publicized event that occurred six months earlier on January 23 when Major Eugene M. Baker and two companies of the Second Cavalry attacked Heavy Runner's peaceful band of Blackfeet and killed 53 women and children. This transpired some 200 miles to the west of the Musselshell. Robert Utley, *Frontier Regulars: The United States Army and the Indian* (New York: Macmillan Publishing Co. 1986) 191. The incident was stressed by Peter Koch in a letter to his uncle written two days earlier. Peter Koch, "Letters from the Musselshell, 1869-1870," *Pacific Northwest Quarterly*, 37 (1936) 330.

51. Her career on the river paralleled that of the *Ida Reese*. The *Viola Bell* experienced four years on the upper river (1867-1870) before sinking near Doniphan, Kansas, August 18, 1871. (Chappell, p.316).

52. The *Bertha* docked at Fort Benton in 1868, '69, and '70; the *Peninah* experienced a longer life than most river steamers. She worked the upper river between 1868 and 1871 and four years later – April 6, 1875 – she suffered the fate of many when she wrecked near Sioux City (Chappell, p.315; *Collections*, MHS, 1, 285-287; 3, 352-358.

53. In an account published 26 years after the affair, Peter Koch still distinctly remembered the rutting bison on the Musselshell and being "frequently kept awake at night by their incessant bellowing, pawing and fighting" Koch, *Contributions*, MHS, 2, 302.

54. Desertions were common in the post-Civil War Army and in the first ten years following cessation of hostilities between North and South ranged from a low of 9.4 percent (in relation to aggregate strength of the Army) in 1870 to a high of 32.6 percent a year later. Jack Foner, *The United States Soldier Between Two Wars*. (New York: Humanities Press, 1970) 223.

55. This is Clendenin's trading post. The abbreviations refer to Thomas C. Power and Company.

56. Several of the early buildings in Montana were built with the Spanish adobe block; most notable were Fort Owen in the Bitterroot Valley and Fort Benton on the Missouri.

57. The Patent Office Annual Reports, 1849-1881, do not indicate any patents issued to CM. Lee (Commissioner of Patents and Trademarks, Washington, D.C.).

58. A rationalistic theology that affirmed the idea of progress and rejected the idea of eternal punishment.

59. Squaw Creek entered the Missouri from the south, several miles below the Musselshell.

60. See entry of January 13, 1871.

61. The *Ida Stockdale* was on the river for five years, 1867 to 1871. She is listed as being sunk at Bismarck in 1871 (Chappell, p.314).

62. The *Nellie Peck* made her last landing at Ft. Benton in 1880. *Contributions,* MHS, 3, p.335.

63. This is the second *Far West* on the upper river. The first operated 1834-1836, the second 1871-1883, according to Chappell. In 1872 she held the record for the fastest trip between Sioux City and Ft. Benton: 17 days and 20 hours. See also, *Contributions*, MHS, 1, 287.

64. This was apparently the only trip to Ft. Benton by the *Flirt*. *Ibid.*, 286.

65. This was the last year for the *Silver lake*. The boat had been active on the river since 1868.

66. The *Miner* first carried freight to Ft. Benton in 1866 and continued on the river until 1872.

67. Records indicate that the *Andrew Ackley* made trips to Ft. Benton in 1868 and 1869 and that she only reached Cow Island on this trip. *Ibid.*, 286.

68. This could have been in response to the February 23 entry of "answering advertisements in Harpers Weekly." *Sketches of Creation* by Alexander Winchell, a professor of geology and zoology at the University of Michigan, became a popular science book advocating a rational religious belief and urging the acceptance of Darwinian science. First published in 1870 by Harper and Brothers, it was reissued 35 years later.

69. The agency had been moved from Fort Benton in 1869 to its new site on the Teton River some 7.5 miles northwest of Benton. In 1875, the government moved the agency 50 miles further north to Badger Creek John Ewers, *The Blackfeet: Raiders on the Northwestern Plains*, (Norman: University of Oklahoma Press, 1958) 275.

70. Any of Lee's suppositions may have been correct. The diary contains no further mention of Harry Woodward.

71. Lee's diary ends with this last entry. As indicated in the Introduction, he evidently used all of his ink early in December. The entries from December 12 to April 19 are in pencil. He also ran out of journal. The March and April entries are on the Journal's back and front covers. Subsequent Lee journals detailing his later years may surface in the future; I hope they do, and if so, I can only apologize here for not having found them.

Appendix

Life at Muscleshell in 1869 and 1870.*
BY PETER KOCH.

The writer spent the greater part of the year 1869-70 at and about the mouth of Muscleshell on the Upper Missouri. It is but a few years ago, and yet at that time conditions of life prevailed in that region, which have already greatly changed, and of which in a few years hardly a trace will be left. From Fort Benton to the Yellowstone the country along both sides of the Missouri was as wild as when Lewis and Clark first stemmed its turbid current. It is true that a few trading posts were planted along its banks, that a number of steamboats yearly made their difficult way between and over its sand-bars to Fort Benton or Cow Island, that at rare intervals a clearing had been made around a woodyard in one of the densely wooded points. But the steamboat passed, and when the sound of its whistle was beyond hearing no sign of its passage was left. The woodchoppers' clearing meant only so much wood cut. No scythe and reaping hook followed his axe, and his solitary cabin never became surrounded with barns and granaries, but was soon left to decay or to be washed into the river, unless its logs were sold for firewood to the steamboat which carried the wood-chopper away at the end of the season. The trading post did not become the nucleus of a village or a centre for spreading civilization. It was simply a place to accumulate robes, skins and furs, and the less civilization there was in the surrounding country, the more profitable the trade was apt to be.

The few whites scattered along the river belonged to three classes, and all made their living from the natural products of the country: the wood-choppers from the Cottonwood and pine along the river banks, the wolfers and trappers from the wolves of the prairie and the beaver of the streams, the traders from the Indians.

Through the greater part of the year these men were scattered singly or in small bands throughout the country; but when the river broke up in the spring, many of them gathered at the trading posts to await the arrival of the first boat. This was the great event of the year. The trader was then to receive his new stock and to ship the robes and peltries of last season's trade. The woodchopper was to dispose of his wood, the wolfer was to market his wolf skins. Then were the scenes of the old trappers' rendezvous enacted over again, although on a smaller scale. Gambling and carousing were the order of the clay, a year's earnings were spent in a few weeks, and when the time came to prepare for another season's work, few were those who had money left to pay cash for their outfit.

The center of this life on the upper part of the river was the trading post at Muscleshell. To those who landed there early in June, 1869, the place presented a characteristic sight. It enjoyed at that time its greatest prosperity and formed quite a little village. There were two trading establishments. One belonged to the Montana Hide and Fur Co. (which failed that year), the other to George Clendenin, Jr. and T. C. Power. There was a gunshop, [This was Cornelius Lee's establishment] two saloons (although it was in the heart of the Indian country) and perhaps a dozen other log-cabins, all built at intervals along the high bluff bank of the river with stockades around the stores. The settlement was ambitious and aspired to become a city. A townsite was laid out, and hopes were entertained, that a military post would be established, and that this would be made the shipping point for Montana freights instead of Fort Benton on account of the difficulties of navigation on the upper river. But all those ambitions were destined to disappointment. No military post was established. The Indian trade declined for various reasons. With the completion of the Union Pacific Railroad the river route lost importance for a time, and when it was revived not Muscleshell but Carroll was selected as the shipping point. When I left the place the Missouri had already undermined some of the houses, and today not a vestige is left to show where the settlement once stood. It has shared the fate of de Soto; the muddy waters of the Missouri roll over its grave.

The settlement and surrounding desolate, sage-brush covered plain did not usually offer many points of interest to the travelers on the steamboats, except the usual features of a village on the extreme frontier, here perhaps somewhat exaggerated: but when the Huntsville landed there at the time referred to, a sight met her passengers which was certainly calculated to shock the nerves of any eastern tenderfoot. Along the brink of the river bank on both sides of the landing a row of stakes was planted, and each stake carried a white, grinning Indian skull. They were evidently the pride of the inhabitants, and a little to one side, as if guarding them, stood a trapper, well known throughout eastern Montana, by the sobriquet of "Liver-eating Johnson." He was leaning on a crutch, with one leg bandaged, and the day being hot his entire dress consisted in a scant, much shrunken, red undershirt, reaching just below his hips. His matted hair and bushy beard fluttered in the breeze, and his giant frame and limbs, so freely exposed to view, formed an exceedingly impressive and characteristic picture.

But while the exhibition of these skulls did not indicate any high degree of civilization on the part of the inhabitants, the manner in which they had been procured showed at least that they possessed the courage and enterprise so necessary in the dangerous and exposed life led by them. For several years the country around Muscleshell had become more and more dangerous. The Sioux were feeling the pressure of the advancing settlements in Minnesota and Dakota, and different bands were pushing up the Missouri and crowding into the country claimed by the Crows and other upper Missouri Indians. They were intensely hostile to the whites, and as the principal trading post was at Muscleshell that became naturally the chief objective point of their raids, although they did not disdain to attack a wood yard when occasion served, or to take the scalp of a solitary wolfer when they could take him unawares. But the large war parties did nearly always start for Muscleshell, and the men at that point had suffered greatly from their depredations. It happened that about the first of May nearly fifty men, mostly wolfers and woodchoppers, were gathered, there waiting for the arrival of the first boat. They were partly at the trading posts on the south side of the Missouri and partly at two wood yards in the point opposite. There were two squaws stopping at one of the stores, and early one morning they went out towards the Muscleshell River to gather dry wood. Here they were attacked by a band of Sioux, but escaped to the houses, one of them wounded. As a matter of course every man turned out with his rifle, when he heard the shooting, and a number of shots were exchanged, but without casualty on either side, as the Indians were a quarter of a mile distant and dodging behind the cottonwood trees, while the whites were protected by the houses and stockades. Ordinarily this would have ended the affair, as the Sioux always left as soon as they were discovered, and the whites were usually perfectly willing to have them do so. But this time the issue was different. Never before had so large a number of men been together at Muscleshell, and this was too good a chance to get even with the Indians to let the opportunity slip. Thirty or forty of the boys therefore sallied forth to follow the Indians and give them a lesson they would remember.

The accompanying sketch-map will show the situation better than I can describe it. The sage brush on the plain was very dense and breast high, and only towards the Muscleshell River was there a scattered growth of large cottonwood trees. On the east side of the Muscleshell the bank was covered with a very dense growth of small willows. The boys advanced cautiously through the sage brush towards and up the Muscleshell which runs here under a cut bank ten to twenty feet high. This bank could be climbed with difficulty, the earth crumbling easily, except where it was cut by short coulees, running back fifty to a hundred feet. As the hunters approached one of these and were within about fifty yards of it, nearly a hundred Indians rose suddenly out of it and with a yell fired a volley into the whites. One man, Jake Leader, was instantly killed and another, Greenwood, wounded. This checked the whites and they scattered for shelter behind the few trees. For a considerable time a desultory fire was kept up on both sides. The Indians did not dare to expose themselves, but would hold up their guns and fire without any particular aim, and the whites could not see their enemies, sheltered in the coulee which was about fifteen feet deep with steeply sloping sides. So far the hunters had had the worst of it, and it seemed as if nothing could prevent the Indians from holding their position till dark and then escaping to their brethren, of whom several hundred were singing and yelling in the woods some distance up the river, but not daring to come to the rescue. The boys were seriously discussing the plan of rushing up to the brink of the coulee, firing down among the Indians and thus taking their position by storm; but it would undoubtedly have entailed a serious loss of life on the part of the assailants, and yet that seemed the only alternative to allowing them to escape.

There was one point, however, from which an effective attack might be made, the mouth of the coulee; but in front of that the Muscleshell River was rushing at the height of the spring flood, an impassable torrent. Finally Frank Smith, Jim Wells, Henry McDonald and Joe Bush-away succeeded in crossing the river some distance below and made their way carefully through the willow thicket until they were opposite the mouth of the coulee which ran straight back from the river. They were armed with Henry rifles and had the Indians at their mercy. When the first bullet struck among the latter they saw that the game was up, and there was no way of escape. In front was the river and all around them on the plain above men were scattered whose rifles they could not hope to elude. In vain did they seek to dig a shelter in the banks with their butcher knives. One after another fell before the fatal bullets from the unseen rifles in the willows opposite. A dash for life must be made, although almost a hopeless one. First the pipe was lighted and passed around, while they sang their death song, and then *sauve qui peut*. Some leapt from the coulee and tried to escape through the encircling enemies, others ran along under the bank in the edge of the water, while many threw themselves into the water and swam to the willow thicket opposite. The whites might have killed them all, but they seem to have become somewhat excited, and a part of them came under the fire of the others and had to seek shelter and stop shooting. Yet

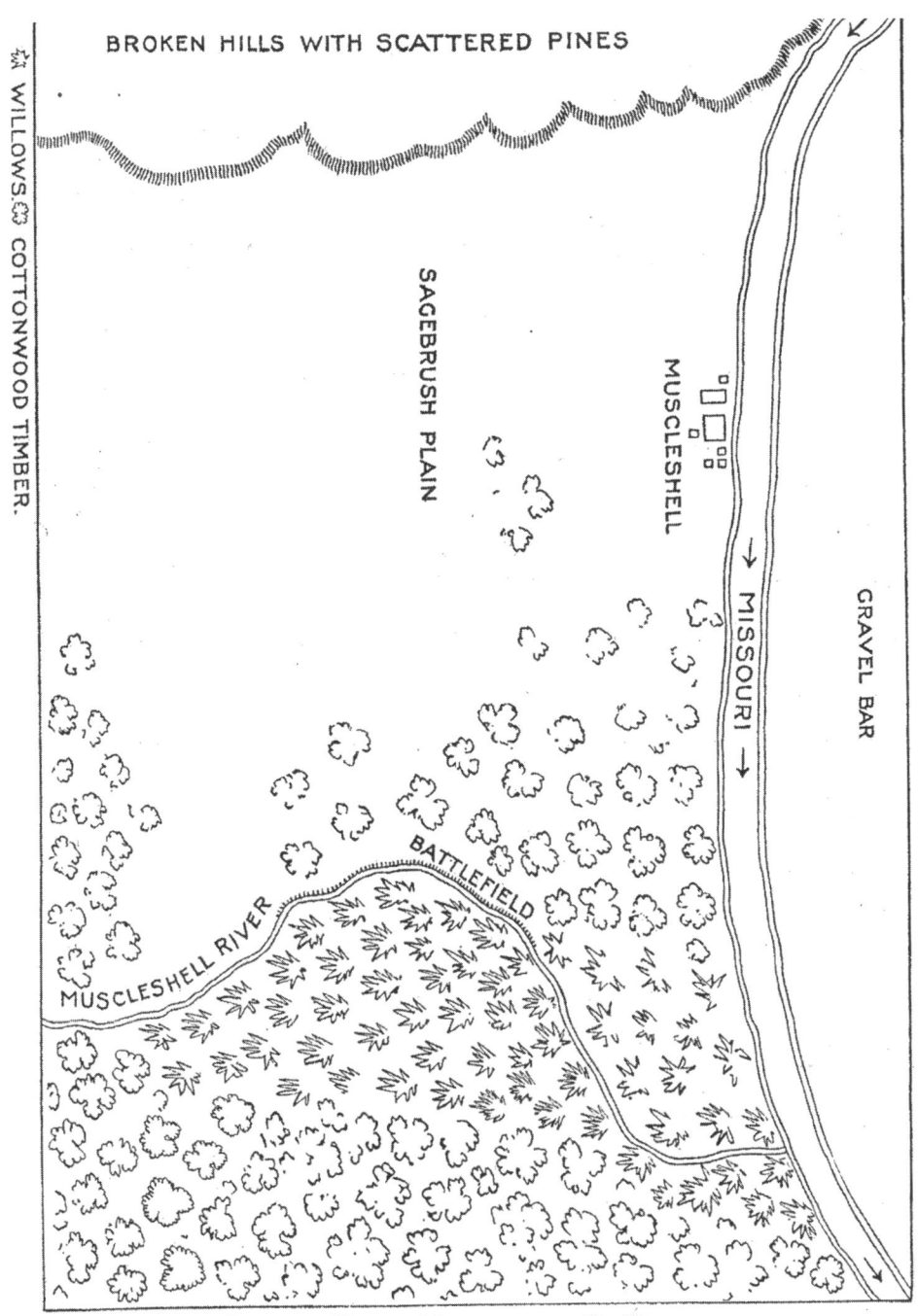

Sketch from Memory by P. Koch.

the Indians suffered greatly and nearly twenty corpses were found on the battlefield.

The survivors made their way to the agency at Fort Peck, and according to their own story thirty-three were killed outright or died from their wounds on the way, while only two Indians escaped without a wound of the ninety-eight who had taken part in the fight. Breech-loaders had just been introduced on the river, and most of the whites were armed with Henry and Spencer rifles, which were as yet unknown to the Indians, who declared with great emphasis that Muscleshell was bad medicine, as the men there could fire their guns right along without reloading or even taking them from their shoulders.

From that day the Sioux swore eternal vengeance against Muscleshell, and numerous war parties started from Fort Peck or from Sitting Bull's camp on the Dry Fork of the Missouri with the avowed purpose of capturing that place. This made it a very dangerous residence, and to the day of its abandonment its inhabitants were never safe, although no serious attempt to capture or burn it was ever made.

The trade at Muscleshell was principally with the River Crows and upper Gros Ventres. The River Crows were a band of the Crow tribe of Indians, in no way different from the mountain Crows who made their home on the Yellowstone, except in their inordinate love of whiskey which the mountain Crows would not admit into their camp. When the two bands met, it was easy to see the ill effect of that curse of the Indians on the River Crows. They were much poorer than their brethren of the mountains, had fewer horses, fewer good arms and took much less pride in their dress and general appearance.

The Gros Ventres of the prairie must not be confounded with the Gros Ventres of the river or Minnetarees who lived below the mouth of the Yellowstone, although now nearly extinct. The latter were a branch of the Crows and belonged to the great Dakota family, while the former were an offshoot of the Arrapahoes who lived on the Sweet Water and other headwaters of the Platte. While I was on the Missouri, an epidemic of smallpox came among the Gros Ventres, and probably two-thirds of them perished. They were camped on Milk River at the time and nearly all who were attacked died, as they treated it with their usual cure-all, the sweat-bath, followed by a plunge into ice-cold water. Quite a number committed suicide from fear of the disease. Finally the camp became panic stricken, and the Indians scattered to the mountains, each lodge by itself. At last the epidemic wore itself out, but I was told that it was no uncommon thing to find lodges standing in the mountains, all their former inhabitants lying dead around them. Many of the whites along the river took the disease, but all in a mild form. Infected robes which found their way east are said to have caused the outbreak of smallpox which occurred the following year at Philadelphia and other points.

The Gros Ventres were a very peaceable tribe and friendly to the whites, differing in that respect greatly from their cousins, the Arrapahoes; but they were poor and suffered greatly in their constant warfare with the Blackfeet who have been a perpetual scourge to all their neighbors, whether red or white. The Crows were less tractable. They were apt to be insolent and overbearing, when they felt they had the upper hand, and, while they might hesitate to kill a white man, they did not scruple to set him a-foot and strip him of everything he had when they thought they could do it in safety.

At that time the trade was yet carried on in the old way. One or more robes were traded for one kind of goods only, such as a robe's worth of sugar or a robe's worth of cotton cloth. The Indian had not learned to divide up the value of the robe, which was the unit of trade, so as to take for instance half of its value in coffee and half in flour. This simplified the trade very much, and when business was lively, a great many robes could be bartered in a day. When the Indian came to trade, he was usually followed by his squaw who entered the room staggering under the load of a dozen or more robes. These were thrown over the counter one by one, and the Indian would call out what he wanted. Half a dozen or more would go for a gun and a saddle, as many more for blankets, generally one was traded for coffee and several for sugar. These articles were measured out in a tin cup and simply poured into a corner of the squaw's skin-dress. When the goods had been measured out and handed over, "tail" was thrown in, corresponding to the amount of the trade, and the trader was ready for the next Indian. Profits were large when I first came on the river. A robe was bought with three cups of coffee, or six cups of sugar, or ten cups of flour. A red three-point Mackinaw blanket cost three robes and all other goods in proportion. beads and other fancy goods afforded the largest profit. I remember one particular kind of pale blue necklace beads to which the Indians took a great fancy, and the robes purchased with them cost just sixteen cents apiece. It is curious that while it is a generally accepted truism that the most glaring colors are the most acceptable to uncivilized people, the Crows will not buy or use bright beads. Almost without an exception their favorite beads are pale, dull colors, and the squaws are as particular in choosing and matching them as a white woman with her ribbons. The pale blue seed-beads are their favorites for embroidering, and the squaws will invariably throw out any bunch which is the least off color. Fashions in beads and fancy goods of all kinds change rapidly with them also, and it is very important that they be selected by someone familiar with their tastes, as they will not accept for a gift beads of a color which does not strike their fancy.

A great deal of whiskey was sold to the Indians in defiance of the United States laws. As there was profit in it, it could not be otherwise. There were no officers within several hundred miles to enforce the law, and as far as there was any public opinion it sustained the whiskey traffic. I say whiskey, but it is only by a euphuism [sic] that the vile stuff on which the Indians got drunk can be called by that name. The recipe for its manufacture was something like this: 1 quart alcohol,1 pound rank, black chewing tobacco, 1 handful red peppers, 1 bottle Jamaica ginger, 1 quart black molasses, Water from the Missouri *ad libitum*. Mix well and boil till all the strength is drawn from the tobacco and peppers.

The Indian who had consumed a bottle of this stuff must have sighed sadly for soda-water next morning; but it is possible that it did not do as much harm after all as a stronger and purer article would have done.

Hostile Indians came around so often that no horses could be kept, unless guarded constantly, and whenever the attempt was made they were invariably stolen sooner or later. It was almost impossible to cut hay even, as the Indians nearly always burned it. The Blackfeet did not trouble us much; but it seemed that whenever the Sioux had nothing better to do, they made up a war party for an attack on Muscleshell. The Assinniboine, Yanctonnais, Tetons, Cut-throats and other bands all took a hand in the fun. The agency for most of these Indians was at Fort Peck, near the mouth of Milk River, and we were several times warned from that point that a war party had started for Muscleshell before the party reached that place and made their attack. Their usual road lay up the river. Sitting Bull's bands came from the Yellowstone or the Dry Fork of the Missouri and followed a trail which led over the high table land between the Yellowstone and Missouri Rivers and struck the latter at the mouth of Squaw Creek a few miles below Muscleshell. The war parties varied greatly in size, sometimes numbering only eight or ten and again several hundred. Their habit was to lie in wait for days or even weeks for a chance to take someone unawares. But that could not often be done; for everyone was constantly on the alert. Not a step was taken without a breech-loading rifle, a revolver and a well-filled cartridge belt. Even when going from one house to another at Muscleshell, the gun was taken along as an alarm might come at any moment, and no one left the house a hundred yards without throwing a cartridge into his rifle.

As soon as the Indians were discovered, they went away after exchanging a number of shots, whether anyone was killed on either side, or not. During the summer a raid might be expected about every two weeks. In winter and during the highest water we were comparatively safe. Since leaving the place I have often wondered that we were not all killed. We never hesitated to go out hunting or wherever else we wanted to go, and I can only account for our safety by the fact of our never being caught napping, and the extreme reluctance of the Indians to make an attack when they were almost certain to lose some of their own number. I could fill this volume with stories of narrow escapes; but I will mention only a few cases in which white men's lives were lost. They occurred in the winter and spring of 1870-71, for, curiously, during the eighteen months the writer spent at Muscleshell not a white man was even wounded in all the skirmishes which took place, although on several occasions some of the Sioux were transformed into "good" Indians.

At that time Thomas Bogy (since dead) was in charge of the trading post at Muscleshell in the absence of George Clendenin, Jr. at Fort Ellis, where he had the appointment of post-trader. About the first of January, 1871, he sent two employees – Ross, an old mountaineer, and Charles MacKnight, a young man lately from the states – across the river to secure some ash timber for the repair of a wagon. Night came and the men did not return. Early the next morning a search party went out and found both men killed. It was a time of year when all felt comparatively safe, and they had probably omitted the usual precautions, as the Indians had evidently surrounded the gulch in which they were chopping and taken them by surprise.

The other instance showed unusual pluck on behalf of the Indians. Three men, Lee, Drew and Thompson, were on their way from Muscleshell to Little Rocky woodyard about forty miles above. Some distance above Fort Hawley they saw fresh signs of a numerous party of Indians. They made at once for the dense willow brush along the river, confident that no Indians would follow three well armed men into such a place. But for once they were mistaken. The Indians had already discovered them and contrary to their usual custom determined on an attack. They belonged to the Yanctonnais tribe of Sioux, which band is superior in daring and enterprise to any of their brethren. The fight was described to me as a most desperate one. The thicket was almost impenetrable, and it was possible to see only a few feet. The men lay down behind drift-wood logs, but the Indians followed them so closely, that at times only a log was between them and their assailants. Lee was killed. Drew was shot in the breast, but the bullet was stopped by a package of letters which he carried in the breast pocket of his hunting shirt. Thompson was wounded in the shoulder. The fight lasted nearly all day, and eight or ten Indians were killed. At nightfall Drew and Thompson succeeded in reaching the bank of the river, rolling in a log and by means of it swimming across to the opposite bank, whence they made their escape.

To the middle of this century the warfare of the Crows was directed principally against the Blackfeet and Cheyennes. The only Sioux with whom they came in contact were the Assiniboines who lived above Fort Union, north of the Missouri. Only when parties went to visit their relatives, the Gros Ventres of the river, did they come across the Arickarees and the main bands of the Sioux. But these Indians were gradually being pushed westward by the advancing civilization. The bulk of them crossed the Missouri and occupied the country of the Gros Ventres and the Mandans after nearly exterminating these tribes. The Crows used to range down to the mouth of the Yellowstone and came often to Fort Union to trade, but at the time I refer to they did not often venture below the mouth of the Big Horn or the big bend of the Muscleshell. They were carrying on a constant warfare with the Sioux, and although far inferior in numbers managed to hold their own quite well, as they were much better armed and equipped and on the whole better fighters. They realized their precarious situation, and I am confident that to this fact only did we owe it that they refrained from open depredations on the whites. The whites were enemies of the Sioux, equally with themselves, and only through their help could the Crows hope to escape extermination.

Usually their warfare was not very bloody. I witnessed once a battle between a small band of River Crows who were camped at Muscleshell and a war party of about twenty-five Sioux who were discovered in the broken bluffs on the north side of the Missouri. The Crows mustered for the battle with the utmost activity and prodigious din. With great ardor and apparently an unquenchable determination to do or die did they plunge into the river and swim across. At full gallop did they charge up the heights, yelling and shooting. The Sioux were posted on the brow of the bluff. They wavered a moment then turned and fled, the Crows in close pursuit. But hardly had they gone out of sight before they returned pell-mell, their positions reversed. It was now the turn of the Sioux, and they chased the enemy half way down the bluff, when the Crows rallied and in their turn drove the Sioux. These furious charges and counter-charges were kept up through a whole afternoon with a mighty expenditure of ammunition. Not less than a thousand shots were fired and the casualties [sic] were – one Sioux horse. At last the Sioux grew tired and withdrew, and the Crows returned, singing a song of triumph and claiming a feast as a reward for their valor.

But there were exceptions to this usually bloodless character of their engagements. In the fall of 1869 a war party of thirty-two young River Crow warriors went to the Dry Fork of the Missouri to steal horses from the Sioux. They were prowling around a large camp when they were discovered. They fled, but were overtaken and compelled to take refuge on the top of a small, isolated butte, where they threw up stone breastworks. The entire Sioux camp with several thousand fighting men surrounded them. The Crows held them at bay here several days, until their ammunition and arrows were exhausted. Then, shouting their death song, they leaped from their breastworks down among their enemies, striking right and left with their knives and battle-axes. They fell, but only after killing nearly a hundred Sioux. Two only were captured alive, and such was the admiration of the Sioux for their bravery, that they permitted them to go unharmed. The next winter a party of Crows went to the battlefield and gathered the bones of the slain. I was in the Crow camp when they returned, and their expressions of grief were a more sickening sight than the slaughter itself can have been. All the squaws had their faces blackened, dozens of fingers were cut off, and all related to the dead in any way slashed and stabbed their arms, breasts and thighs, until they were covered with a mixture of blood and black paint. Add to this their doleful cries and piercing screams, and it would be hard to imagine a more horrible scene.

Wolfing will soon be one of the lost arts, because no wolves will be left to poison. It may therefor be worth while to describe the wolfer's *modus operandi*. As soon as cold weather began, he would start into his chosen field. Generally two went together for company and greater safety. Their outfit consisted of their blankets, coffee, sugar, flour and a liberal supply of ammunition and strychnine. It was necessary to go to the buffalo country, because the wolves followed the buffalo herd, and yet, if possible, the place selected must be one where the Indians do not hunt much, or too many carcasses would be left lying around on the prairie. The first thing to do was to put out baits in convenient places; where buffalo were killed. These were partly skinned and three or four bottles of strychnine, containing one-eighth ounce each, were sprinkled over the carcass after gashing it well with the knife, and the strychnine was rubbed into the flesh and the blood with the hands and then left. Another buffalo was killed a mile or two from the first and prepared in the same way and so on, until frequently thirty or forty baits were put out, generally forming a circle. During mild weather it was necessary to visit the baits every few days to skin the poisoned wolves, or the hide would become loose and the skins spoil. Where the country was not too dangerous the wolfer managed to take advantage of mild spells throughout the winter and keep his wolves well skinned up; but if he couldn't do that, the dead wolves, when frozen stiff, were piled up to protect them as far as possible from the magpies, which birds spoiled many skins in spite of all precautions. Towards spring a final visit was paid to the baits, all the wolves skinned and the furs carried to the nearest trading post, where each skin was worth about three dollars. The most profitable wolfing country, however, was infested by hostile Indians, and there different tactics were pursued. Three or four wolfers went together and put out their baits in November and December, then they returned to a safer place and did not go to their baits again until spring, when the weather became soft enough to skin the wolves. It was an exceedingly rough and dangerous life, but for that reason all the more attractive to the class of men engaged in it, and a successful wolfer made considerable money. When the poisoned buffalo carcasses were frozen hard, a very small quantity of meat sufficed to kill a wolf, and more than a hundred wolf skins have been taken at a single bait. But it happened frequently that the Indians became so dangerous that it was found impossible to go to the baits in the spring, and then a whole winter's work was lost. At the time of the Fort Pease expedition in 1875, a great many baits were put out north of the Yellowstone. The country was alive with wolves, and during the winter thousands of them were seen lying dead around the baits; but in the spring it was worth a man's life to leave the fort half a mile, and even the hardy wolfers, inured to danger as they were, dared not attempt it, so that hardly a wolf skin was saved. The wolfers were never on good terms with the friendly Indians even, as these always had many of their dogs poisoned when moving their camps through a country in which baits had been put out, and they cut up the wolf skins whenever they had a chance, and annoyed the wolfers in every possible way, so that many a fracas took place between them.

Frequently the wolfer was "set a-foot" (i. e. had his horse stolen) on the prairie and then had to make his way to the nearest post, as best he could. His work was mostly in the open plains country, where he suffered greatly from the winter blizzards. I have heard many tales of frightful sufferings and know of several instances, where the hapless wolfer was reduced to feeding on the carcasses of the poisoned wolves. Strangely enough I have known several old wolfers who always fried their batter-cakes in wolf fat, when obtainable, alleging that it gave a much finer flavor to the cakes than if fried in any other kind of grease.

The wolves have shared the fate of the buffalo, and of the large prairie wolves few are now left; but in 1869-70 Muscleshell was in the heart of the buffalo country, and there seemed then no end to either buffalo or wolves. In March, 1870, I traveled from Muscleshell to Fort Browning on Milk River, and for a distance of forty miles I do not think we were ever out of easy rifle shot of buffalo. Our trail led along a low ridge through a gently undulating country, and we could see many miles on either side; but turn where we would, the eye only met herd after herd of grazing and slowly moving buffalo. We did not disturb them, and they moved barely far enough to one side to let us pass. Three days later I passed over the same trail on my return trip, and the vast herds had disappeared as if by magic. Only two or three old bulls were still wandering over the prairie; but the grass was cut as close as if fed over by sheep, and immense quantities of *bois de vache* were left for the convenience of later travelers over these treeless plains. At Muscleshell it was no uncommon thing to shoot bulls from the doors of our cabins, and during the rutting season we were frequently kept awake at night by their incessant bellowing, pawing and fighting. Elk, deer and antelope were also abundant along the Missouri at that time, and although we depended on game altogether for our meat supply we had usually more than we could possibly use.

At the time I refer to steamboats had to tie up and cut their own wood throughout the Sioux country, except in a few places, such as Fort Peck, where wood-yards were established in the immediate neighborhood of the trading posts. But from Muscleshell to Fort Benton wood-yards were found in abundance, wherever there was any accessible timber. Cottonwood sold for five and six dollars per cord on the bank of the river, pine and cedar from eight to twenty dollars according to the difficulty of getting it and the necessity of the steamboat. Considerable money had been made in the wood business; but my own experience was rather unfortunate. 1870 was the year of the completion of the Union Pacific Railroad, and the number of steamboats on the upper Missouri dropped from forty in 1869 to eight in 1870. Consequently wood was a drug in the market and could not be sold at any price. Out of several hundred cords which my partner and I banked we sold less than twenty-five cords, and before the summer was over the Indians burned the remainder.

Even as high up as Muscleshell wood chopping was a dangerous business. We never worked without a man on guard and our rifles leaning against the nearest stump. And even with all possible precaution men were killed nearly every season. Hardly a "point" but had its rudely marked grave and its tale of battle and death. But lower down the river the business was still more risky and had been almost entirely abandoned. In

1868 a party of eight young men came out from St. Louis and went ashore near Spread Eagle bar above Fort Union to establish a wood yard. They were told it was almost sure death, but they were inexperienced and thought they could conciliate the Indians and insisted on carrying out their purpose. A few weeks later the boat on which they had come up the river returned from Fort Benton just in time to bury their bones.

A party of Sioux had come up to them, played friendly, mingled among them without suspicion, been allowed to examine their Henry rifles and finally killed them with their own guns. After plundering the cabin they set it on fire, and the logs were still smouldering when the steamboat, arrived. Truly the banks of the Missouri are bloody ground.

I must not close this sketch without mention of the one white woman at that time living on the upper Missouri below Fort Benton. Her name was Jennie, by courtesy called Mrs.Smith, but better known throughout Montana under a sobriquet not fit for polite ears. She lived with a man by the name of Frank Smith, who went to Michigan with her in 1870 and there married her. While at Muscleshell she lost her scalp. One day she was carrying dinner out to some men hauling wood in the hills, when a war party of Indians surprised her, shot her through the neck and, supposing her dead, scalped her before any one could come to the rescue. The Indians were soon driven off and it was found that, except for losing her scalp, she had suffered no serious injury. When I saw her she was apparently none the worse for her adventure.

Such was life on the Missouri fifteen years ago, full of danger and exposure and apparently with few attractions to relieve its rude and repulsive features. Yet so easy is it for man to relapse into barbarism that even now men of education and refinement become infatuated with its untrammeled freedom and find it difficult to tear themselves away after once becoming accustomed to it.

Contributions to the Historical Society of Montana, 2, (1896) 292-303.
*Various spellings of the Musselshell began with Lewis and Clark.

ACCOUNT OF THE ATTEMPTS TO BUILD A TOWN AT THE MOUTH OF THE MUSSELSHELL RIVER.
BY LIEUT. JAMES H. BRADLEY
(AUTHORITY—COL. GEORGE CLENDENNIN.)

The advantages presented by the mouth of the Musselshell River for the location of a town, were early to attract attention after the settlement of Montana. The Missouri River above this point presents a difficult navigation in consequence of its swift current and numerous rapids, and late in July or early in August generally becomes too shallow to admit of navigation at all by the class of boats usually employed; while, until late in October, little difficulty is experienced in ascending to this point. Again, above the mouth of the Musselshell, the Missouri describes a wide circle to the north-west, while a practicable land route exists by the short arc drawn from this point to the settlements in the mining regions. It was believed that a successful rival to Fort Benton might be-here established, and the broad and beautiful valley presented by the receding bluffs and the abundant timber in the vicinity were additional arguments in favor of the selection of this point. As the fine and fertile basin of the Judith, through which the road would pass, is suited to agriculture and naturally dependent upon a town thus located, it was hoped that a numerous population would ere long resort hither and thus advance materially the importance and prosperity of the place. Then passing into the realms of conjecture, as the surrounding mountains had never been thoroughly prospected, it was believed by many that paying gold fields would eventually be found there, and thus a new and mighty impulse be given to a town so conveniently located with reference to them as the one projected.

Influenced by such considerations, a number of gentlemen associated themselves as the Rocky Mountain Wagon Road Company and in 1866 opened a route across the mountains south of the Missouri River, from the mining regions of Montana to the mouth of the Musselshell, at which point a townsite was selected. An old steamboat captain named Kerchival had been among the first to advocate the route, and was one of the partners in the company, and in his honor the place was given the name of Kerchival City. The company put up a log cabin which was occupied by its employees; but two years passed, the town did not grow, the freighting business did not flourish in consequence of powerful opposition, and presently the encroaching waters of the river swept the establishment of the Rocky Mountain Wagon Road Company into the stream, and Kerchival City passed into the catalogue of towns that were but are not.

In 1868 the attempt was renewed under the auspices of the Montana Hide and Fur Company, of Helena, which dispatched a party of nine men under James Brewer to take post at the mouth of the Musselshell and build a warehouse. They arrived in March, 1808, laid out a town on the south bank of the Missouri and called it Musselshell. Soon afterward they were joined by Colonel George Clendennin with his brother Richard, and James McGinniss, from Grand Island, where this gentleman had opened a woodyard while awaiting the developments respecting the new town. He at once began the construction of buildings for the purpose of engaging in trade. In the course of the season a number of people flocked to the new town from the mountains and up and down the river; and before the following winter eight buildings were ranged in line fronting the river bank, while some fifty people were gathered in the vicinity. A company of troops, commanded by Captain Nugent of the 13th Infantry, came down from Camp Cooke and took post there, building a stockade with bastions just below the town within whose walls they pitched their tents, giving to the place the name of Camp Reeve. The friendly tribes of Gros Ventres and Crows resorted to the place in large numbers to trade; and thus during the summer of 1868 all was bustle and activity at the mouth of the Musselshell.

Things thus looked prosperous for the new town. If so much was accomplished in one summer with the disadvantages of making a beginning, what might not be reasonably looked for in succeeding years now that so imposing a nucleus was fairly established? To this question a prompt if not satisfactory answer was given. Hostile Sioux at once environed the town, swept down upon and scooped up, in the adjacent valley, the grazing herds of the townsfolk and killed two soldiers of the garrison. In the fall of 1868 the troops were withdrawn to Camp Cooke.

Musselshell was destined, in the course of its brief existence, to be the center of considerable Indian adventure, and, ere the summer of 1868 passed by, the first scene in the drama had been enacted. But before proceeding to its narration, let us inform the reader of an event of previous occurrence that, though not properly connected with the history of Musselshell, paved the way to the incident we propose to relate. During the year 1867 the government let a contract for the establishment of a pony mail route from St. Paul, Minnesota, to Helena, Montana; Fort Hawley being one of the stations, and the point of departure from the Missouri River for Diamond City. The service, however, was very ill-performed, and a measure that might have been of great benefit to the country became a positive detriment from the repeated losses of the mail matter forwarded by the route. The pony-riders had long and difficult journeys to make between the different stations, they found fuel scarce and newspapers heavy, and with happy ingenuity got over both difficulties by burning the papers, and developing still farther their inventive talent made excellent cigar lighters out of the letters in the mail sack. To receive a letter over the route at all soon became a matter of surprise, and at last the government refused payment for the ill-performed services and the route was abandoned.

In the spring of 1868, Al. Bradbury, superintendent of the western section of the route – which, we will remark, was exceptionally well conducted – arrived at Musselshell, having been engaged in collecting the material of the company and closing up its affairs. About the middle of April he set out for Helena accompanied by Henry McDonald, a daring and successful rider on the route, and four other men, the party having it its possession some five or six horses. The route chosen led them over the Judith Mountains, and, as they neared their base, they discovered at a distance a party of about thirty Sioux Indians whose movements were threatening and the party sought a commanding knoll and prepared for defense by digging small rifle pits with their butcher knives. The Indians came up and attacked them vigorously, making repeated charges against their position, which were all repulsed. Here, under a hot fire, they maintained a stubborn defense for two hours, when night fell.

They had lost all their horses, killed in the course of the attack, and two of the men were wounded though not disabled. As soon as the darkness screened their movements they abandoned their position and were enabled to elude the vigilance of the savages, and Bradbury with four of his companions subsequently reached the settlements without further adventure. But not so the other, named Dennis. During the night he became separated from his companions and with all his efforts was unable to rejoin them. He floundered about in the darkness in a state of no little anxiety, and when morning broke discovered to his dismay that the Indians were upon his trail. He fled at his best speed, but found that he was being rapidly overtaken. Escape now seemed impossible, but with the desperation of despair he pressed on.

He was now entangled in the "bad-lands" prevalent in that region, which is seamed and scarred by the combined action of wind and water until it presents an illimitable dismal prospect of barren mounds, naked ridges and deep, steep-walled ravines, difficult to traverse and almost completely shunned by every form of animal and vegetable life. As he struggled on he came upon one of those sinks, so common in such regions, where the water has worn a subterranean channel from the high ground to the bottom of some ravine. The Indians were now close at hand and into this he plunged, crawling forward till he found an indentation in the side, into which he sank and lay motionless. The Indians were not long in reaching the spot and discovered his hiding place. The winding course of the hole hid the white man from their view and they hesitated to follow him into his cavern. But one could advance at a time, and should the white man be armed – as seemed probable – the leader at least must be killed. It was a desperate enterprise and all shrank from it.

But at last they discovered the exit of the sink in the ravine below. An entrance here was less perilous, as it was supposed the white man's attention would be directed to the other opening and he might be surprised by a cautious advance. Three young warriors stripped and entered. As they crept slowly and noiselessly up the narrow way, by an instinctive feeling Dennis became aware of their approach. He was armed with a revolver, and shrinking close in his little cavern he nerved himself for a desperate defense. He was unaware of the number of his foes; but resolved if the leader passed him without discovery to permit him to do so, and thus get two in range before firing. On they came, and as Dennis had hoped, the foremost savage, peering straight forward, glided by on his hands and knees as noiselessly as a mouse. Close behind him followed a second and aiming as well as he could through the intense gloom, Dennis pulled the trigger. Before the savage who had passed him could recover from his astonishment Dennis fired another shot with the muzzle almost touching the body of his foe. Then all was still except the hurried scrambling of the rearmost Indian as he retreated by the way he had come, leaving Dennis alone with the motionless forms of his two victims.

The shots came to the ears of the Indians above, and they anxiously awaited the result. But no shout of triumph came from their comrades in the sink and presently the sole survivor of the three rejoined them with the story of his companions' probable fate. Then a yell of rage and lamentation went up outside, and Dennis listened in trembling apprehension lest the desire of revenge should urge them to a still more desperate effort against his life. But it was not made. Their "medicine" proved too weak and they sought their recompense of scalps in the pursuit of some less hazardous enterprise.

All day Dennis remained in his cavern, tortured with suspense, listening for the movements of his foes without, but for hours all was still. When night came he crept past the bodies of his victims and ventured forth, choosing the outlet into the ravine. To his great joy the enemy was gone, and he lost no time in putting all possible distance between himself and the scene of so much mental suffering. But his troubles were not over, for during two days he wandered without food or water, and then had the good fortune to reach a camp of Crow Indians, where he obtained refreshment and repose and the next day made his way to Musselshell.

This story is given as narrated by himself, but circumstances afford it corroboration; and the writer, in common with the well-known and highly esteemed gentleman who is his informant, deems it as much entitled to credit as the wonderful escapes of Colter, Clyburne and others, that upon similar evidence are now accepted as facts of frontier history. Indeed, a majority of the most intensely interesting incidents of personal adventure are based upon the unsupported statements of the parties themselves, and were all such to be erased from the pages of frontier history, it would almost bankrupt them in interest, and leave but little indeed to animate youth to deeds of daring and rouse anew the sluggish blood in the veins of age.

The spring of 1869 brought some encouragement to the enterprising inhabitants of Musselshell. General Hancock, commanding the department of Dakota in which Montana was embraced, directed the survey of a military road from Fort Ellis to the mouth of the Musselshell River and the selection of a suitable military reservation in the vicinity of the latter point. This work was performed under the superintendence of Captain Clift of the 30th Infantry, the reservation chosen being about a mile square, bordering to the north upon the Missouri River and embracing both banks of the Musselshell. This seemed to portend the establishment of a military post, and, as Camp Cooke was badly located and its abandonment about to take place, it was hoped that the garrison might take post at the new town. But this was a hope not destined to fulfillment [sic] while meantime the settlement was beset with Indian alarms.

In March, 1869, a considerable war party of Sioux advanced against the place. Passing up the river they attacked a party of four wood-choppers at the mouth of Fourchette Creek who were at work near their cabin. Three were killed, but the fourth, though wounded, reached that shelter, his retreat being covered by a comrade, who was himself suffering from a previous wound and hence had remained in the cabin. The two maintained a successful resistance, and when the savages left remained till their wounds permitted them to travel, when they made their way to the settlement. Arriving at Musselshell the Indians placed themselves in ambush on the morning of March twenty-second, within a quarter of a mile of town. Two wagons were occupied in hauling logs from the adjacent woods, one coming as the other went, and thus meeting at every trip. In one of the trips a white woman of the town and two Crow squaws were riding in one of the wagons, when it met the other in the midst of the ambuscade. At this moment the Indians opened fire. The wagon containing the women was overturned, the white woman was shot through the neck and scalped after nearly reaching town, while the rest of the party fled, one of the squaws receiving a bullet through the leg.

The firing alarmed the town and the citizens turned out under arms. As Colonel Clendennin turned the corner of his store he saw an Indian leaping about in the sage brush about one hundred and fifty yards distant, and gave him the benefit of several shots, but without effect. It was at this place that the wounded white woman was found, who was brought in, and who finally recovered, minus her scalp. All but one of the remainder of the attacked party reached town in safety. This one, old Captain Andrews, a well-known miner of Montana, was some distance off and calling for help, as the Indians were in the sage brush between him and town. A party advanced to his aid in skirmish order and effected his rescue.

As Colonel Clendinnin had some cattle in the woods he called for volunteers to assist him in bringing them in. A number joined him and they pushed on rapidly into the woods. As they advanced, some Indians on the hills were seen calling out and making signs, as if to warn their comrades in the timber. Soon afterward, when the party were about three-fourths of a mile from town, two Indians appeared through the timber driving the cattle before them. They approached with confidence until within one hundred and fifty yards of the party, when with a start of surprise they turned and fled. The whites had not fired, as the unconcerned approach of the Indians led to the belief that they were part of some friendly band endeavoring to do a service, but the Indians at first had evidently taken them for their own party, not dreaming that the whites would thus boldly seek them in the timber. They were fired upon as they fled, but without effect.

But this affair was only the prelude to one of a more serious character. On the morning of the ninth of May, 1869, a man named Davis and his squaw, started down the Missouri toward the Musselshell for fuel. As they approached the bank of the latter stream an Indian rose and fired upon them, the bullet passing through the clothes of the squaw between the arm and the body. The alarm was instantly communicated to the town, and as every man's weapon was always ready, in a few moments some twenty armed men were advancing in skirmish order in the direction of the enemy.

Colonel Clendennin was on the left of the line next to the Missouri, and, as the steep bank of the Musselshell afforded the Indians excellent cover, he proposed that he should first reconnoitre [sic] their position by keeping along down the Missouri till he reached the mouth of the Musselshell when he would be enabled to get a good view of them up the valley. Acting upon this idea he discovered a numerous body of Indians running along under the bank and turning the point beyond, while about half a dozen were seen to enter a small ravine as if to shelter themselves from the fire he had instantly opened upon them from a repeating rifle. Informing the whites of the situation, the whole party advanced against the ravine, hoping to capture or kill the small force seen to enter it.

As they approached, however, a heavy fire was opened from the ravine and continued with great rapidity, which compelled the whites to halt and lie down in the shelter of the sage brush. In this position both parties remained for some time, exchanging shots whenever a mark was presented. In the meantime Jacob Leader, a German employed by Colonel Clendennin as a Crow interpreter, joined the line and rashly advanced against the ravine. Stimulated by his example the entire party rose and moved forward, but a hot fire was poured into their faces and in a moment Leader fell, with a shot that entered the center of his nose and came out at the back of his head. This checked the advance, and the whites again sought the shelter of the sage brush.

The determination with which the Indians maintained their position in the ravine led the whites to believe that they had wounded comrades there whom they sought to defend; and notwithstanding a heavy rainstorm had set in, it was resolved to continue the attack and afford no opportunity for their removal. In the meantime a reinforcement of about twenty men joined the whites from the other side of the river, but even with this increase of force it was not deemed prudent to advance directly against the ravine, as it was evident several lives must be sacrificed.

Finally Jim Wells, Frank Smith and a man called "Frenchy," proposed to cross the Mussellshell at a point below, and, following up the farther bank under cover of the willows to a point opposite the Indian position, secure a flank fire upon the enemy in the ravine. The remainder of the force was to await the result of the attempt and press the attack as soon as the Indians were thrown into confusion.

The plan was well conceived, and it was boldly executed. The valiant little flanking party advanced cautiously on its dangerous mission, arrived opposite the ravine, parted the willows carefully and to their consternation found the ravine swarming with Indians. Instead of the expected six there were not less than sixty. This explained the great weight and rapidity of their fire, and proved that the ravine must have been already filled with Indians when it was reconnoitred [sic] by Colonel Clendennin. Nothing daunted by their close proximity to such an overwhelming force, Wells's party opened fire. Amazed at such audacity the Indians returned the fire. But as the rain had soaked their bowstrings and the pans of the flint-lock guns with which many of them were armed, their resistance was feeble and they finally broke. The main body now charged them on the other bank, and routed at all points the Indians, not less than two hundred in number, fled the field, leaving in the hands of the whites thirteen of their number dead or wounded, and bearing with them a large number of wounded, of whom twenty-one afterwards died, many of them immediately after the battle. The whites lost Leader killed and a man named Greenwood wounded in the shoulder. The fight began at half-past seven in the morning and terminated at noon, and may safely be pronounced one of the most hotly contested ever fought with Indians in Montana.

The wounded Indians left upon the field were at once dispatched, and the bodies scalped and in one case otherwise shamefully mutilated. The following day Captain Andrews retaliated for the loss of his oxen in the affair of March twenty-second, by removing the heads from ten of the bodies of the slain Indians, cutting off and preserving the ears, and boiling the heads till the skulls could be cleaned, which he then placed on exhibition and finally carried east.

Soon after the battle a steamboat arrived from below, and it then appeared that the Indians had found means to avenge in part their severe defeat upon this occasion. The boat had touched at a woodyard near Round Butte, about fifty miles below Musselshell, and there found the remains of seven woodchoppers recently killed, scalped and horribly mutilated. It was undoubtedly the work of the party which attacked Musselshell, either before or after the battle.

Musselshell passed through the remainder of the year 1869 without any episode of importance, but no further accessions were made to its population. It began to appear that as a freighting town it was a failure, as out of the huge fleet of steamboats (unparalleled in the history of the river) that this year sought the upper Missouri, only one discharged freight at this point – about eighty tons – which was the only freight ever forwarded over the new road. The surrounding country was undeveloped, furnishing no other local business than the trade of the desultory bands of Crows and Gros Ventres, who came in fear and trembling of their dreaded enemies, the Sioux. In this year, too, the Pacific railroad completed its embrace of the continent and the new channel thus created for the flow of Montana traffic, was far from strengthening the foundations upon which the prosperity of Musselshell was to reach its grand proportions. Still the town held bravely on, and if it did not this year increase in population it at least suffered no material diminution, but when the winter of 1869-70 settled down upon the aspiring *entre pot* to Montana, giving the inhabitants rest from toil and turmoil and affording opportunity for reflection, the most sanguine were unable to extract from the situation much comfort for the ensuing season.

As usual, Sioux war parties followed in the train of the year (1870) and the familiar crack of the rifle and the savage war whoop again resounded in the valley. No serious engagement ensued, and no inhabitant of the town was killed, but it was believed that the better handled rifles of the townspeople made occasional vacancies in the prowling squads of Sioux warriors. A new feature was this year introduced into the skirmishes at Musselshell. A three-inch smooth-bore iron cannon was loaned to the inhabitants by General Hancock, with an abundant supply of solid shot, shell and cannister; and its thunders occasionally echoed through the valley, dispersing in disorder the impudent bands of savages that congregated upon Sioux Hill, from which with impunity they had formerly signaled defiance to the town.

But notwithstanding the cannon, the Indians had found means to observe that a party of the citizens returned at about a certain hour every day to work at a cellar in course of excavation in the suburbs: and on the night of the third of July, 1870, a numerous party crept to the place under cover of the darkness and, concealing themselves in the cellar, prepared to give the working party a bit of a surprise when they appeared at the usual hour in the morning. The next day, however, was the Fourth of July, and the patriotism of the cellar diggers induced them to pass the day in recreation and repose. The ambuscading warriors awaited their appearance in vain, being for a good part of the day dissatisfied and disappointed spectators of the festivities in town. At last Mr. Halvor Olson crossed from the opposite side of the river, and passed sufficiently near the ambuscade to induce the Indians to fire. Fortunately, however, he escaped unharmed, and the discomfited savages fled with increased respect for the protecting influences of the white peoples' great "medicine day," leaving one of their number killed. His body was brought into town, tied on a log and rolled into the river. The patriotism of the cellar diggers saved their lives, and it is seldom that a better argument is presented for the observance of our great national holiday.

But a still more wonderful escape occurred this year a little earlier in the season. An eccentric and restless Frenchman arrived from Helena for the purpose of taking passage down the river by the first boat. After waiting at Musselshell for some time he grew discontented, and after a period of fretfulness set out on foot alone to return to Helena. Finding no inns or habitations by the way where he could refresh himself, he was glad to retrace his steps, and, as he was without food and the country he traversed was destitute of water, he arrived at Musselshell nearly exhausted. Untaught by this experience he concluded to attempt a return by the "Benton trail" and again set forth.

Soon after his departure an alarm of Indians was raised in town, and the inhabitants turned out under arms. The Indians were seen dashing on horseback through the skirt of the timber, from which they proceeded at full speed by a roundabout course to the top of the hill by which the Benton trail ascended from the valley. Here they posted themselves so as to be screened from the view of anyone ascending by the trail. Meantime the Frenchman, unconscious of his peril, tramped on and began to climb the hill. He was in full view of the assembled villagers, who sought by every means to attract his attention and warn him of his danger, but unhearing or unheeding he kept on his way. Thwarted in their efforts to warn him and powerless to aid him, the townspeople remained for some moments anxious spectators of his movements.

As they saw the deliberate preparations of the savages to take the Frenchman's life and the rapidly lessening distance between them and their intended victim, the excitement became intense; and at last almost by a common impulse they levelled their guns and opened fire. Upon the Indians? No, that would have been futile; but upon the Frenchman. His destruction seemed inevitable, and it was thought better that a friendly hand should speed the bolt and disappoint the exultant savages of their anticipated triumph. It is seldom that such a sight is witnessed.

The bullets rattled around the Frenchman like hail, but he seemed to wear a charmed life, for though good shots were handling many of the rifles not one took effect. In spite of the fire he kept steadily on, and soon rising above the ridge found himself face to face with the expectant savages. Then for the first time he paused, gazing at them in bewilderment. They might have killed him at once, but withheld their fire to count their coups. With this object they dashed upon him as he stood spellbound and irresolute and in a moment he was surrounded. The leading Indian counted his coup by dealing him a heavy blow with the flat of a saber across the face. The stroke roused the Frenchman from his stupor, and with a tremendous bound he cleared the throng and dashed down the hill. Never was such speed made before by human feet and his steps when subsequently measured were something wonderful. Not an Indian dared urge his horse down the steep hill at sufficient pace to overtake him.

The villagers had turned their fire upon the Indians when they exposed themselves, and had continued it briskly during the episode on the hill. This checked their pursuit, and they contented themselves with delivering a rapid fire after the retreating Frenchman while he continued within range, when they moved off. The same miracle seemed to protect him under the fire of the Indians, for it was as unavailing as had been that of the villagers, and after running such a gauntlet as friend and foe have seldom combined to prepare for a man, he reached the town in safety. After this "affair" he was enabled to restrain his impetuosity until the arrival of a boat.

While these events were transpiring the waning confidence in their enterprise upon the part of the founders of Musselshell reached fruition. In the spring of 1870 the Montana Hide and Fur Company closed its affairs there and abandoned the place; and throughout the season desertions occurred one by one, until Colonel Clendennin found himself, about the close of August, alone with his employees and establishment. Musselshell as a town was no more.

This gentleman resolved to remain, for the purpose of carrying on an Indian trade, and with this view took down the abandoned houses, made considerable additions to his buildings and connected them with a stockade, making a compact and handsome fort to which he gave the name of Fort Sheridan. For four years he remained resolutely in this dangerous region with a garrison of from five to eight men, trading with the Indians and keeping a woodyard for the convenience of steamboats. His customers were the Sioux, who upon the abandonment of the town ceased open hostilities against the place and agreed to remain peaceable, as they wished to make the fort a point to trade. Standing Buffalo with a numerous band was the first to appear, in the spring of 1871, but though similar bands visited the fort in succeeding years, the trade was never extensive or profitable. The Crows and Gros Ventres ceased their trading visits when the town was abandoned, but the surrounding region was a standing battle ground between them and the Sioux to which few but war parties resorted.

Although, during the existence of Fort Sheridan, the Sioux exhibited no open hostility in that vicinity, they continued to steal horses when opportunity offered, and upon two occasions added to the list of murders perpetrated there. On the fifth of January, 1871, two employees of the fort, Charles B. McKnight and John Ross, were surprised and killed by the Santee Sioux within a mile and a half of the fort while in the woods looking for ash timber. The following year a white man named Hunter, accompanied by three Assiniboine squaws, was attacked by the Unc-papas while looking over the battle ground of May ninth, 1869. The squaws were all killed under the supposition that they were Crows, but Hunter escaped with a severe wound.

Upon the founding of Carroll in the spring of 1874, Colonel Clendennin broke up his establishment at the mouth of the Musselshell and in May of that year removed to the new town. Fort Sheridan was dismantled and the available material transferred to Carroll, the cannon contributed by General Hancock being returned to Fort Buford. About two hundred cords of wood valued at $4.50 per cord were left behind at the landing and was burned by the Sioux the June following. In July, Christopher Gates and Patrick Vaughan were dispatched by Colonel Clendennin to take down the remaining buildings at Fort Sheridan and cut up the material into steamboat wood. While thus engaged they were surprised by the Sioux, who seemed to haunt the place with relentless hatred. From the indications it appeared that Gates was killed, while Vaughan had sought refuge in one of the buildings, which was then fired by the Indians and he perished in the flames.

Contributions to the Historical Society of Montana, 2, (1896) 304-313.

Bibliography

Unpublished Materials

Bogy, Thomas Diary of Thomas Bogy at Ft. Belknap, 1874-79. Special Collection 150 (Hereafter, SC), Montana Historical Society (Hereafter, MHS).
Brewer, James S. Reminiscences. SC64. MHS.
Canfield, Andrew N. Diary MF73. MHS.
Clendenin, George. Clendenin File. Archives Vertical File. MHS.
Davis, George R. Autobiographical Sketch. MC64. MHS.
Grinnell, George B. Letters. MHS.
Healy, John J. Typescript of interview. MF 64. MHS.
Heberle, Lawrence S. History of Broadwater County. Mss #878. Special Collections. Montana State University.
Marsh, Grant. P. Marsh File. Archives Vertical File. MHS.
McKnight, Joseph H. J. H. McKnight Papers. MC56. MHS.
McNeal, Eli W. Reminiscences. Typescript. SC258. MHS.
Pony Express Courier, Vertical File, MHS.
Power, Thomas C. Thomas C. Power Papers. MS55. MHS.
Skelton, William. Reminiscences. Typescript. Archives Vertical File. MHS.
Stuart, James. Diary of James Stuart at Ft. Browning. MHS.
Town, George. Reminiscences. MC64. MHS.
Wells, James A. Reminiscences. Interview conducted by William F. Wheeler at Fort Benton, 1884. SC 978, MHS.
Wheeler, William F. William F. Wheeler Papers. MC65. MHS.
Worthen, Clifton B. Judith Basin in Central Montana. Mss#760. Special Collections. Montana State University.

Documents

Barry, Edward E. The Fort Belknap Indian Reservation: The First One Hundred Years, 1855-1955. Report Prepared for the Indian Claims Commission, Docket No. 279-C. (Ms in Special Collections, Montana State University, Bozeman, Montana.
Howell, Captain C. W. Improvements of the Missouri River, *House Executive Document* 136, 40th Congress, 2d Session, SN 1337.
Fisk, James. Expedition from Ft. Abercrombie to Fort Benton in 1862, *House Executive Document* 80, 37th Congress, 3rd Session, SN 1164.
Foley, Micael F. An Historical Analysis of the Administration of the Fort Belknap Indian Reservation. Report Prepared for the Indian Claims Commission, Docket 279-C. (Ms. In Special Collections, Montana State University, Bozeman, Montana.
United States Census, Population Statistics for Montana, Idaho and Iowa. 1870, 1880.
Sketch furnished to U. S. Engineers Office, Glasgow, Montana, by David Hilger, State Historical Library.
Letter, A. J. Simmons, Agent, Milk River Agency to J.A. Viall, Superintendent,

Montana, June 20, 1871, in *House Executive Document* 23, 42d Congress, 2d Session, Serial 1510.

Letter, M. M. McCauley, Agent for the Blackfeet, to E. S. Parker, Commissioner of Indian Affairs, Feb. 13,1871, *House Executive Document* 15, 42d Congress, 1st Session, 2, Serial 1471

Newspapers (Specific articles)

Bozeman Courier, June 4, 1937. Article Re: House and Woody.
Dillon Examiner, September 29, 1920. Re: Ft. Browning, by M. E. Plassman.
Forsyth Independent, no date, Re: Liver-Eating Johnson, by S. Panton
Fort Benton *Record,* May 15 and March ll, 1875, Re: George Theodore and M. C. Thum.
Great Falls Tribune, January 21, 1903. Obituary of J. H. McKnight.
Great Falls Tribune, July 5, 1914. Re: Joe Kipp, by James Willard Schultz.
Great Falls Tribune, March 24, 1931. Obituary of Joe Butch.
Great Falls Tribune, August, 20, 1937. Re: J. H. McKnight, by Joe Ford.
Great Falls Tribune-Leader, July 23, 1963. Re: Ft. Hawley.
Hardin Tribune Herald, May 8, 1931. Re: Mitch Bouyer, by W. H. Banfill.
Hardin Tribune Herald, December 18, 1931. Re: Mary L. Doane and Ft. Ellis.
Hardin Tribune Herald, no date, Re: Musselshell. Reel 17, Clipping File. K. Ross Toole Archives, University of Montana
Jefferson Valley News, no date, Re: Life at Ft. Pouchette. Reel 7 Clipping File, K. Ross Toole Archives, University of Montana.
Joliet Independent, no date, Re: Ft. Browning. Reel 7, Clipping File, K. Ross Toole Archives, University of Montana.
Kalispell Times, June 14, 1934. Re: Grant P. Marsh.
Kalispell Times, March 1935. Re: Musselshell, by A. J. Jordan.
Meagher County News, January 25, 1950. Re: A. S. Reed, by Oscar Mueller.
Mineral Independent, August 1, 1929. Re: Henry Keiser and Liver-Eating Johnson, by Lou Grill.
Mineral Independent, June 2, 1932. Re: Liver-Eating Johnson, by W. H. Banfill.
Mineral Independent, October 1, 1936. Re: Crow Davis.
Mineral Independent, no date, Re: C. W. Cook, by Grace Stone Coates
Mineral Independent, April 27, 1936. Re: W. G. Dexter and A. H. Wilkins.
Montana Journal, November 1987. Re: burials at Musselshell.
Montana Post, June 8, 1867. Re: Diamond City.
Philipsburg Mail, April 4, 1921. Re: W. O Dexter
Phillips County News, July 4, 1963. Re: Musselshell, by Gladys Costello.
Pony Express Courier, July 1943, August 1943. Autobiography of Edward Swan.
River Press, Febuary 15, 1882. George Clendenin obituary.
River Press, March 18, 1931. Re: Henry McDonald, by Grace Stone Coates.
*Rocky Mountain Weekly Gazette (*Helena) Aug. 20, 1873, Re: Mountain Charley.

Articles

Aitkins, C. J. Log of the Steamer Bertha from Sioux City, Iowa to Fort Benton, Montana. *Collections*, State Historical Society of North Dakota, 2. (1908) 359-370.

Allen, Robert S. Witness to Murder: The Cypress Hills Massacre and the Conflict of Attitudes Toward the Native Peoples of the Canadian-American West During the 1870, in Getty, Ian A. L. and Antoine S. Lussler, eds, *As Long as the Sun Shines and the Water Flows: A Reader in Canadian Native Studies*. (Vancouver: University of British Columbia Press, 1983) 229-246.

Anderson, Gary C. Early Dakota Migration and Intertribal Warfare, *Western Historical Quarterly 11 (1980) 17-36*.

Bradley, James H. Account of the Attempts to Build a Town at the Mouth of the Musselshell River. *Contributions,* Historical Society of Montana, 2 (1896) 304-313.

Bradley, James H. Affairs at Fort Benton. *Contributions, Historical Society* of Montana, 3, (1900) 201-287.

Bradley, James H. Miscellaneous Events at Fort Benton, *Contributions,* Historical Society of Montana, 8, (1917) 127-130.

Barry, Edward E. "From Buffalo to Beef: Assimilation on Fort Belknap Reservation," *Montana, The Magazine of Western History,* 26 (1) (1976) 38-51.

Chappell, Philip. History of the Missouri River. And Missouri River Steamboats. *Transactions,* of the Kansas State Historical Society. 9, (1905-1906) 237-315.

Chouteau, Charles P. Early Navigation of the Upper Missouri. *Contributions*, Historical Society of Montana, 7, (1910) 253-256.

Cone, Carl B. (ed.). Letters from the Musselshell, 1869-1870. *Pacific Northwest Quarterly*, 37 (4) (1936) 313-335.

Davison, Stanley. White Hopes of the Big Muddy, *Montana, The Magazine of Western History. 9 (2) (1959) 2-15*

Ege, Robert. Braves of All Colors: The Story of Issiah Dorman. *Montana, The Magazine of Western History*, 16, (1) (1966) 35-40.

Ewers, John. Intertribal Warfare as a Precursor to Indian-White Warfare on the Northern Plains, *Western Historical Quarterly 6 (4) (1975)397-410.*

Golding, P. The Cypress Hills Massacre: A Century Retrospect, *Saskatchewan History 26, 81-102*.

Gray, John. Northern Overland Express. *Montana, The Magazine of Western History*, 16, (4) (1966) 58-73.

Gray, John. George Boyd, Montana Frontiersman, Chicago Westerners *Brand Book*, 22 (5) (1965) 33-40.

Haines, Aubrey. Ed. Voyage to Montana, *Montana, The Magazine of Western History* 49 (4) 16-29; 50 (1) 18-27.

Hedges, Cornelius. Life of William F. Wheeler. *Contributions*, Historical Society of Montana, 3, (1900) 27-32.

Hiady, W. M. Indian Migrations in Manitoba and the West, *Papers* of the Manitoba Historical and Scientific Society, 2d Series, 17 2-35.

Holmes, Oliver W. Diary of James A. Garfield Trip to Montana in 1872, *Montana, The Magazine of Western History*, 6 (4) (1956).

Kane, Lucille. New Light on the Northwestern Fur Company, *Minnesota History* 31

(1955) 93-99.

Koch, Peter. Life at Musselshell in 1869-1870. *Contributions*, Historical Society of Montana. 2, (1896) 292-303.

Krieg, Frederick C. Chief Plenty Coups, The Final Dignity, *Montana, The Magazine of Western History* 16 (4) (1966) 28-39.

Kroeber, Alfred L. Ethnology of the Gros Ventre, *Anthropological Papers* of the American Museum of Natural History (1908) 1 145-281.

Lass, William E. Steamboating on the Missouri, Journal of the West, 6 (1) (1967) 53-67.

Lass, William E. Elias H. Durfee and Campbell K. Peck: Indian Traders on the Upper Missouri Frontier. *Journal of the West*. 43 (2) (2004) 9-19.

Logan, Herschel. H. E. Dimick of St. Louis. *American Rifleman*, 106, (1958).

McElroy, Harold. Mercurial Military; A Study of the Central Montana Frontier Army Policy, *Montana, The Magazine of Western History 4 (4)* 9-23.

McDonald, Henry. An Ill-Fated Settlement, *Forest and Stream* (August 2,9,23,1888).

McMillan, Marilyn An Eldorado of Ease and Elegance, *Montana, The Magazine of Western History 35 (2) (1985) 36-49.*

Olch, Peter. Treading the Elephant's Tail; Medical Problems on the Overland Trail, *Bulletin* of the History of Medicine 59 (2) (1985) 196-212.

Oviatt, Alton B. Steamboat Traffic on the Upper Missouri River,1859-1869, *Pacific Northwest Quarterly* 40 (1949)

Peterson, William. Log of the Henry Shreve to Fort Benton, 1869, *Mississippi Valley Historical Review* 31 (4) (1945) 537-578.

Point, Nicholas. Journey in a Barge on the Missouri from the Fort of the Blackfeet to That of the Assiniboines, *Mid-America* 13 (1931)

Saindon, Bob and Bunky Sullivan. Taming the Missouri and Treating Depression; Ft. Peck Dam, *Montana, The Magazine of Western History* 27 (3) (1977) 34-57.

Senieur, Matilda. Bismark to Fort Benton by Steamboat in the Year 1869, *Montana, The Magazine of Western History, 2 (2) (1952) 55-59.*

Sharrock, Susan R. Crees, Cre-Assiniboines and Assiniboines: Interethnic Social Organization on the Far Northern Plains, *Ethnohistory 21 (2) (1974) 95-122.*

Slaughter, Linda Fort Abercrombie, *Collections*, State Historical Society of North Dakota 1 (1906) 412-423.

Weisel, George F. Journey to Benton, *Montana, The Magazine of Western History 1 (3) (1951) 5-13.*

West, Helen B. Tragedy on the Teton: 1881, *Montana, The Magazine of Western History* 12 (3) (1962) 21-23.

White, Richard. The Winning of the West: The Expansion of the Sioux in the 18th and 19th Centuries, *Journal of American History* 65 (2) (1978) 319-345.

Books

Abbott, E. C. and Helena Huntington Smith *We Pointed Them North* (Chicago: R. R. Donnelley & Sons Company, 1991)

Athearn, Robert G. *Forts of the Upper Missouri* (Englewood Cliffs: Prentice Hall, 1967)

Banks, Eleanor M. *Wandersong* (Caldwell: Caxton Printers, 1950)

Barbour, Barton H. *Fort Union and the Upper Missouri Fur Trade (*Norman: University of Oklahoma Press, 2001)

Barry, Edward E. *The Ft. Belknap Indian Reservation: The First Hundred Years, 1855-1955* (Bozeman: Montana State University, 1974)

Brown, Mark H. *Plainsmen of the Yellowstone*: A History of the Yellowstone Basin (New York: Putnam, 1961)

Burlingame, Merril G. *The Montana Frontier* (Helena: State Printing Company, 1942)

Cheney, Roberta C. *Names on the Face of Montana* (Missoula: University of Montana Press, 1971)

Chittenden, Hiram. *The American Fur Trade of the Far West* 3 vol. (New York: Francis Harper, 1902)

Cowie, Isaac. The Company of Adventurers (Toronto: William Briggs, 1913)

Crawford, L. F. *Rekindling Camp Fires* (Bismark: Capital Book Company, 1926)

Denig, Edwin T. *Five Indian Tribes of the Upper Missouri* (Norman: Oklahoma University Press, 1961)

Denton Heritage Committee. *Homestead Fever: History of Denter-Danvers-Coffee Creek (*Great Falls: Blue Print and Letter Company, 1977)

Downs, Winfield S., ed*., Encyclopedia of Northwest Biography (New York: The American Historical Company, 1941)*

Drips, J. H. *Three Years Among the Indians in Dakota* (New York: S. Lewis, 1974)

Ewers, John C. *The Blackfeet: Raiders on the Northwestern Plains* (Norman: University of Oklahoma Press, 1958)

Fahey, John. *The Flathead Indians* (Norman: University of Oklahoma, 1974)

Foner, Jack. *The United States Soldier Between Two Wars* (New York: Humanities Press, 1970)

Grey, John*. Custer's Last Campaign: Mitch Boyer and the Little Big Horn* (Lincoln: University of Nebraska Press, 1991)

Grinnell, George B. The Passing of the Great West: Selected Papers of George Bird *Grinnell* ed. John Reiger (New York: Scribners 1972)

Guerin, E. J. *Mountain Charley* (Norman: University of Oklahoma Press, 1968)

Hafen, Leroy. Ed. *The Mountain Men and the Fur Trade of the Far West,* 10 vol. (Glendale: Arthur H. Clark, 1965-1972)

Hafen, Leroy and Ann Hafen, Eds. *Powder River Campaigns and Sawyer Expedition of 1865* (Glendale: Arthur H. Clark, 1961)

Hamilton, James M. *From Wilderness to Statehood: A History of Montana, 1805-1900* (Portland: Binfords and Mort, 1957)

Hanson, Joseph M. *The Conquest of the Missouri* (Chicago: A. C. McClurg and Company, 1909)

Heitman, Francis B. *Historical Register and Directory of the United States Army, 1789-1903* (Washington: Government Printing Office, 1903)

Highland, Geneva, *Big Sky Country* (Billings: Billings Print Company c1960)

Hodge, Frederick. *Handbook of the American Indians,* 2 v. (Washington: Government Printing Office 1907-1910, 1965 Reprint)

Jacobs, Charles M. *Horizons O'r the Musselshell* (Missouri Valley Pioneer Club,

1974)

Jordan, Arthur J. *Jordan* (Missoula: Mountain Press, 1984)

Kelly, Luther S. *Yellowstone Kelly: Memoirs*. Ed. M. M. Quaife, (New Haven: Yale University Press, 1926)

Larpenteur, Charles. *Forty Years a Fur Trader on the Upper Missouri* (Chicago: Lakeside Press, 1933)

Lass, William E. *A History of Steamboating on the Upper Missouri* (Lincoln: University of Nebraska Press, 1962)

Lass, William E. *Navigating the Missouri* (Norman: Arthur H. Clark Company, 2008)

Lawrence, Lou. *Pioneer Days at Big Sandy*, Montana. (Big Sandy: ? 1963)

Leeson, Michael A. Ed. *History of Montana: 1739-1885*. (Chicago: Warner, Beers and Company, 1885)

Lepley, John. *Packets to Paradise*. (Missoula, Montana: Pictorial Histories Publishing Co, 2001

Long, J. Larpenteur. *The Assiniboines* (Norman: University of Oklahoma Press, 1961)

Lowie, Robert. *The Crow Indians* (New York: Rinehart and Company, 1935)

Malone, Michael and Richard Roeder, *Montana: A History of Two Centuries* (Seattle: University of Washington Press, 1976)

Marquis, Thomas B. *Memories of a White Crow Indian* (Lincoln: University of Nebraska Press, 1928)

McGinnis, Anthony. *Counting Coup and Cutting Horses: Intertribal Warfare on the Northern Plains* (Evergreen: Cordillera Press, 1990)

McLaughlin, James. *My Friend the Indian* (Boston: Houghton Mifflin, 1910)

Miller, David, Dennis Smith, Joseph R. McGeshick, James Shanley and Caleb Shields. *The History of the Assiniboine and Sioux Tribes of the Fort Peck Indian Reservation, Montana, 1800-2000* (Poplar: Fort Peck Community College, 2008)

Miller, Joaquin. *An Illustrated History of the State of Montana* (Chicago: Lewis Publishing Company, 1894)

Milner, Clyde A. and Carol A. O'Conner. *As Big As The West: The Pioneer Life of Granville Stuart* (New York, Oxford University Press, 2009)

Nabakov, Peter, *Two Leggings; the Making of a Crow Warrior* (New York: Crowell, 1967)

Noyes, A. J. *In the Land of the Chinook: The Story of Blaine County* (Helena: Montana State Publishing Company, 1917)

Oehler, C. M. *The Great Sioux Uprising* (New York: Oxford University Press, 1959)

Oglesby, Richard. *Manuel Lisa and the Opening of the Missouri Fur Trade* (Norman: University of Oklahoma Press, 1963)

Overholser, Joel. *Fort Benton: the World's Innermost Port* (Fort Benton: Joel Overholser, 1987)

Phillips, Paul C. *The Fur Trade* (2 vols.; Norman: University of Oklahoma Press, 1961)

Phillips, Paul C. *Medicine in the Making of Montana* (Missoula: Montana State University Press, 1962)

Progressive Men of the State of Montana (Chicago: A. W. Bowen and Company, 1901)

Prucha, Paul. *Guide to the Military Posts of the United States* (Milwaukee: State Historical Society of Wisconsin, 1964)

Prucha, Paul. *The Great Father: The United States Army and the Indian, 1866-1890* (Lincoln: University of Nebraska Press, 1986)

Raymer, Robert G. *Montana: The Land and People* (3 vols., Chicago: Lewis Publishing Company, 1930)

Rodnick, David. *The Fort Belknap Assiniboines of Montana* (New Haven: Yale University Press, 1938)

Rowe, C. J. *Mountains and Meadows: Pioneer History of Cascade, Chesnut Valley, Hardy, St. Peter Mission and Castner Falls, 1805-1925* (Great Falls: Blue Print and Letters, c.1970)

Sanders, Helen F. *A History of Montana* (3 vols. Chicago: Lewis Publishing Company, 1913)

Schultz, James W. *Friends of My Life as an Indian* (New York: Forest and Stream Publishing Company, 1913)

Sharp, Paul. *Whoop-Up Country: The Canadian-American West, 1865-1885* (Norman: University of Oklahoma Press, 1955)

Spence, Clark. *Territorial Politics and Government in Montana, 1864-1889* (Urbana: University of Illinois Press, 1975)

Stearns, Harold J. *A History of the Upper Musselshell Valley of Montana, to 1920* (Harlowtown: Times-Clarion, 1966)

Stewart, Edgar I. *Custer's Luck* (Norman: University of Oklahoma Press, 1955)

Stout, Tom. Ed., *Montana, Its Story and Biography* (Chicago: American Historical Society, 1921)

Stuart, Granville. *Forty Years on the Frontier* (2 vols., Ed. by Paul Phillips, Cleveland: Arthur H. Clark and Company, 1925)

Sturtevant, William C., Ed., *Handbook of the North American Indians* vol. 13 (Washington: Smithsonian Institution, 2001)

Sunder, John E. *The Fur Trade on the Upper Missouri, 1840-1865* (Norman: University of Oklahoma Press, 1965)

Taylor, Joseph H. *Sketches of Frontier and Indian Life on the Upper Missouri and Great Plains,* Washburn, North Dakota, the author, 1895

Thorp, Raymond., and Robert Benker.*Crow Killer: The Saga of Liver-Eating Johnson* (Bloomington: Indiana University Press, 1969)

Utley, Robert M. *Frontier Regulars: The United States Army and the Indian, 1866-1890* (New York: Macmillan Publishing Company, 1973)

Vaughn, Robert. *Then and Now, or Thirty-Six Years in the Rockies* (Minneapolis Printing Company, 1900)

Weist, Tom *A History of the Cheyenne People* (Billings, Montana Council for Indian Education, 1977)

Winchell, Alexander. *Sketches of Creation* (New York: Harper and Brothers, 1870)

Wolle, Muriel S. *Montana Paydirt* (Denver: Sage Books, 1963)

Afterword

When referring to the general landscape of the Musselshell Country described by C.M. Lee in his journal and in which the tales recounted therein unfolded, it's tempting to say that little has changed since the time he lived there – but that isn't really true. In 2011 it's still a fundamentally wild and largely undeveloped part of the Missouri and Musselshell Rivers landscape in that part of Montana, but time has brought not just subtle alterations to the area but profound sociological and physical developments that have made it a much different place than that encountered by those who lived and toiled there in the time period covered by Lee's journals.

Three fundamental considerations come to mind. Most profound, of course, are the sociological changes. The frontier culture present at that time no longer exists. Nor are the limitations of travel and commerce imposed on the inhabitants of that time the same. Modern, paved highways and vastly improved roadways course much of the area, at least giving incredible human access to the vast portions of the rugged terrain found in that part of a rugged, broken landscape. Thirdly, the exact site where this tale unfolded – the junction of the Musselshell and Missouri Rivers where Fort Musselshell was located – lies under the surface of one of America's most famous water development projects, the reservoir created by the Fort Peck Dam, built in the late 1930s.

And yet, in many ways, the Missouri-Musselshell country is as it was in C.M. Lee's period of time. Weather-wise, it's much the same as it was in 1869-1872. Cold in winter, hot in the summer, teeming with wildlife, particularly mule deer and antelope, except when severe blizzards decimate their numbers as they did in the winter of 2010-2011. The area, in fact, is a landscape so productive of wildlife even today that it boggles the mind. Certainly the wanton slaughter of bison (we'll call them buffalo) and antelope described by C.M. Lee in his journals played a part in the drastic decline of the buffalo in that area and elsewhere in the American West, but with the exception of the buffalo, the wolf and the black-footed ferret, most wildlife species have continued to thrive in this nutrient-rich if harsh landscape. The prevalence of bird species is amazing. A recent survey, for example, identified more than two hundred species of birds in the area.

A trip to the Musselshell-Missouri country today where C.M. Lee and his compatriots lived is still awe-inspiring. It is, by and large, a landscape that speaks to you at any point in time on its own terms, just as it did to C.M. Lee and others who frequented the area in 1869-1872. Large tracts of land are little changed from Lee's time. Difficult; even brutal weather conditions still prevail. As one person put it in a recent talk about the area: "It's a land of absolute extremes. Too hot, too cold, too wet, too dry, too windy and much too windy." A sparse, even diminishing, human population exists over the greater area involved. Scattered agricultural enterprises exist, largely based on surviving in a dry-land environment. It's also the site of something new, however. A fledgling organization called the American Prairie Foundation is attempting to piece together, through a long-term land acquisition project, a restoration, just to the north of the Missouri-Musselshell convergence, of the vast tract of native prairie that prevailed there until recent times. With that project, over time, would also come a limited but nonetheless significant restoration of a major component of Lee's landscape that has been, until recently at least, nonexistent there: a substantial herd of wild bison, the buffalo. This awesome symbol of the American West largely disappeared, right along with much of the North American prairie environment, since Lee's time. Now the American Prairie Foundation, in its own words, has underway a mission "to create and manage a prairie-based wildlife reserve that, when combined with public lands already devoted to wildlife, will protect a unique natural habitat, provide lasting economic benefits, and improve public access to and enjoyment of the prairie landscape." That's a concept that no one in Lee's time could possibly have envisioned, except for maintaining the natural habitat and enjoying the prairie landscape. They had to have liked it, and the lifestyle it gave them, or they could never have persevered to follow their dream to its end.

LISTING OF BOOKS

Additional copies of **H. Duane Hampton's book – Life and Death at the Mouth of the Musselshell** and many other of Stoneydale Press' books on history, outdoor recreation, big game hunting, or historical reminisces centered around the Northern Rocky Mountain region, are available at many book stores, gift shops, and sporting goods stores, or direct from Stoneydale Press. If you'd like more information, you can contact us by calling a Toll Free Number, 1-800-735-7006, by writing to the address at the bottom of the page, or checking us out on our website at www.stoneydale.com. Here's a partial listing of some of the books that are available.

Historical, Outdoors, Hunting Reminisces

Montana Ghost Towns and Gold Camps: A Pictorial Guide, By William W. Whitfield. The author describes 71 historic locations in special commentary and with 450 crisp photographs to provide this guide to Montana's rich ghost town heritage. 8 1/2 by 11-inch format, 240 pages, softcover.

First Roots: The Story of Stevensville, Montana's Oldest Community, By The Discovery Writers. Chronicles in incredible detail, in text, photographs and drawings, the story of the founding of the town of Stevensville, Montana's oldest permanent settlement in 1841. 6x9-inch format, softcover.

Men of the Mission: In The Shadow of Old St. Mary's, By Jeanne O'Neill. Features the stories of the Jesuit priests and workers who served at the Historic St. Mary's Mission in Stevensville, Montana, from its founding in 1841 through the end of its mission era. 5 1/2 by 8 1/2-inch format, 96 pages, numerous illustrations and photographs.

Will to Live: A Saga of Survival, by Gary S. Edinger. Tells the story of a Wisconsin logger who miraculously, some say heroically, survived a woods accident in 2007 when a falling tree sheared off his left leg below the knee at a worksite too far distant from help for him to survive. A saga of what he (Edinger) believes enabled him to survive an impossible situation. 6x9-inch format, 192 pages, many photographs.

Hikes and Climbs to Bitterroot Mountain Summits, By Michael Hoyt. A gorgeously-illustrated, with over 300 color photographs, detailed guide for beginning and intermediate climbers and hikers to 50 mountains and 60 routes in the Bitterroot Mountains of western Montana and neighboring Idaho. 384 pages, 5½ by 8½-inch format, extra-durable softcover

Dale Burk's Montana, By Dale A. Burk. In vibrant text covering the full story of Montana and stunning color photographs, the author takes you into the heart and soul of wild Montana. 8x10-inch format, 150 color photographs. Hardcover and softcover editions.

Colter's Run, By Stephen T. Gough. A stirring novel of famous early-day frontiersman John Colter and the time he spent in the headwaters of the Missouri River, the Three Forks country, trapping, fighting with and eluding the dreaded Blackfeet Indians, all the while trying to live up to forces within himself that compelled him to face constant threat of death. What he accomplished is legendary, that he survived that experience is miraculous. 6x9-inch format, 392 pages, softcover.

Reflections From the Golden Era of Hunting, By Fred S. Scott. As one of Idaho's most famous hunting figures, Fred Scott has pulled together 63 stories of big game hunting for elk, bear, deer and antelope as a companion book to his earlier "Memories of Hunting Idaho's Golden Era. 256 pages, 6x9-inch format, softcover.

Memories of Hunting Idaho's Golden Era, By Fred S. Scott. Experience, through the stories of this book by one of Idaho's most revered big game hunters and master storytellers the saga of a lifetime spent in quest of elk, deer, bear and other game species in the wilds of Idaho. 64 chapter, many photographs, 256 pages, 6x9-inch format. Softcover.

From Cottontails to Kudu, By Mitch Rohlfs, Ph.D. The tradition of a life being shaped by the rigors, challenges and joys of hunting looms large in this book, which details the transformation of a young boy on his first rabbit hunt into an international big game hunter and accomplished upland bird hunter. 6x9-inch format, hardcover, 256 pages, dozens of photographs.

The Trail of a Sportsman, By Duane Bernard. Follow the author on a life-long quest to hunt big game across the world and to achieve what is called Oregon's "Super Slam" on a working man's budget. Go with him on adventures to Montana, Idaho, British Columbia, New Mexico, Alaska, Quebec, South Africa, Zimbabwe and Namibka, as well as in his native Oregon. 6x9-inch format, 154 pages, many photographs.

Cow Range and Hunting Trail, By Malcolm S. Mackay. An expanded new edition of the early-day Montana classic first issued in 1925, written by legendary rancher-outdoorsman Malcolm S. Mackay and illustrated by famed cowboy artist Charles M. Russell. 256 pages, 35 photographs, a new long-lost chapter added to marvelous stories of ranching and big game hunting in the West. This book is a reprint of a national best-seller from 75 years ago.

They Left Their Tracks, By Howard Copenhaver, Recollections of Sixty Years as a Wilderness Outfitter. Gripping tales laced with humor as only a master storyteller can create. Touches on a lifetime spent in the wilderness, in constant contact with wild creatures like the elk and grizzly bear, plus his experiences sharing the wilderness with clients over a span of sixty and more years. 192 pages, softcover edition. (One of our all-time most popular books.)

Copenhaver Country, By Howard Copenhaver, the latest collection of humorous storiesby a master storyteller. Contains rich humor and studied observations of a land Howard loves and the people he met along the way in a lifetime spent in the wilds. 160 pages, many photographs.

More Tracks, By Howard Copenhaver, 78 Years of Mountains, People & Happiness, Tales of Howard and his family on their early-day ranch near Ovando, Montana, and the Bob Marshall Wilderness. 180 pages, clothbound or softcover editions.

Mule Tracks: The Last of The Story, By Howard Copenhaver. As one of Montana's most revered storytellers and honored outfitters, Howard spent years leading his mule packstrings through the Bob Marshall Wilderness. Read here of his adventures, misadventures and other wild tales of mules in the wild country. 176 pages, hardcover and softcover editions.

Indian Trails & Grizzly Tales, By Bud Cheff Sr. A wonderful collection of stories taken from a lifetime outfitting in Montana's Bob Marshall and Mission Mountain Wilderness areas, by a master woodsman. 232 pages, available in softcover edition.

Sometimes Only Horses to Eat: David Thompson – The Saleesh House Period 1807-1812, By Carl W. Haywood. Covers the time Thompson spent developing the fur trade in northwestern Montana, northern Idaho and northeastern Washington (1807-1812). Based on Thompson's journals, a thoroughly researched and crafted in a way to shed light on Thompson's day-to-day activities. Many illustrations, phtographs and maps. 6x9-inch format, 392 pages, softcover.

Untold Tales of Bison Range Trails, By Ernie Kraft. The full saga of the exciting story of the heralded National Bison Range at Moiese, Montana, told by an "insider" who worked at the Bison Range for thirty years. 8 1/2 by 11-inch format, 228 pages, 60 photographs and a dozen illustration.

Flames and Courage, Saga of the 1910 Fires, By Helen Meadows and Sandra Gubel, Illustrations by Marjorie Griffin. A timely historical children's book of how families caught in the path of the catastrophic forest fires of 1910 survived, told by those who survived and their descendants. 8 1/2 by 11-inch format, 100 illustrations., softcover.

Hunting Books

The Packer's Field Manual, By Bob Hoverson. Featuring use of the Decker Pack Saddle, this manual written by one of the top experts in the country will literally provide you with every detail necessary to successfully pack with the Decker Pack Saddle. 6x9-inch softcover format, 192 pages, many photographs and illustrations by Roger Inghram.

Hunting Chukar, By Richard O'Toole. This authoritative and detailed guide to hunting the West's most elusive game bird, the chukar, provides both experience and knowledge taken from 35-plus years of experience. Chapters on locating birds, tactics used in hunting them, gear, the choice and use of dogs, and many photographs. 6x9-inch format, softcover, 12 chapters and an appendix.

Radical Elk Hunting Strategies, By Mike Lapinski. In clear and lucid text, expert Lapinski takes up elk hunting where other writers leave off – the secrets of calling elk in close. This book literally develops a very aggressive concept of hunting big bull elk by urging the hunter to do things the elk don't expect a hunter to do. 6x9-inch format, 192 pages, 60 photographs, softcover.

Solving Elk Hunting Problems, By Mike Lapinski. Subtitled "Simple Solutions to The Elk Hunting Riddle," this book, in 15 chapters and more than 80 photographs tells you now to cope with specific problems you'll encounter in the field – a hung-up bull, changes in elk behavior under heavy hunting pressure, peak rut activity, and so on. 6x9-inch format, both softcover and hardcover editions.

High Pressure Elk Hunting, By Mike Lapinski. The latest book available on hunting elk that have become educated to the presence of more hunters working them. Lots of info on hunting these elk. 192 pages, many photographs, hardcover or softcover.

Bugling for Elk, By Dwight Schuh, the bible on hunting early-season elk. A recognized classic, 164 pages, softcover edition only.

A Hunt For the Great Northern, By Herb Neils. This acclaimed novel utilizes the drama of a hunting camp as the setting for a story of intrigue, mystery, adventure and great challenge set in the woods of northwestern Montana. 204 pages, softcover.

Ghost of The Wilderness, By James "Mac" Mackee. A dramatic story of the pursuit of the mountain lion, the Ghost of The Wilderness. A tremendous tale of what Jim MacKee went through over several seasons in his quest for a trophy mountain lion in the wilds of Montana. 160 pages, softcover.

The Woodsman And His Hatchet, By Bud Cheff. Subtitled "Eighty Years on Wilderness Survival," this book gives you practical, common sense advice on survival under emergency conditions in the wilderness, written by an expert with eight decades of experience in Montana's Bob Marshall Wilderness. Softcover.

STONEYDALE PRESS PUBLISHING COMPANY
523 Main Street • Box 188
Stevensville, Montana 59870
Phone: 406-777-2729
Website: www.stoneydale.com